Marriage in Contemporary Japan

The phenomenon of *bankonka* – 'postponement of marriage' – is increasingly reported in contemporary Japanese media, clearly illustrating the changing patterns of modern lifestyles and attitudes towards marriage, personal obligation, and ambition. This is the first book in recent years to explore the contemporary state of marriage in Japanese society. Setting out the different perceptions and expectations of marriage in today's Japan, the book discusses how economic issues and the family impact on marital behaviour. Contrary to the views of some feminists that young women have no interest in improving their status and position, this book argues that, by delaying marriage and childrearing, young women can be seen as 'rebels' challenging Japanese patriarchal society. Unlike many other studies, it gives equal attention to male gender roles and masculinity, exploring what constitutes being a 'real man' in Japan – through the analysis of mainstream and non-mainstream conceptions of masculinity that co-exist in contemporary Japan, and considers the implications of such different roles for the institution of marriage. It investigates the roles of wife and mother, articulating why the strict division of labour defining men as breadwinners and women as homemakers became popular. Moreover, it describes the changing character of courtship relationships, explaining why the norm has shifted from arranged marriages pre-1945 to love marriages after that period. Finally, it puts the Japanese experience into a cross-cultural, international context with a series of comparisons with marriage elsewhere both in Asia – including Korea and Hong Kong – and in western countries such as France, Sweden, Italy, and the United States.

Yoko Tokuhiro is a Lecturer at The Center for Liberal Arts, Meiji Gakuin University, Japan. Her research interests include the anthropology of Japan, marriage, family, and gender.

Routledge Contemporary Japan Series

A Japanese Company in Crisis
Ideology, strategy, and narrative
Fiona Graham

Japan's Foreign Aid
Old continuities and new directions
Edited by David Arase

Japanese Apologies for World War II
A rhetorical study
Jane W. Yamazaki

**Linguistic Stereotyping and Minority Groups
in Japan**
Nanette Gottlieb

Shinkansen
From bullet train to symbol of modern Japan
Christopher P. Hood

Small Firms and Innovation Policy in Japan
Edited by Cornelia Storz

**Cities, Autonomy and Decentralization
in Japan**
Edited by Carola Hein and Philippe Pelletier

The Changing Japanese Family
Edited by Marcus Rebick and Ayumi Takenaka

Adoption in Japan
Comparing policies for children in need
Peter Hayes and Toshie Habu

**The Ethics of Aesthetics in Japanese Cinema
and Literature**
Polygraphic desire
Nina Cornyetz

**Institutional and Technological Change in
Japan's Economy**
Past and present
Edited by Janet Hunter and Cornelia Storz

Political Reform in Japan
Leadership looming large
Alisa Gaunder

Civil Society and the Internet in Japan
Isa Ducke

Japan's Contested War Memories
The 'memory rifts' in historical consciousness
of World War II
Philip A. Seaton

Japanese Love Hotels
A cultural history
Sarah Chaplin

**Population Decline and Ageing in Japan –
The Social Consequences**
Florian Coulmas

Zainichi Korean Identity and Ethnicity
David Chapman

A Japanese Joint Venture in the Pacific
Foreign bodies in tinned Tuna
Kate Barclay

Japanese–Russian Relations, 1907–2007
Joseph P. Ferguson

**War Memory, Nationalism and Education in
Post-War Japan, 1945–2007**
The Japanese history textbook controversy and
Ienaga Saburo's court challenges
Yoshiko Nozaki

A New Japan for the Twenty-First Century
An inside overview of current fundamental
changes and problems
Edited by Rien T. Segers

A Life Adrift
Soeda Azembo, popular song and modern mass
culture in Japan
Translated by Michael Lewis

The Novels of Oe Kenzaburo
Yasuko Claremont

Perversion in Modern Japan
Psychoanalysis, literature, culture
Edited by Nina Cornyetz and J. Keith Vincent

**Homosexuality and Manliness in Postwar
Japan**
Jonathan D. Mackintosh

Marriage in Contemporary Japan
Yoko Tokuhiro

Marriage in Contemporary Japan

Yoko Tokuhiro

LONDON AND NEW YORK

First published 2010
by Routledge
2 Park Square, Milton Park, Abingdon, Oxon, OX14 4RN

Simultaneously published in the USA and Canada
by Routledge
711 Third Avenue, New York, NY 10017

*Routledge is an imprint of the Taylor & Francis Group, an informa
business*

First issued in paperback 2011

© 2010 Yoko Tokuhiro

Typeset in Times New Roman by
Keyword Group Ltd

British Library Cataloguing in Publication Data
A catalogue record for this book is available
from the British Library

Library of Congress Cataloging in Publication Data
Tokuhiro, Yoko.
Marriage in contemporary Japan / Yoko Tokuhiro.
p. cm.—(Routledge contemporary Japan series ; 26)
Includes bibliographical references and index.
ISBN-13: 978-0-415-44110-0 (cloth : alk. paper)
ISBN-10: 0-415-44110-2 (hardback)
ISBN-13: 978-0-203-87118-8 (e-book)
ISBN-10: 0-203-87118-9 (e-book)
1. Marriage—Japan. 2. Sex role—Japan. I. Title.
HQ682.T628 2009
306.810952—dc22
2009009310

ISBN 10: 0-415-44110-2 (hbk)
ISBN 10: 0-415-67370-4 (pbk)
ISBN 10: 0-203-87118-9 (ebk)

ISBN 13: 978-0-415-44110-0 (hbk)
ISBN 13: 978-0-415-67370-9 (pbk)
ISBN 13: 978-0-203-87118-8 (ebk)

Contents

Acknowledgements   vi
Explanatory note   vii
List of tables and figures   viii

Introduction   1

1 Perceptions and expectations of marriage in Japan   16

2 The impact of feminist discourses on marriage and fertility 28

3 Male gender roles and masculinity   54

4 Gender roles: The roles of wife and mother   73

5 Changes in courtship practices   89

6 Beyond Japan: Crossnational comparisons   116

   Conclusion   130

   Appendices   134

Notes   138
Bibliography   143
Index   161

Acknowledgements

I am extremely grateful for having been given the opportunity to undertake this research, thanks to a PhD studentship at the University of Hong Kong.

I am indebted to many people for their assistance and support during this research. First I would like to thank my PhD supervisors – Professor Kirsten Refsing and Dr Peter Cave. Professor Refsing's enthusiasm for the topic sustained me through a long and difficult process. Dr. Cave gave thoughtful and critical advice throughout all the stages of this project. I cannot thank him enough for his invaluable assistance.

Gratitude is also due to many other people, including the staff members of the Japan Youth Foundation, especially Yoko Itamoto, for allowing me to take part in their programmes during my fieldwork. I am deeply indebted and grateful to my informants in Japan, who shared so much about their lives and experiences with me. Many thanks also to all of my dear friends for their critical and thoughtful advice and who combined patience with a sense of humour including Alex Ham, Ekaterina Korobtseva, Paul Rosta, Takako Yoshimura and Yukie Tsuzuki. I would also like to express my great appreciation to Tom Gill who helped me in the editorial process, and my editor at Routledge, Peter Sowden, for his professionalism. And thanks to the anonymous reader of the manuscript, for many valuable comments which helped to improve this book.

It goes without saying that any remaining errors of content or style remain solely my own responsibility.

Lastly, no words will adequately express my gratitude to all members of my family, especially my husband Yuji Tokuhiro and my parents, Hiroshi and Rei Suzuki. I am deeply grateful to them for sharing this long journey with me.

Explanatory note

This book originated in a PhD thesis, the research for which was completed in 2004. I have updated survey material where possible. The ages given for my informants are as of the date I interviewed them, mostly around 2000.

All Japanese words are romanized according to the modified Hepburn system used in Kenkyusha's New Japanese–English Dictionary (Masuda, 1974). With the exception of people's names, famous place names (e.g. Tokyo), and some words which have become part of the English language (e.g. Bushido), macrons are used in Japanese words to indicate long vowels. People's names are given in the English order, with the surname following the given name.

Figures

1	Average age at first marriage 1960–2005	3
2	Proportion of men and women who have never married by age	5
4.1	Trends in female labour force participation rates	74
4.2	Age-specific female labour force participation rates in Japan by birth cohort	75
4.3	Age-specific female labour force participation rates and reasons for female employees to quit their jobs	81
4.4	Changes in number of female employees based on marital status in the non-agricultural sector	84
4.5	Reasons for choosing to work part-time	84
5.1	Annual trends in arranged and love marriages	98

Tables

5.1	Summary of where love match couples met	102
5.2	Methods or places of couples meeting – average age of first encounter, first marriage and years of dating period in Japan	113
5.3	Average age at first encounter, first marriage and years of dating period in Japan	114
6.1	Singulate mean age at marriage, by sex, 1955–1995	118
6.2	Marriage prevalence – percentages ever married at age 50, by sex, 1955–1995	118
6.3	The share of arranged marriages in the three regions	123
	(a) Percentages of arranged marriages among Japanese women by age group	123
	(b) Percentages of arranged marriages among Hong Kong women by birth cohort and age group	123
	(c) Percentages of arranged marriages among Korean women by marriage cohort	123
6.4	Singulate mean age at marriage by sex: Europe and US, 1950/51–1980/81	125
6.5	Marriage prevalence	126

Introduction

The story of Sayuri[1]

My interest in researching the field of marital behaviour in Japan originally came about through one of my Japanese girlfriends, named Sayuri (39), who is currently working as an associate professor at a women's junior college in Japan. When I first met her, more than a decade ago, she was cohabiting with her boyfriend and at that time she did not see the point in getting officially married.

Sayuri was brought up in an 'upper-middle class' Japanese family. Her father had conservative values concerning gender roles and wanted his daughter to lead an 'ordinary' life and eventually get married. Through home discipline and education, he attempted to raise Sayuri with 'traditional' expectations. For instance, Sayuri mentioned to me once that when she was a small girl she was repeatedly told: 'You are a girl so you should line up your shoes properly'. Yet, Sayuri, who was very sceptical about her parent's gender-differential discipline, always wondered why only girls had to behave this way and thought she would have been more willing to follow her parent's discipline if they had told her to behave well as *an individual*. As she grew older, her father enthusiastically tried to persuade Sayuri to go to one of the prominent private women's colleges in Tokyo to become a 'qualified' bride. By this time, Sayuri had become even more doubtful about her father's expectations and instead went to one of the most prestigious state universities in Japan. Instead of feeling proud of his daughter's accomplishment, her father was seriously concerned that she would find great difficulty in finding a prospective partner because her academic background would be too high *for a woman*.

As mentioned earlier, Sayuri was living with her boyfriend and had no intention of getting married. This was mainly because she was (and still is) against conventional *ie* ideas based on the feudalistic family structure known as the *ie* system.[2] For instance, Sayuri believes her family name constitutes part of her identity and individuality and she wishes to maintain her surname for the rest of her life. The marriage law today, however, requires a couple to choose one common surname, either the husband's or wife's, prior to marriage; today almost all couples (97 per cent) choose the husband's surname (Nishikawa and Nishikawa 2001). Sayuri perceives the convention whereby most Japanese women change their family name at the time of marriage as problematic, because it perpetuates the conventional normalcy of a bride entering into her husband's family.

Sayuri and her partner had continued their relationship for about seven years without incident. This changed when Sayuri was 36 years old, and became pregnant. The couple believed that their child would be socially stigmatized if they remained unmarried. Thus they decided to become legally married and needed to decide which surname to take. As the decision should be made based on fairness and equality, they decided that the winner of '*janken*' or the game of 'rock, paper, scissors' would keep their surname while the loser would give up theirs. Sayuri won the game and they currently have their marriage registered under Sayuri's family name. Her father who has no son was extremely grateful when he heard about the couple's decision. For Sayuri's partner, however, becoming a husband in order that his child would not be illegitimate meant surrendering his family name. Sayuri believes that the loss of his surname was a blow to her husband and has tactfully refrained from discussing the matter with him ever since.

This case provides an example of two independent individuals seeking to build a more egalitarian relationship, thus illustrating shifting attitudes towards marriage. Through some casual conversations with other unmarried Japanese acquaintances, I became more interested in marital behaviour, especially in changing attitudes towards marriage in contemporary Japan within the broader framework of gender roles and the meaning of marriage in Japanese culture. Along the way, I asked myself, how does Japanese culture or the norms surrounding marriage affect ordinary people's way of life or, more specifically, how is the institution of marriage associated with people's lives in regard to retaining their self-respect in contemporary Japanese society?

To date, there have been many studies focused on women's roles or femininity, compared with relatively few studies of men's roles or masculinity in Japan. Since the scope of my research embraces both sexes, it will illuminate the relatively unexplored area of masculinity as well as exploring the significance of possible changes in women's consciousness and aspirations in terms of gender, family, and marriage in Japan.

Description of the current situation

Although Japan can still be regarded as a '*kaikon shakai*' – a society where marriage is the norm – the number of young people delaying marriage is sharply rising. This shifting marriage pattern suggests changing perceptions and expectations of marriage, which I hope to elucidate in this book.

The phenomenon of *bankonka* or 'the postponement of marriage' is a topic frequently covered by the contemporary Japanese media. The number of articles that have appeared in the press in recent years confirms the general public interest in this phenomenon. It has also attracted a great amount of attention from a wide range of people including sociologists, demographers, commentators, and essayists due to *bankonka*'s illustration of the changing pattern of modern life styles and changing attitudes towards marriage, personal obligation, and ambition.

Documentary writer Yumiko Suzuki (1995) has written that although the phenomenon of *nōka no yomebusoku* or 'farmers unable to find a bride' has existed in Japan since the 1960s, the issue was not widely taken up by the media until more recently. It only became prominent when young men living in urban areas began to face similar difficulties in getting married. In the early 1980s it was then referred to as *dansei kekko-nan jidai* or 'the era of marriage difficulties for men'. The debate on the delay of marriage culminated when many scholars started to assert that the postponement of marriage played a principal role in accounting for the recent decline in the birthrate. The reason, it was argued, was that the delay of marriage directly resulted in the delayed beginning of women's reproductive lifespan (Ogawa and Hodge 1991; Yamada 1996). This has led to the topic being discussed even more in the context of 'the childless society' (Jolivet 1997).

The average age at first marriage was stable between 1960 and 1975 (see Figure I.1) and during this period the variance was low. In fact, as most women married by the age of 25, marriageable women in Japan used to be compared to Christmas cakes, which were eaten on the 25th and not after. This suggested the difficulties faced by women in finding a partner after 25 years of age. Emiko Ochiai calls it 'a nightmarish era which imposed a uniform life course on every man and every woman' (1997: 55). However, statistics show that since 1975 the average age at first marriage has risen, reaching 29.8 years of age for men and 28.0 years of age for women in 2005 (Statistics and Information Department, Ministry of Health, Labour and Welfare 2006). At the same time there has been a marked difference between marriage trends for men and women. As Shirahase

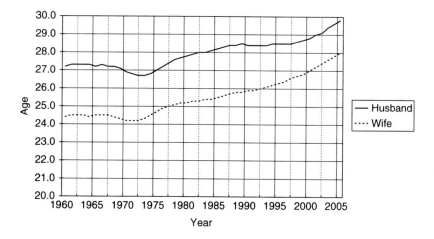

Figure I.1 Average age at first marriage 1960–2005.
Source: Statistics and Information Department, Ministry of Health, Labour and Welfare, *Jinkō Dōtai Tōkei* (Statistics of Population Dynamics), 2006.

(2008) points out, women with high levels of education and men with low levels of education tend to have particular difficulty in securing marriage partners – a trend she dates to the mid-1990s and associates with the bursting of the bubble economy and rising rates of male unemployment.

Clearly, then, this phenomenon has changed and developed over a period of several decades. It is thus important to note here that when I discuss the recent phenomenon of delayed marriage, I am generally referring to the period from 1975 to 2005.

The average age at first marriage, however, represents only those who married in a particular year, but not those who avoid marriage. In other words, this graph does not show whether the proportion of people actually getting married is increasing or decreasing. Therefore, these figures could be misleading in understanding family formation patterns if the proportion of those who stay single for life is increasing. Xerox (1992) suggests that, 'It has been a commonsense deduction that celibacy emerges in association with a late marriage pattern – that late marriage and nonmarriage result from the same underlying changes' (p. 21). Thus, under the circumstances, one should also look at the changes in the proportion of men and women who are not married.

Figure I.2 shows the percentage of people who are unmarried according to age-group, sex, and year; these statistics show that since around the mid-1970s, growing numbers of men and women have remained single, probably leading to an increase in persons who stay single for life.

These two charts also show an interesting disparity between the sexes developing since the mid-1970s. In 1975, the percentage of women who had never married at age 50 was 4.3 per cent, more than double the figure for men (2.1 per cent). Thirty years later, in 2005, the pattern was reversed, with 15.4 per cent of men still never married at age 50, against 6.8 per cent for women. The numbers for both sexes showed an increase in not getting married, but the pace of increase for men far outstripped that for women.

According to the National Institute of Population and Social Security Research (personal communication, 18 August 2008), there are three main reasons for this striking trend.

First, there is a sex imbalance built into the population, with roughly six per cent more boys than girls being born each year.[3] This imbalance used to be offset by a higher male death rate, resulting from war fatalities and a higher vulnerability to diseases such as tuberculosis, pneumonia etc., but these factors have shown less influence in recent years. Second, the tendency for men to marry women on average several years younger than themselves led to a skewing of the marriage market in the 1970s, when the so-called *dankai* (baby-boom) generation born in the immediate postwar years reached marriageable age. The large number of men in the baby-boom generation tended to marry women from slightly younger, post-baby-boom age cohorts. This meant, first, that *dankai* men had a smaller pool of marriage partners to choose from; and second, that a shortage of marriage partners developed for men in those slightly younger post-*dankai* cohorts.

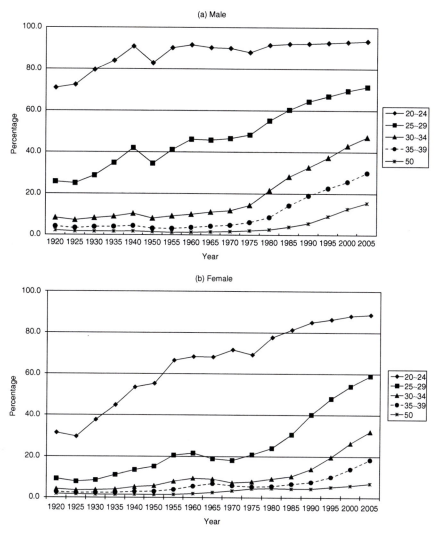

Figure I.2 Proportion of men and women who have never married by age.
Source: Calculated by the author based on figures obtained from the Statistics Bureau, Ministry of Internal Affairs and Communications, *Kokusei Chōsa* (Population Census), 2005.

Third, the divorce rate has been rising in recent years, and among Japanese divorcees, men are more likely than women to remarry. Hence the rising divorce rate is also increasing the number of divorced men who remarry, while the reluctance of divorced women to remarry is reducing the number of women in the marriage market.[4]

Marriage and gender in theoretical and comparative perspective

Defining marriage

Marriage is a topic of deep and wide concern in many societies, but at the same time, there has been and continues to be arguments about its definition and universality. Tovar in the *Routledge International Encyclopedia of Women* defines marriage as

> a culturally approved relationship that legitimizes a sexual and economic union, usually between a man and a woman. All national states have definitions of what constitutes a legal marriage and under what circumstances it can be lawfully dissolved; indeed, there may be as many definitions of marriage as there are cultures and legislatures (2000: 1301).

Many anthropologists have delineated the wide variety of forms that marriage can take, so that it has become difficult (if not impossible) to arrive at a universal definition that is satisfactory for all societies. Thus it is not surprising to find different approaches or different aspects of marriage being highlighted in its various definitions. For example, while George Murdock (1949: 8) stresses the interpersonal aspects of marriage: 'marriage exists only when the economic and the sexual are united into one relationship', Ward H. Goodenough (1970: 4) highlights the contractual or legal rights aspects of marriage by defining it as '[it is] a contractual union of a man and a woman and involves sexual privilege, economic cooperation, cohabitation, the production of children, and responsibility for the children's care, socialization, and education'.

Peter Riviere, another anthropologist, argues that marriage is 'one of the socially approved and recognized relationships between the conceptual roles of male and female' (1971: 66). He is extremely cautious in his approach to marriage, saying that this statement is neither a definition nor an explanation but nonetheless allows us to view marriage 'as a category of the total male/female relationship' (1971: 66).

Riviere's point of view is basically structuralist – he looks at society and sees it as a set of ordering relations, in other words social relations are part of a deep order that involve not only society but also the human mind. His standpoint contrasts with the 'functionalist' way of looking at society, which analyzes social relations in terms of their functions, or the role they play in maintaining or perpetuating the society and its culture. Riviere is not trying to define marriage or to say that it plays this role or that role in society; indeed he says that such an approach leads to a situation where 'the marital institution and its function are being used to define each other' (1971: 62). He gives an example saying that if the function of marriage is to legitimatize offspring, then this automatically means that the legitimacy of the offspring depends on marriage. This explains why he notes, 'if we are not to condemn ourselves for ever to the tautologies of functionalist explanations we must come to realize that marriage as an isolable phenomenon to study is a misleading illusion' (1971: 57). Therefore Riviere argues that 'the only escape from this sterile predicament' is 'to recognize both marriage and its function as expressions or statements about the order of things' (1971: 62).

In addition to Riviere's discussion, one can probably argue that the increasingly diverse arrangements being made around relationships in modern industrial capitalist societies show that attempts to define marriage are probably doomed to failure, and it is more sensible to look at the issue in terms of the various arrangements that societies have for creating a legitimate social order and in particular legitimate sexual and family relationships. In this book I have therefore taken the position that conflicting ideas about what kinds of social order, personal relationship, and life pattern are *legitimate and acceptable* – to individuals as well as society – are at the heart of the issue of delayed marriage in contemporary Japan.

Nonetheless, despite the potential problems in defining marriage from an anthropological, cross-cultural perspective, marriage relationships in various forms have been, and continue to be, a very important part of social order and personal life in much of the world, and consequently, defining marriage arouses great and widespread interest and passionate debate. A large number of people wish to secure control over marriage practices, by ideological, economic, legal or even forcible means, because they are so crucial not only to individuals, but also to the social order (or at least to the understandings of the social order), in all sorts of forms – for example, gender and sexual order, socialization and child-rearing, and demographics and economics.

Changes in the institutions of marriage and family in industrialized countries

Many people – including sociologists, anthropologists, and economists – have questioned the long-term future of marriage as an institution. They point to phenomena, in the West in particular, like the lingering elements of inequality in the male/female power relationship within marriage, the increasing number of divorces and extra-marital births, cohabitation as a substitute for marriage, postponement of marriage, and lifelong singlehood. How did these changes occur in the West and in industrial societies in general?

The principal argument is provided by Goode (1982 [1964]) who points out that as societies modernize, young people gain more freedom and independence through the introduction of wage labour. As wage labour starts to dominate in the economic system, young people gain more opportunities to obtain tangible (as well as intangible) benefits outside the family unit, and they are freed from their kin, especially parents. This increases the independence of children while it decreases parental control over children, with consequent loss of influence over marital issues, including mate selection. This is the context in which the idea of romantic love gains greater importance in the selection of future mates. More and more people seek intimacy and personal fulfilment from marriage.

Equally important is the notion that marriage should be based on equality between the spouses. However, there are more than enough case studies illustrating that the spousal relationship remains unequal. Beck and Beck-Gernsheim (1995) argue that gender inequalities are not a thing of the past but rather the basis of industrial society. They assert that there is a conflict between the desire for a successful and fulfilling career and the altruism necessary for being a good home-maker and parent. In other words, there are contradictions between personal freedom and family demands. Beck and Beck-Gernsheim note (1995: 2)

> Women and men are currently compulsively on the search for the right way to live, trying out cohabitation, divorce or contractual marriage, struggling to coordinate family and career, love and marriage, 'new' motherhood and fatherhood, friendship and acquaintance. This movement is under way, and there is no stopping it.

They continue that 'In many people's view . . . the individualists themselves are the problem, their wants and discontent, their thirst for excitement and diminishing willingness to fit in with others, to subordinate themselves or do without' (1995: 3).

The growth of individualism

Indeed, it has become widely accepted by academics that increased individualism is an important explanation for marital and family changes. An extensively used textbook on the family by Burgess and Locke (1945: 527) states the following.

> The concept of familism previously defined as an ideal type signifies that the interest of the family as a group is paramount to the interests of its individual members. The concept of individualism by contrast means that the continuity and welfare of the family is no longer the chief social aim but rather the personality development of its members. In the modern period the stress is increasingly upon the individual and upon the personality development of family members. The trend is away from regarding the family as an end in itself and toward evaluating it in terms of the happiness and the welfare of its members. Individualism may even go to the logical extreme of a person deciding not to marry in order to be free from the responsibilities of family life and to retain a maximum of personal freedom.

The growth of individualism 'is believed to have undermined commitment in intimate relationships' (Lewis 2001: 8), and has raised concerns about the potential lack of permanence and stability of the institutions of marriage and family. There seems to be a contradiction, or at least tension, between the pursuit of one's own happiness and loyalty to marriage. Lewis (2001) illustrates this aspect by saying that individualism is at the heart of the idea of romantic love but this could just as easily slip into adultery as into monogamy. Moreover, exclusive sexual intimacy has become more and more important within marriage, while sex has become more widely available. Thus, she argues that the ideal of romantic love, which contains strong elements of individualism, does not necessarily lead unproblematically to companionate marriage.

This is exactly why some demographers stressed the importance of taking into account the more individualistic values that have been accompanying demographic changes. Van de Kaa's (1987) theory of 'Europe's Second Demographic Transition', which he argues began in the 1960s, emphasizes this point. He notes that there has been a dramatic shift in norms towards progressiveness and individualism, emphasizing rights and self-fulfilment. This has taken the form of the separation of sex and marriage and cohabitation and out-of-wedlock fertility have become increasingly acceptable.

Since we now have a general picture of the issues associated with the causes of change in the institution of marriage, I will now focus on its consequences. Lewis (2001) explains how both British and American sociologists and psychologists have, in the last 20 years, noted the negative effects of divorce on children. Research findings in the 1950s and 1960s appeared to show that divorce might be better for children than living with parents in conflict. At that time it was still possible to be reasonably optimistic about the institution of marriage because the number of divorces as well as of out-of-wedlock children was relatively low. However, Lewis continues, by the 1980s, with the rapid increase in both the divorce rate and the extra-marital birth rate, scholars drew much more pessimistic conclusions. The high divorce rate is particularly problematic in industrial societies where childcare is heavily dependent on the nuclear family. In a conventional society, children were often looked after by extended family, even if the marriage had ended. In this way, marriage in modern societies is becoming increasingly important, while at the same time, it is becoming less stable as an agency for bringing up children (Davis 1985).

Is gender inequality within marriage an inescapable phenomenon?

In her well-known book *The Future of Marriage* (1976 [1972]) Jessie Bernard argues that there is a difference in how men and women experience marriage. She referred to it as 'his' and 'her' marriages, saying that marriage has a beneficial effect for the well-being of both men and women but nonetheless it works better for men. Bernard notes that 'Husbands enter marriage with an initial advantage in the institutional prescription of superiority to them' (1976: 144), suggesting that people play socially prescribed roles that they learn in their status as males or females. Furthermore, in the section titled, 'The housewife syndrome' she describes how housewives who play this socially defined marital role could face the symptoms of psychological stress. Full-time homemakers suffer from these symptoms because, she argues, they are committed to a dead-end job and are socially and emotionally isolated from the outside world.

Three decades have already passed since Bernard's book was first published. This continuing inequality is still to be found between husband and wife. This indicates a deeply rooted patriarchal structure within the private sphere which is complexly interconnected with the rest of society. A growing number of women today work outside the home and they contribute to the overall family income. Ironically, though, many researchers report that wives still spend more hours caring for the family than their husbands, a situation Arlie Hochschild referred to as *The Second Shift* (1990).

Before I continue with the further analysis of gender inequality in society, it is essential to discuss the concept and meaning of gender itself. At the extremes, it is possible to concentrate either on the biological or on the social explanations for gender differences. Is gender a stable property of individuals, or is it a result of learning through interaction with others? Money and Ehrhardt (1972: 1) point out that 'In the theory of psychosexual differentiation, it is now outmoded to juxtapose nature versus nurture, the genetic versus the environmental, the innate versus the acquired, the biological versus the psychological, or the instinctive versus the learned. Modern genetic theory avoids these antiquated dichotomies.' Underlying this statement is a warning to those who separate biology and environment, underestimating or totally ignoring the connections between them. In other words there is probably some truth in both biological and environmental approaches. One can argue that people do develop a basic gender identity when very young, but that there is a lot of room for the content of that gender identity to change and vary over time. In other words, most people remain quite sure that they are men or women, yet what is permissible (i.e. legitimate, to use Riviere's term) for men or women can change overtime and can also vary according to the situation they are in.

In this regard, Amy S. Wharton (1995) provides a useful explanation of how, broadly speaking, conceptions of gender can be divided in two: a conceptualization that sees gender as a characteristic belonging to individuals and emphasizes the role of socialization in leading to the internalization of gender identity, and an alternative conceptualization that perceives gender as a result of social interaction occurring in particular situations. The second conceptualization sees gender as more fluid. Kondo, in her work *Crafting Selves: Power, Gender, and Discourses of Identity in a Japanese Workplace* (1990), introduces the related idea. Based on her ethnographic study in Japan, she argues, using feminist and poststructuralist theories, that *the self is not a static truth* – people shift their identities, including gender identities, in contradictory and multiple ways and they even possess the power to create and construct their selves. Kondo emphasizes that as people interact with one another, the people involved are all affected, and their behaviour and attitudes can vary according to the situation they are in. In this way, she challenges the kind of anthropology, as well as the particular bias in the West in general, which assumes the existence of an immutable identity to be studied, and a correspondingly static notion of the empirical observer. As she notes 'identity is not a static *object*, but a creative *process*' and its concept 'is inevitably implicated in relations of power' (1990: 43).[5]

A further aspect of gender identity is how people see and understand their own gender identity, i.e. how they define themselves as men or women. What do they think it means to be a man or a woman – and what does it mean for them? How flexible or fluid is that identity as far as they are concerned? What range of behaviour does the identity 'man' or 'woman' involve? How important is the identity to them? This issue will be dealt with throughout the book.

Feminism, and feminist scholarship in particular, has had a great deal to say about marriage as well as issues concerning gender. This work has been very influential, certainly in the scholarly world and to some extent also in society more generally. The women's movement and feminist scholars have paid a great deal of attention to trying to understand how social attitudes and institutions influence women's position, and moreover feminists have been trying to find a way to change oppressive structures within society. Feminists may differ in their views regarding the genesis of gender inequality and the way in which unequal gender systems are maintained. However, there are several general views shared by most feminists. While feminists may acknowledge the importance of both biological and sociocultural factors in producing gender differences, most of them share the basic assumption that gender is socially produced and culturally organized. This is because our genetic endowment can, to a considerable extent, be modified by environmental factors.

Sherry B. Ortner, who has made significant contributions to the work of feminist anthropology, dealt with the issue of the universality of female subordination in a now classic essay 'Is Female to Male as Nature is to Culture?' (1972). She argued that the social perception of women's involvement with nurturing and domestic roles leads to the identification of women as being closer to 'nature', while men supposedly represent 'culture', which is seen as superior. Ortner's view of the nature/culture dichotomy, strongly influenced by Levi-Strauss' structuralism, gained popularity, especially among feminists in the 1970s, because it supported the notion of universal male domination. In later years, more and more researchers began to emphasize cultural particularity rather than universality. For example, Karen Sacks, in her work, *Sisters and Wives: The Past and Future of Sexual Equality* (1979), points out that female subordination is not inevitable, nor is it the same always and everywhere. She argues that it is affected by the economic organization of societies. In this way, Ortner's binary view based on Levi-Strauss' structuralism lost currency because it failed to take into account variable cultural as well as historical realities.

In later work Ortner breaks away from the tradition of Levi-Straussian structuralism. In a 1981 essay, she argues that 'certain nongender-based principles of social organization take precedence over gender itself as a principle of social organization' (1981: 396) in hierarchical societies. As a result, Ortner continues, 'men's and women's statuses are more similar to one another's than to persons of either sex at other levels' (1981: 397). This explains why Sacks concludes that 'women's gender identities are not analytically separable from their racial and class identities' and advocates a theoretical framework that would 'comprehend class, race and gender oppression as parts of a unitary system' (1989: 545–6). These discussions also illustrated the fact that the conceptualization of gender identity formation could not be simply reduced to class; the classical Marxist approach was too narrow and ethnocentric. It required a broader framework in order to tackle the issue of gender identity. Most feminists today therefore acknowledge the importance of taking into account various types of inequalities, such as racism, class inequality, ageism, and discrimination against gays and lesbians.

Joy Hendry (1985) refers to the importance of considering the diversity of gender relations and marriage across cultures. First, she provides useful insights into the extent to which the Japanese case resembles or follows the trend in other industrialized societies. While she acknowledges that all industrialized societies share numerous common features in their marriage trends, she also emphasizes that the Japanese case is characterized by some persistent basic differences. 'Kingsley Davis suggests that marriage in Japan is some thirty years behind that of the United States, but evidence shows that the situation may be more complex' (Hendry 1985: 197).

The common features include medical progress, increased life expectancies and reliable birth control. These have led to later marriage and to a decline in fertility. Also, the growing number of married women in the labour force is closely linked to increased domestic efficiency (vacuum cleaners, washing machines, dish washers, and so on). And just like other industrialized societies, the trend in Japan is towards the nuclear family, rather than three- and four-generational families, because industrialized societies require flexibility and mobility.

On the other hand, Hendry continues, the ideology of marriage in Japan is fundamentally different from those seen in other countries, in terms of spouse selection and marital behaviour. For example, she points out the different connotations attached to individualism and notes that 'The Japanese word for individualism hardly escapes the connotations of the word for selfishness' (1985: 198). In theory, the current Japanese Constitution, based on the Western ideology of individualism, guarantees equal rights between husbands and wives. Marriage concerns only the two parties involved. However, in practice, Hendry suggests, marriage is still very much a family matter. She also notes that in the early part of the twentieth century marriages based on emotional attachment were considered foolish. Hendry thus points out that in order to understand the present situation or the future of marriage, it is essential to incorporate a historical dimension (1985: 199).

I agree with Hendry's view that historical and cultural perspectives are essential for the understanding of changes in marital behaviour. In other words, Hendry's discussion rightly emphasizes the role of culture in creating men and women through the prevailing gender ideologies at particular points of time in history. However, particularly in recent years, researchers have shifted their emphasis to the idea of how men and women manipulate and/or conquer culture. Ortner (1996) argues that there are hegemonic gender beliefs which mould men and women, but that not every aspect of human behaviour is determined by these. She notes 'whatever the hegemonic order of gender relations may be . . . it never exhausts what is going on. There are always sites, and sometimes large sites, of alternative practices and perspectives available, and these may become the bases of resistance and transformation' (1996: 18). Ortner promotes practice theory which 'seeks to explain the relationship(s) that obtain between human action, on the one hand, and some global entity which we call "the system," on the other' (1984: 148). Based on this theory, she argues that human beings, at least to some extent, have the power to transform 'the system' or the world they live in. In her words, they are 'actors [who] play with skill, intention, wit, knowledge, intelligence' (Ortner 1996: 12) – are capable of moulding their own destinies.

To return to Hendry's view on individualism in Japan, she suggests that the idea of individualism is not prevalent in Japanese society because the concepts of individualism and selfishness are closely related in the Japanese mind and language. Her work was published in 1985, and it is arguable whether her analysis still applies almost 20 years on. Even if there is ambivalence about the value of individualism at the level of public discourse, there is considerable evidence suggesting that 'individualism' of a kind (e.g. expecting personal satisfaction) seems to be quite widespread in Japanese society, particularly in the very recent decades.

A similar argument about individualism is made in *Onnatachi no Shizukana Kakumei: 'Ko' no Jidai ga Hajimaru* (Women's Quiet Revolution: The Dawn of the 'Individualist' Era). The book was published in 1998 by the *Nihon Keizai Shinbun*, the leading Japanese financial newspaper. The authors of the book argue that women in particular show a tendency to take a more individualistic approach to life by emphasizing their own values, and that 'a quiet revolution' is already taking place in areas such as the workplace, marriage, childbirth, and childrearing. They assert that this quiet revolution, emphasizing 'individualism' rather than simply accepting 'collectivism' or group-oriented thinking, will restore vitality to society. And in fact during the past few decades, Japanese women have been more eager to lead a lifestyle which emphasizes personal satisfaction. The recent trend in the postponement of marriage is a manifestation of this phenomenon and my case studies in the following chapters provide further examples.

Methodology and the field

I have used two main procedures in examining the issue: literature review and fieldwork. First, I reviewed the literature on Japanese marriage practices in both English and Japanese, including social scientific writing, newspapers, and journals. Several topics of my book have been examined through some literature that provided historical and/or comparative perspectives. These approaches have been extremely useful in obtaining insights into the norms and values held by people living in specific social and cultural contexts at particular points of time in history. Also, these perspectives have been effective in elucidating different human behaviours and experiences built into the systems of various cultures. I have also used material taken from Japanese popular culture such as films, magazines, and marriage sites on the internet. In this book, material obtained from popular culture has been especially constructive and helpful on the theme of masculinity to encapsulate how Japanese men conceptualize the idea of 'manliness'.

In addition to this literary research, I carried out fieldwork in Tokyo for about three months in total during 1999 and 2000. I first visited an institution called the Japan Youth Foundation[6] where a programme called '99 Tokyo 21st Century

College' was held in 1999. This was formerly known as '*Hanamuko Gakkō*' or 'Bridegroom School', and the programmes were primarily designed to educate men of all age groups, to become eligible bachelors or better husbands. I have tried to encapsulate the school's methods and the light that they shed on marriage behaviour in contemporary Japan. I also examined the participants' perceptions and expectations of marriage through a series of interviews. There were about 40 participants in total, of whom I was able to interview six unmarried individuals (one man and five women) who were aged in their 30s, either working or living in the Tokyo Metropolitan area. I then asked the six to introduce me to friends in similar situations. This snowball approach generated a total of 29 interviews, including 13 men and 16 women (see Appendix 1). Each of the 29 interviewees contributed a 2–5 hour-long interview, with the average interview lasting 3.5 hours. I tape-recorded some of the interviews in order to concentrate on the topics and the dynamics of the interview, followed by subsequent transcription. In some cases, the informants felt uncomfortable with my use of a tape recorder, in which case the method of note taking was chosen. I continuously kept contact with some of my interviewees through e-mails.

All of my interviews were carried out with an interview guide containing questions (see Appendix 2). The questions were designed to find out how unmarried young Japanese people perceive marriage and alternatives to it. Yet the study of marriage, including the issues concerning delay or avoidance of marriage, is such a broad theme that it was essential to focus on certain topics. Consequently the main questions were focused on the interviewees' values and beliefs, including their expectations of marriage and their ideal images of prospective partners, as well as their personal relationship patterns; for instance, how and with whom they actually spent their free time. Semi-structured interviews consisting of main and subsidiary questions were used. This allowed me to abandon the script in order to follow up on what people said with questions that I did not necessarily plan. In this way, I could explore what appeared to be meaningful to each participant, which resulted in my obtaining some most informative responses.

As mentioned earlier, the recent issue of '*kekkon-nan*' or 'difficulties in getting married' first appeared among farmers living in rural areas but the problem has also extended to those living in the urban areas. I focused on people in the Tokyo area because it is in urban areas that changes of attitudes about marriage *per se* have been most pronounced, whereas in rural areas the '*kekkon-nan*' may result at least in part from the lack of appeal to women of a rural way of life. Also, I decided to interview people aged in their 30s, because this group has shown one of the most rapid increases in the proportion of never-married men and women since 1975. The Population Census by the Ministry of Internal Affairs and Communications reports that only 14.4 per cent of men and 7.7 per cent of women were not married in the 30–34 age group in 1975, whereas by 2005 the figures had risen sharply to 47.1 per cent for men and 32 per cent for women. People aged in their 30s are of special significance in that they may still be seriously interested in marriage and are not completely out of the marriage market, yet they have not conformed to mainstream social expectations and are thus pushing up the age of marriage and the proportion of never-married people. Silverman points out that purposive sampling allows a researcher to choose a case because it illustrates some feature or process in which he or she is interested. He warns, however, that this does not in itself justify the selection of that case. 'Rather,' Silverman argues, 'purposive sampling demands that we think critically about the parameters of the population we are interested in and choose our sample case carefully on this basis' (2000: 104).

1   Perceptions and expectations of marriage in Japan

Introduction

One day when I was travelling on the Tokyo subway, I picked up a free magazine titled *L25* published by a company called Recruit.[1] The magazine is targeted at those so called 'OL' (office ladies) between the ages of 25 and 34 working in the Tokyo Metropolitan area. A small column reads '*Dekichatta [kek]kon tte dō omou?*' (What do you think about shotgun weddings?) The magazine reports that such marriages are on the rise. The Japanese Ministry of Health, Labour, and Welfare (2005a) also reports that in 2000, 26 per cent of first-born babies were conceived before marriage, which is a 100 per cent increase over the 13 per cent recorded in 1980. The rise has been even more dramatic among younger women, as 58 per cent of first-born babies delivered in 2000 to women aged 20–24 were conceived before marriage, compared with 20 per cent in 1980 (Ministry of Health, Labour, and Welfare 2005a).

The rapid increase in pregnant brides has opened a new market for some companies. One insurance company, AIU, started a new type of travel insurance that covers pregnant brides going abroad for their honeymoon. Wacoal, a female underwear manufacturer, saw potential for profits in producing wedding dresses for pregnant brides, using the slogan 'beautiful yet gentle dresses for the maternal body' in an advertisement.

These news items show the extremes to which Japanese couples will go to avoid giving birth out of wedlock. Indeed, the rate of children born out of wedlock remains extremely low in Japan, running consistently at only about 1 to 2 per cent of total births since around 1960 (National Institute of Population and Social Security Research 2003). This reveals a strong normative tie between legal marriage and reproduction. Countries in the West show a weaker tie, and according to Ochiai (1997: 173) the extra-marital birth rate in Japan is one-tenth that of Germany, one-twentieth that of Britain, and less than one-fortieth that of Scandinavian countries.

The prevalence of extra-marital births in the West, especially the northern and western European countries is closely associated with a high prevalence of unmarried cohabitation. Leaving home before marriage is supposed to encourage both formal marriage and cohabitation, but a large proportion of unmarried people in Japan live with their parents, a phenomenon often condemned by conservative Japanese social commentators. Suzuki, for instance, says that it 'discourages autonomy and decision making ability in their own lives' (2006: 23). In 2005, for instance, 70.3 per cent of unmarried Japanese men and 76.4 per cent of unmarried Japanese women between the ages of 18 and 34 still lived with their parents (National Institute of Population and Social Security Research 2007a). What is intriguing is the fact that a large number of unmarried Japanese are delaying their marriage without forming any kind of consensual or 'paperless' unions.

In order better to understand this and other aspects of contemporary Japanese views of marriages, the next section will briefly discuss the cultural-historical background.

Cultural-historical background

Pre-war

The *ie seido* or 'family system' was considered a cornerstone of Japanese society until the end of the Second World War. The family system was hierarchical in structure, providing priority to family members based on gender, age, and birth. It was based on the Confucian ethic that supported a patriarchal family, which directed people as a 'conscience-driven guide' especially among the Samurai (warrior) class and some rich merchants during the Tokugawa feudal period (1603–1868). As discussed in more detail in a later chapter, the Confucian doctrine was not pervasive among the majority social group – the farming class – until the Edo period. Thus Wagatsuma and De Vos (1984) note that relationships between family members among the rural peasants seemed to be more intimate and egalitarian than among the Samurai class. However, the Confucian ethic and its values permeated the whole of society during the Meiji period (1868–1912) as the government promoted the idea of Confucian ethics as the basis of national moral education.

Confucian values stressed the subordination of the individual to a larger group and directly affected mate selection. Individual decision-making by people of a lower class also came to be viewed as improper and rebellious with regard to both family and society. The prime objective of marriage was the continuation of lineage and therefore mate-selection was controlled by family members through a form of arranged marriage (*miai*). Dore states that

> 'Arranged marriage' means that the parties were brought together expressly for the purpose of marriage on the initiative of parents, a friend of the family or a go-between. It means also that the initial criteria of selection were objective ones. (1999: 167)

The patriarchal family system was officially supported by the Meiji Civil Code, which legitimized the power of the head of the family over other family members, and made women legally inferior to men. All this brought about changes in the concept of, and attitude towards, marriage among the majority population, i.e. the farmers (Wagatsuma and De Vos 1984).

When the prime objective of marriage was the continuity of family lines, parenthood played a significant role not only in terms of continuation of lineage but also to provide emotional fulfilment, especially among women, who were placed in an inferior situation.

> For those who are married according to arrangement, the marriage does not become complete until they produce children. The arrival of the first child is the consummation of the marriage, the fulfilment of the expected function of the marriage. In other words, they get married not so much for the purpose of becoming husband and wife as for becoming father and mother.
>
> (Blood 1967: 82)

Furthermore, many couples in arranged marriages, finding a lack of genuine affection in the relationship, gained something emotionally from the arrival of the first child. This was probably more so among women. Many who felt dissatisfied with their husbands actually looked forward to becoming mothers through which they gained emotional satisfaction and social acceptance (Sechiyama 1996; Blood 1967).

Post-war

After the war, the *ie seido* or family system was abolished, through the 1947 Constitution and associated Civil Code. The new constitution assured the freedom of choice of spouses and both men and women became able to marry without the consent of parents. The following is Article 24, regarding marriage:

> Marriage shall be based only on the mutual consent of both sexes and it shall be maintained through mutual cooperation with the equal rights of husband and wife as a basis. With regard to choice of spouse, property rights, inheritance, choice of domicile, divorce and other matters pertaining to marriage and the family, laws shall be enacted from the standpoint of individual dignity and the essential equality of the sexes
>
> (Prime Minister of Japan and His Cabinet).

Edwards notes that all these changes tended to 'weaken the concept of marriage as a duty toward the house' in popular thought (1989: 6).

Despite the revision of the Meiji Civil Code, the statistics clearly reveal that the number of love marriages exceeded the number of arranged marriages only after the late 1960s. This suggests that despite the legal change in the family system, it took some years for the Japanese to adopt the new principle as a new ideal. Wagatsuma and De Vos argue that arranged marriages still continued even among those who expressed a preference for a marriage based on their personal choice and that this was due to deeply rooted social and family pressure. Another possibility could be that arranged marriages were easier to accept psychologically for many young people, as free choice in marriage was often viewed as a form of rebellion towards parents and society. Thus, even after the revision of the Civil Code, arranged marriages dominated as a preferred method of mate-selection (Wagatsuma and De Vos 1984). Cultural constraints imposed on individuals as well as norms surrounding marriage thus affected people's actual behaviour.

Among those constraints we may include the dominant view of human nature that underlies thinking on marriage. It is often asserted that Japanese culture has tended to encourage interdependency. For instance, Walter Edwards describes this interdependent view of marriage as 'complementary incompetencies' which help to hold or bind the marriage together (1989: 120). He argues that the Japanese tend to view themselves as 'incompetent' when alone, and only through marriage or other group association do they become competent. He notes that

> Japanese notions of gender make marriage necessary because individuals – both men and women – are always incomplete; their deficiencies, moreover, are complementary. Men need women to manage both their money and their domestic lives. Women need men to provide economic security and proper representation for the family in the public domain. (1989: 123)

Furthermore, he asserts that in Japan getting married is a basic mark of adulthood, carrying with it social responsibilities and an achievement of independence as a couple. Remaining single 'carries the severe implications of immaturity and lack of moral responsibility' (1989: 124). Although the prejudice against non-marriage seems to be weakening, the view described by Edwards remains influential, informing such phenomena as the denigration of 'parasite singles'[2] that I will discuss later. By the same token, once people have entered into married life, any pursuit of individualism which threatens the harmony of the family is perceived as being selfish in Japanese society. Edwards notes,

> Anyone who asserts he is his own man, complete in himself, is by definition *wagamama* – selfish, heedless of his interdependence with others, unwilling to recognize and accede to the constraints that social relations invariably entail. In short, like the child who thinks only of himself, he is immature.
> (Edwards 1989: 126)

These attitudes are reflected in strong ethical norms regarding the correct approach to marriage – norms that have not necessarily changed that much from the days when arranged marriage was very much expected. A survey conducted by the *Asahi Shinbun* (1 January 1998) asking people for their 'image of marriage' revealed that the most popular keyword among women was '*nintai*' (patience). The most popular answer among men in almost all age groups was '*sekinin*' (responsibility). It can be argued that commitment, especially social commitment defined as 'a sense of obligation to the relationship rather than a positive feeling about the partner' (Kayser 1993: 11), is still one important factor that keeps spouses together in Japan. The belief still persists that marriage is a lifetime commitment, although social pressure and constraint against ending their marriage is somewhat weakening now.[3] People are still quite concerned about how they are viewed by the general public, and at the same time, and the belief that parents should remain together for the sake of the children also remains strong to this day.

Perceptions of marriage in Japan today

With a strong contemporary emphasis on the ideal of romantic love marriages, the number of love marriages came to exceed that of arranged marriages, and today the proportion of love marriages is over 85 per cent (Ministry of Health and Welfare 1996). This indicates that the value of marriage and family has been changing in important ways. This change has been particularly notice-able among women. For example, the White Paper on Social Welfare in 1998 reported that more women are in favour of postponing their marriage 'until they find the ideal person', compared with men, who are more seriously concerned about the *tekireiki* or 'marriageable age' (Ministry of Health and Welfare 1998).[4] Furthermore, a national government survey indicated that changes in women's attitudes towards marriage were the greatest in the 1980s, and by 1990 only 13.8 per cent of Japanese women reported that they viewed marriage as 'a woman's happiness' (*josei no kōfuku*), down from 39.7 per cent in 1972 and 30.4 per cent as recently as 1984 (Ministry of Health and Welfare 1996). Young women today are redefining the concepts of marriage and family and seeking a way to fulfil their aspirations for happiness within marriage. Women are generally rejecting the conventional male norms of leaving women to do domestic chores, being allowed to pursue a career only with the husband's tolerance and consent (Jolivet 1997).

It is important to determine what sort of women are the forerunners in regard to changing views towards marriage. There seem to be three important variables that significantly affect women's age at first marriage, namely women's academic background, regional differences, and age cohort. First, there is a clear correlation between the timing of first marriage and educational attainment. It was reported that in 1997 the average age at first marriage was 22.8 among graduates from junior high school, 25.3 among high school graduates (co-educational only), 26.4 among junior college and vocational school graduates, and 27.4 among four-year college and postgraduates (National Institute of Population and Social Security Research 1998). According to the 1995 National Survey on Lifestyle Preferences by the Economic Planning Agency, women with higher educational achievements tend to support the *jiritsu gata* marriage (in which husband and wife maintain their own independence) rather than *teishu kanpaku gata* (in which the husband leads and dominates the family). This survey reports that 18.8 per cent of junior high graduates, 28.2 per cent of high school graduates, 29.5 per cent of junior college graduates, and 35.4 per cent of four-year college graduates supported *jiritsu gata* while 11.5, 8.6, 6.8 and 2.1 per cent respectively supported *teishu kanpaku gata*. Highly-educated women's attempts to build more egalitar-ian relationships can also be seen from their preference for finding marriage partners whose age is closer to their own. Graduates from junior high school prefer to marry men who are on average 3.35 years older, 2.75 for high school, 2.57 for junior college and vocational school, and 2.37 for four-year college graduates (Institute of Population Problems, Ministry of Health and Welfare 1993). When asked about the role that women themselves value most, the majority of female graduates from four-year colleges continued to place their role as a family member as the first priority (57.4 per cent). Yet, a substantial minority of females in this group (31.3 per cent) supported the idea of pursuing individual goals and purposes, compared to just 14 per cent of high school graduates and 12.1 per cent of junior high school graduates (Economic Planning Agency 1994: 13). These surveys appear to indicate significant changes in the perceptions and expectations of marriage among highly-educated women (especially four-year college graduates).

Second, high educational attainment is usually associated with greater opportunities to increase income. For instance, the average monthly wage of female high school graduates in 2007 was 200,100 yen while four-year college graduates and holders of postgraduate degrees averaged 280,200 yen (Ministry of Health, Labour, and Welfare 2008). This is an important point for this study because in areas of the country where women earn higher salaries which is predominantly in urban areas, there is a tendency to postpone marriage. For instance, in 1995 the three regions with the highest female incomes, Tokyo, Kanagawa, and Chiba, maintained higher female average ages at first marriage, 27.3, 26.7, and 26.5 years of age respectively (Economic Planning Agency 1997), compared to the nationwide average age of 26.3 (National Institute of Population and Social Security Research 2001).

One reason why highly educated women postpone marriage is probably that they are aware they will forego the opportunities for earning such high incomes by staying at home as a result of marriage and/or child-rearing.[5] At the same time, women with higher educational backgrounds perceive careers differently. When female graduates from four-year colleges were asked about the reason for their participation in the labour force in a 1991 survey, most women (53.8 per cent) answered that they wished to make the best use of their abilities and possessed a strong desire to become economically independent. Only 9.9 per cent of junior high graduates, 13.6 per cent of high school graduates, and 34.9 per cent of junior college graduates replied in the same manner (Seimei Hoken Bunka Sentā [Life Insurance Culture Centre] 1992 cited in Toshitani *et al.* 1996).

Third, if women's perceptions of marriage are evaluated and analyzed based on age cohort, women of the younger generation tend to have more egalitarian ideas. In response to a question about ideal family types in a 1998 survey, more people in the younger generation supported *katei nai kyōryoku gata* marriage (husband and wife cooperating with each other) while fewer supported *yakuwari buntan gata* marriage (with a clear division of labour between men as breadwinners and women as housewives) (NHK Broadcasting Culture Research Institute 1998). In short, these data indicate that young urban women with high academic backgrounds are the ones who tend to delay their marriages and have changing perceptions of marriage, education, and career.

In contrast, men's ideas and attitudes towards marriage, 'have evolved much less rapidly than women's' (Jolivet 1997: 165), thus creating discrepancies between the sexes in their attitudes towards marriage (Jolivet 1997; Ohashi 2000; Iwao 1993; Tsuya and Mason 1995). In response to a 1992 survey question about the qualities regarded as the most important in deciding on prospective marriage partners, 80.6 per cent of unmarried women aged in their 20s and 30s replied that compatibility of personality is most important. Nonetheless, only 46.8 per cent of men in the same age group thought that women highly valued this factor. This suggests that men are not fully aware of the factors regarded as most important by women in the selection of their prospective marriage partners. Also, 59.0 per cent of unmarried women in their 20s and 30s believed that women should have careers just like men while only 37.3 per cent of men in the same age group agreed (National Survey on Lifestyle Preferences Fiscal Year 1992, cited in White Paper on the National Lifestyle Fiscal Year, Economic Planning Agency 1995). Despite women's eagerness to build more egalitarian relationships with their future husbands, these surveys show the difficulties women face in finding the 'right' men who are open to such relationships; another important cause of the recent postponement of marriage in Japan.

One possible approach to explaining the changing marriage pattern of Japanese women may be found in the economic theory introduced by Gary Becker (1981). Becker argues that the economic incentive for women to marry has been reduced because of their higher earning capability. Exchange theory also supports his argument, which states that love and attraction are most likely to occur when the people involved perceive an advantage resulting from the contributed and received resources. Becker describes single men and women as potential traders and argues that people marry because each has something different to offer, i.e. women as homemakers and men as providers, creating a mutual dependence between the sexes. Therefore, Becker argues that 'the gain from marriage is reduced by a rise in the earnings and labor force participation of women and by a fall in fertility because a sexual division of labor becomes less advantageous' (Becker 1981: 248). With better levels of education today, more women are capable of finding well-paid jobs, resulting in their no longer being so dependent on men for economic support.

Becker's economic model, however, is open to criticism. Some argue that the theory 'does not recognize collectively generated or agreed-upon norms and sanctions – what other social scientists commonly refer to as "culture"'(Mason and Jensen 1995: 5). There is no doubt that different cultures comprise different values and beliefs, and so people's perception of marriage differs across cultures. In this regard, Mason and Jensen (1995) argue that there is more than enough evidence to prove that while the idea of marriage as a source of economic security has become less important, its value as a source of companionship has been greatly emphasized in the West, especially since the Second World War. They quote an example from Oppenheimer and Lew's (1995) study finding that American women with high education and high earnings do not postpone their marriage and in fact they show a tendency to marry earlier than less-educated and lower-earning American women. 'In sum, greater earned income seems to facilitate marriage formation or to make a young woman a more desirable marriage partner, rather than to be used as the means of "buying out" of marriage' (Oppenheimer and Lew 1995: 131). Therefore Mason and Jensen assert that this phenomenon indicates changing perceptions of marriage in the United States. They go on to examine the Japanese case, quoting Tsuya and Mason's (1995) findings that in contrast to the case of women in the US, increased educational and economic opportunities among young Japanese women provide the most credible reason for the recent postponement of marriage in Japan. Mason and Jensen conclude that the fact that 'highly educated Japanese women marry later than do their less-educated counterparts may reflect the continued traditionality of the Japanese family system – a traditionality that includes evaluating marriage primarily in terms of the division of labour between the spouses' (Mason and Jensen 1995: 6). The comparison between the US and Japan suggests that changing marital behaviour must be considered in context. A single factor cannot be assumed to have identical consequences always and everywhere. Rather, it depends on how it combines with other issues.

Findings from the fieldwork: the lingering popularity of marriage in Japan

Although the phenomenon of late marriage is becoming more apparent, the fact remains that a high proportion of Japanese people do eventually marry – 84.6 per cent of men and 93.2 per cent of women by the age of 50 as of 2005.[6] In a 2005 survey that asked unmarried people about their marital intentions, 87.0 per cent of men and 90.0 per cent of women aged between 18 and 34 responded that they 'intend to get married in the future' (National Institute of Population and Social Security Research 2007a). Compared with some industrialized countries in the West, Japan can still be regarded as a '*kaikon shakai*', a society where marriage is the norm. A question therefore arises. As I noted earlier, a national government survey (1996) suggested that young Japanese women are less attracted to the idea of marriage, with only 13.8 per cent stating that they viewed the idea of marriage and happiness as necessarily related. Why, then, do an overwhelming majority of Japanese women still wish to get married?

In this regard, qualitative research based on interviews with 16 unmarried women in their 30s provided me with some useful insights into how they actually view marriage at a personal level. All were highly educated women who were university graduates, except for one informant who graduated from a women's junior college. They fit into the category identified by Tsuya and Mason (1995), of highly educated Japanese women who tend to marry later than their less-educated sisters. There were many reasons why they remained unmarried, three of which appeared especially salient; (1) When they were in their 20s, many of them were determined to marry only if they could find an ideal partner; (2) others were reluctant to lose the freedom of being single; and (3) others gave their profession priority over marriage. This was made possible by the fact that most informants earned enough money to support themselves and those who earned less still lived with their parents. Under these circumstances, they did not have to marry for financial reasons.

However, 10 of these 16 informants said that they now enthusiastically wished to marry. When they were asked for their reasons, four out of the ten informants said that they simply wanted to gain personal and emotional satisfaction. One informant, Yuki (34), once sent me an e-mail, quoting a *tanka* (a Japanese poem of thirty-one syllables) as a medium to express her feelings. The *tanka* Yuki quoted was written by a female poet of around the same age, named Machi Tawara. It reads: '*Samuineto hanashi kakereba samuineto kotaeru hitono iru atatakasa.*' Slightly abbreviated, this means something like: 'the warmth of having somebody who will say *yes it is cold isn't it* when you say *isn't it cold.*' Yuki portrays herself as searching for someone who can give her the comfort of knowing that there is someone there for her when she needs him. Perhaps Yuki's view is not exactly an ideal of passionate love but rather one of companionship. In a way, her attitude can be seen as containing expectations of marriage that are not very high, though one senses some deep emotions just below the surface.

All informants were asked about their views on cohabitation, an option where one might gain emotional satisfaction simply by living together with one's boyfriend without getting married. Most informants showed a strong preference for legal marriage rather than cohabitation. To most informants, the superiority of marriage to cohabitation was 'common sense' – a matter too obvious to require explanation. One respondent, Ayako (31), verbalized this instinct by saying that she would feel less threatened by the danger of breaking up with the partner once married. Indeed, a marriage contract binds a couple by law and since it is presumed to last forever, the relationship is more difficult to end (Bardwick 1980).

While four of the ten interviewees who wanted to marry simply expressed the desire for emotional fulfilment, the other six replied that they wanted emotional fulfilment and also would like to have children. There was a stronger desire to marry quickly among those women who replied that they wanted to have children. This was because they were seriously concerned about the so-called 'biological clock' and this influenced their behaviour. Shiori, a 32-year old professional woman, working in an Investment Advisory Company as a fund manager, is one example. Her annual income is as much as ¥ 20–30 million (approximately equivalent to US$ 150,000–230,000)[7] and thus she earns more than enough to support herself.

When Shiori was 31 years old, her grandmother passed way. This was the first time she had experienced the death of someone close to her, making her aware of the mortality of her parents and that one day she would have to live alone. From this point, she started to think seriously about marrying and said that she would be able to lead a more emotionally fulfilling life by living with someone intimate.

It proved to be no easy matter to find a partner who could meet her expectations. Even though she said that the man's income was not important as long as there was mutual respect and understanding, she went on to say that she wanted him to be successful and enjoy his work, maybe implying that finance is a consideration. It is possible that because of her personal success she would find it extremely difficult to find the 'perfect' partner. Her expectations might be too high, making it difficult for anyone to come up to her standards and requirements.

Also, before her grandmother died, Shiori was told by her that she should 'at least' bear a child. She feels the same way and strongly wishes to have children now. To the question of how she viewed having extra-marital children, she said that she perceived strong social sanctions against having them. This again reveals a strong normative tie between legal marriage and reproduction – children born out of wedlock in Japan amount to just under 2 per cent of births (National Institute of Population and Social Security Research 2003). In this regard, a country like Sweden shows a great difference as the rate of extra-marital births increased to as high as 51 per cent of all births in 1989, caused by the increase in the number of people cohabiting (Yuzawa 1995). Traditional norms about illegitimacy remain in Japan though gender roles are shifting.

As the interviews progressed, I started to wonder about the nature of inform-ants concerned about the 'biological clock'. They said it was a 'physical' issue but it seemed more like a psychological one, in that they felt compelled to get married. This was likely because they still desired to fulfil social and cultural expectations, one of the most important of which is marriage. The following statements clearly support this argument.

'Normal' to Get Married?

One of the female informants, Ayako (31), said that she felt people around her felt sorry for her as an unmarried woman. She gave the example of an incident at a *gōkon* (joint party which is similar to the idea of a blind date) with some men from one of the largest manufacturing companies in Japan. Four unmarried women who all happened to be 31 years old, and four men, some married and some not, came to this informal party. During the party, one 35-year old married man said to the women; 'If you are all 31 years old, I think it is strange not to find at least one of you married.' Ayako said that she would have been really shocked if she had received this kind of comment at a younger age, but after she had passed the age of 30, she felt with some feelings of resignation that this is how people regard unmarried women over 30.

Yuki (34) also revealed a similar experience. She said that from men's point of view, women's value drops dramatically from the age of around 28 or 29 and when a woman is over 30, she is regarded as 'old'. She furthermore noted that men seem to treat women in their 30s or 40s as 'sexually neutral' ('*chūsei*') and she believed that they only have two categories for women, '*onna no ko* (girls) or *obasan* (middle-aged women)'. In order to clarify the reasons that made her feel this way, she was asked if she could explain this with some concrete examples. She then raised one unpleasant experience when she went to a restau-rant with a subsection chief (*kakarichō*) and a young female colleague. As they were having dinner, the *kakarichō* said to the young girl, 'You should think about getting married soon.' Then she replied, 'Don't you have a daughter of my age?' The man replied, 'Yes, that's right. I am very concerned about her because she is *already 24*.' Yuki believed that this *kakarichō* knew she herself was well beyond that age and unmarried, but he still made such comments in front of her. On another occasion which happened a year previously when she was 33, while she was having a drink with a number of people, one drunk middle-aged man told her that she was '*tō ga tatte iru*'.[8] This means that you have passed the prime of youth. She told me that 'although he said this in a drunken moment, he has no right to say such things and a man like him lacks consciousness of fundamental human rights towards women.'

Another female informant even showed her own bias against people who remain unmarried. Mami (30) works in a small firm where they make and sell novelty goods. She fears that if she remains unmarried, she could become 'bitter'. Mami got this idea from a single female colleague in her 40s who had to quit the firm because of her temper and hysterical manner. Whether this woman really had to quit her job because of her temper is not the main concern here. Rather the way that Mami and most probably the people around her viewed this unmarried woman is of importance. The main issue is the bias and contempt with which Mami and other people viewed the woman because of her age and single status.

Informants seemed to have extremely firm beliefs that it is 'normal' to get married and have children, or that if you are 'normal' it is *atarimae no koto* (a matter of course) to get married and rear children. The prevailing ideology predisposes them to feel this way. Lunsing (2001) describes a similar view based on his ethnographic study of sexual relations in Japan. Lunsing's informants included many homosexual men who nonetheless married women out of deference for social norms. He states, '*Joshiki* [common sense] holds that marriage is what you do and they [his informants] had no reason to question that . . . only after marriage [they] started to wonder whether they took the right step . . . (2001: 84).' People who do not conform to this idea and remain unmarried have to face social stigma from the general public. Many scholars assert that there is a tendency among young Japanese women to place more importance on their personal life and their own independence rather than being concerned about the appropriate age for marriage. This does not mean that they are free from the stress and pressures imposed upon them by a society which still believes that women should be married and have a family by a certain age. To some extent, they even seem to have internalized these ideals. Although these women have economic independence, they still suffer from the 'normal' society's concepts of appropriate behaviour for women.

Conclusion

It should be clear by now that cultural values concerning the institutions of marriage, education, and career often interact to determine age at first marriage. For instance, as mentioned earlier, Japanese women with high educational backgrounds tend to perceive career as a way to fulfil personal desires. This affects their involvement not only in the workplace but also in the institution of marriage. I also discussed how young Japanese women are delaying their marriages because they are unable to find prospective marriage partners who can (or are willing to) live up to their changing perceptions and expectations of marriage based on more egalitarian relationships. This suggests that their ambition to get married has not changed but rather their expectations and perceptions of marriage have altered in important ways. In this regard, the phenomenon of delayed marriage should not simply be seen as a manifestation of a 'retreat from marriage'. Despite the discrepancies between the sexes in attitudes towards marriage, young Japanese women continue to internalize the idea of marriage as an important personal goal. The clue to this issue lies within the realm of culture, in that there is a normative pressure for 'normal' men and women to think that marriage is culturally required rather than a matter of individual choice. Yet while conventional discourses/ cultural ideas remain strong, there is also change, and one major possible cause of that change is the feminist movement. Chapter 2 will therefore examine the way feminism has been affecting Japanese marriage and fertility patterns. This analysis should help us understand why, how, and to what extent women's expectations and perceptions of marriage have shifted in recent decades.

2 The impact of feminist discourses on marriage and fertility

Introduction

It is generally assumed that Japanese women are lagging behind their Western counterparts in terms of their status and position within society. Some observers of Japanese feminism, both in and outside Japan, consider that the women's movement in Japan is too fragile and ineffective to change a society which considers feminism as a Western import without roots in Japanese society. On the other hand, in recent years Japanese feminists have been stressing the importance of indigenous feminism in Japan. They have been trying to identify the specific conditions of its development within the cultural context and to assert that *feminizumu* (feminism) is rooted in Japanese society (Ueno 1996). I believe it is important to acknowledge differences in women's lives cross-culturally and thus Japanese *feminizumu* needs to be considered in its indigenous historical, political, and cultural contexts. At the same time, however, the spread and intermixing of ideas and attitudes can no longer be prevented in a globalizing world and this can provide further strength and depth to Japanese feminism.

> [I]t is time to move beyond thinking strictly in terms of feminisms of nations or feminisms of cultures. *Feminizumu/josei undō* [Feminism/women's movement] is a product of specific historical occurrences both within and beyond Japan in the past several centuries. It is neither determined solely by culture or nation, nor is it free of the issues and values of Japanese culture.
>
> (White 1999: 38–9)

It is hard to deny the limitations of Japanese feminism which will be discussed later in this chapter. Recent years, however, have seen a significant cultural change in how women in Japan regard marriage. More women have been exposed to the analysis of women's issues through the emergence of women's studies, since about 1978, and the lively debates on feminism carried out, by and large, by a group of 'celebrity feminists' from about 1983 up to the present (White 1999). Yumiko Ehara, a Japanese feminist scholar, also notes that the changes of the 1970s and 1980s can be observed in the shift away from special interest groups to the domain of mainstream research and media (1993: 50).

Feminism in Japan has entered the lives of ordinary women to a greater or lesser degree and the changing attitudes of many young Japanese women towards women's issues have been influenced by these feminist ideals. I argue that while there have been *josei undō* or women's movements working on a global level, a defining characteristic of Japanese feminism today is its individual rather than movement-oriented approach.

One can posit that the ranks of feminists (or rather 'crypto-feminists') in Japan today could include those millions of young women who by delaying marriage and childbearing are changing Japanese society. Increasing numbers of young women, especially the highly educated, are postponing marriage because they resist their typical feminine gender roles as wives and mothers. They are far from 'typical feminists' and would not consider themselves as such, but they can be seen as 'crypto-feminists' who choose those elements of feminism that suit them. As Unger and Crawford say in relation to feminist influence more generally 'Even though not all young women label themselves feminists, the idea that women can and should have aspirations other than wife and mother has been widely accepted' (1992: 364). In this regard what is important is not whether they recognize themselves as feminists or not, but rather how they view issues concerning women and, more importantly, how they define themselves as 'women'. Furthermore, in her book *The Changing Meaning of Feminism: Life Cycle and Career Implications from a Sociological Perspective*, Peterson notes, 'Even if women individually define feminism, there will be common ground and issues that surface over and over again' (1998: 4). Indeed, there are many problems they face and share as 'women' and their growing liberal attitudes are likely to further aggravate their problems.

From these perspectives, I would accept Peterson's division of feminism into two basic approaches, of equal significance, and would support its definition in these broad terms: 'Feminism represents views and teachings about women who take either a movement-oriented approach in which people form groups and caucuses on behalf of women, or an individual-oriented approach where a woman defines her own ideas about being a woman' (Peterson 1998: 2). The second approach is extremely important for the understanding of the situation of Japanese single women today because 'it [feminism] is not a movement that reflects the reality here [Japan]' (Ueno 1997: 291). By contrast, the individual-based interpretation of feminism legitimately includes women who simply decide their own fates as women – and their decisions to delay marriage can cause major social consequences. The unprecedented fall in the birthrate is one of them. This fall will have a dramatic effect on the existing economic and social structure, including, to name but two, an aging society and a shrinking labour force.

The historical background to Japanese feminism

I would argue that Ueno's argument, that feminism in Japan is to be found more in the individual consciousness than in movements, is broadly correct. Nevertheless, there is a distinct tradition of a feminism movement in Japanese history, which is undoubtedly among the factors influencing the consciousness of Japanese women today. In this section I will briefly review the history of that movement. The analysis begins with the Meiji period which laid the foundations of modern Japan. It is followed by a discussion of two periods which saw the establishment of Japanese feminism on firmer ground: the early period of women's liberation in Japan between 1970 and 1975, and the period since 1975 up to the present. These two periods have shown significant cultural changes concerning women's issues, including the recent delayed marriage syndrome.

The Meiji period – the continued exclusion of women from politics

During the Meiji period (1868–1912) a dramatic transformation in the political, economic, social and legal spheres was required to modernize the country in order to prevent domination from the West. 'The Meiji government abolished hereditary restrictions on occupation and residence in 1868. During the 1870s the government abolished the hereditary military class and instituted a system of prefectures staffed by imperial appointees' (Nolte and Hastings 1991: 155). However, although the process of establishing a legal and institutional system in Japan brought some benefits to women, ironically, it also brought some new legal controls over women's rights. Although male suffrage was slowly extended in the growing democracy, women were excluded from it. Instead, women were pushed into the private sphere and were taught to be '*ryōsai kenbo*' or 'good wives and wise mothers'. This issue will be discussed in detail in Chapter 4.

There were some women who tried to improve the status of women in this era. They include the pioneering female activists of the Popular Rights Movement, Christian women, and Socialist women. These groups of women, each in their own way, worked enthusiastically to solve problems by means such as organizing campaigns against prostitution and concubines. Their activities also included campaigns for women's political rights. They attempted to reform Article 5 of the Public Peace Policy Law which prohibited women from convening, attending or speaking at political meetings or joining political organizations. Through their efforts the reform attempts passed the Lower House, only to fail in the House of Peers (Mackie 2003).

One reason for this failure was that these three prominent groups of women of the Meiji era, i.e. the female activists of the Popular Rights Movement, the Christian women, and the Socialist women, never consolidated their energies to work together to improve the status of women. Tokuza notes that 'class and ideological differences between the women of these three groups precluded their cooperation with one another; as a result, all the groups failed to achieve organizational connections with the huge constituency of working women' (1999: 56).

The plunge into militarism

The first issue of *Seitō* (Bluestocking) – a literary monthly magazine written, edited and published entirely by women – was published in 1911. At first *Seitō* approached women's problems from a literary angle, through poetry, drama and prose. Then the journal became more radical, openly criticized Japanese society and began to advocate women's liberation from oppression. *Seitō* created great controversy by claiming autonomy for women and challenging the Japanese family system. However, it had to cease publication in 1916 because of financial problems and changes in editorial policy as well as pressure from the government (Tokuza 1999). Overall, as Mackie (1996: 263) notes, *Seitō* was the most significant feminist manifestation in Japanese history up to the Second World War. The members continued their feminist activities, each in their own way, including the women's suffrage movement in the New Women's Organization or *Shin Fujin Kyōkai*.

The New Women's Organization – the first women's suffrage group – was founded by Raicho Hiratsuka, Fusae Ichikawa, and Mumeo Oku in 1920. The organization soon increased its membership to more than 200. Their first aim was the rescinding of Article 5 of the Public Peace Policy Law of 1900 which prohibited women's political activities. They managed to win a revision of Article 5 in 1922 and as a result women were allowed to attend, and participate in, political gatherings. Despite the continuing efforts of these feminists, as well as of many other women in various organizations, women had to wait until 1945 to enjoy full political participation (Sievers 1983).

The social climate changed after the Manchurian Incident in September 1931, when militarists and nationalists seized power in Japan. The government started to control all political and social groups advocating civil rights and this made it extremely difficult for feminists to continue their activities. The government, at the same time, successfully encouraged women to join national patriotic societies. These societies included *Aikoku Fujin no Kai* or the Patriotic Women's Society, founded in 1901, and *Dainihon Kokubō Fujin no Kai* or the Greater Japan Women's Defence Society, founded in 1932, which increased its membership from 40 in 1932 to 10 million in 1941 (Ikegami 1984). For the first time, the existing women's organizations were merged into a single organization, known as the Greater Japan Women's Association, under government guidance. These women were asked to show their 'patriotism': they sent off soldiers, helped injured soldiers and bereaved families, distributed food and supplies, and entered formal employment (Ikegami 1984). One of Japan's most famous feminists of the time, Itsue Takamure, was co-opted into the war effort, enthusiastically calling on women to spread Japan's 'matrilineal society' to other parts of the world (Oguma, 2002). Working women were even seen in the war-related heavy and machine industries. In this way, women displayed their talents and their ability to work in jobs formerly occupied by men. Unfortunately, however, their contribution also strengthened Japanese nationalism, militarism and overseas conquests.

Under occupation

After defeat in the war, Japan was put under US occupation until the peace treaty of San Francisco in September 1952. The American authorities began to democratize and demilitarize the country and they brought dramatic changes for Japanese women. All women over the age of 20 were finally given the right to vote in 1945, and in the following year women over the age of 25 were allowed to stand for office. These changes were based on the assumption that 'women would be more "peace loving" and challenge the militarist traditions of the pre-war state' (Mackie 1996: 266). Furthermore, the new constitution of 1947 which emphasized equality and individual rights tremendously improved women's positions. This historical background tends to portray female suffrage and women's individual rights in Japan as simply having been granted 'from above'. However, this perception neglects the efforts made by many Japanese suffragists and feminists in the pre-war period. Because of their assiduous efforts, Japanese women were able to take advantage of these legal changes in the immediate postwar period and move on to further improve their status during the second wave of feminism in the 1970s.

In the immediate postwar period, women's political activities can be best described as 'connecting politics and the kitchen'. Their political activities were focused on issues directly relevant to women's positions as housewives and mothers, such as pollution, consumer issues, and peace movements. However, the very fact of being involved in politics led women to a deeper awareness of the importance of power, and/or the lack of it. Thus they eventually began to examine gender relations – the power of men and of their institutional dominations over women – more critically and radically.

The Women's Liberation Movement in the 1970s

A new generation of feminists started to emerge in the late 1960s – Buckley (1994) notes that by the 1970s there were about 37,000 women's groups active in Japan. She also notes that these organizations often employed the strategies of nonaffiliation, decentralization, and local activity: this frequently led Western feminists to underestimate the ability of women in Japan for large-scale political action. Many of these Japanese activists were extremely wary of governmental support because of their experience during the war period: pre-war women's groups had been absorbed by the state, and co-opted for the war effort. Buckley adds that many Japanese feminists would argue that in Japan, a country where the state is strong and can get stronger through the co-option of large-scale movements, decentralization and fragmentation are the appropriate strategies for the success of women's liberation. These decentralized organizations of women published newsletters which came to be known as *minikomi* (mini-communications): media produced by individuals or small groups, as opposed to *masukomi* (mass communications, i.e. mass media). The *minikomi* functioned as an important network, closely connecting these small organizations, while each maintained its independence, focusing on its own activities (Buckley 1994: 157–8).

Several classic books of Western feminism were translated into Japanese during the 1970s and this had a significant impact on feminism in Japan. This does not simply mean that feminism was just another import from the West; rather it shows that there were similar problems shared by women in the West and in Japan. For these books to be translated into Japanese and published in Japan (let alone sold and read), there had to be people in Japan who had the will and desire to actually do that work – which they presumably would not have done without a sense of a shared common problem. Mackie (1996: 270) notes that 'In all of the advanced capitalist nations women were experiencing the contradiction of an education which seemed to promise self-fulfilment, and a labour market based on inequalities of class and gender.' Japanese women in *ūman ribu* or women's liberation, like their American counterparts, started to examine the conventions of their sexual behaviour and analyzed how they came to internalize sexual mores that emphasized women's passivity. They criticized the institution of marriage and some even began to experiment with new lifestyles including cohabitation or bearing illegitimate children (Tanaka, Y. 1995).

Scholars of Japanese feminism as well as those who were involved in the women's lib movement have distinguished the period of the early years of the movement (1970–75) from the *feminizumu* of today (White 1999). Many members of the women's liberation movement had been involved in the student movement of the 1960s and had become disillusioned by a leftism dominated by men. These activists thought that they were doubly oppressed, both by the rules of class and by men who controlled the system. This suspicion about hierarchical systems remains one of the most important features of the Japanese women's movement.

In the early 1970s there were attempts by conservative groups to prohibit abortions, previously allowed for economic reasons.[1] In fact, women in Japan were given access to abortion relatively earlier than in many countries of the West. This was because the immediate postwar government partially legalized abortion in 1948 in order to control the size of the population. Kanai argues that this effective legalization meant that freedom of abortion did not become a political issue in the feminist movement until there was a proposal to amend the Eugenics Protection Act to remove the economic reasons clause (Kanai 1996: 15). This was the social context behind the most fundamental demand of the women's liberation movement in the 1970s – for the recognition of the rights of women over their own bodies. That struggle developed very differently over the two key reproductive issues of abortion and the pill. Norgren (2001), in her book *Abortion before Birth Control: The Politics of Reproduction in Postwar Japan*, describes how medical and family planning organizations neatly engineered the legalization of abortion law and obstructed legalization of the contraceptive pill in order to enhance their own interests.

Mitsu Tanaka, formerly involved in the student movement, became a leading figure of this era. She formed the *Tatakau Onnatachi* or Fighting Women group in the early 1970s (Mackie 1996) to protect women's right to have abortions. This group was largely in charge of a *ribu taikai* or women's liberation rally held in August 1971. The rally was successful in that it attracted a large number of women from different social backgrounds yearning for social and political changes, and in this regard this rally was a 'turning point in the history of the Japanese women's liberation movement' (Tanaka, Y. 1995: 144). The early phase of the women's liberation movement can be characterized as grassroots consciousness-raising. Another *ribu taikai* was held in 1972. This rally led to the

establishment of *Ribu Sentā* or the Centre for Women's Liberation, which oper-
ated from September 1972 to May 1977 in Tokyo. The Centre had two major
objectives: to provide a place to exchange views among feminists, and to provide
a refuge for women in need of help (Mackie 2003).

Despite the activities carried out by many women's groups like the Fighting
Women, their behaviour became overshadowed by the guerrilla tactics used by
some flamboyant groups like *Chūpiren* or Alliance for Abortion and the Pill.
Chūpiren, led by Misako Enoki, used some exuberant strategies: these included
the occupation of public and corporate buildings to demand access to legalized
contraceptive pills (their use was banned at that time), and appearing in pink
helmets in the offices of unfaithful men. These incidents were widely ridiculed
by the mass media and their pink helmets soon came to symbolize the eccentricity
of the women's movement. Eventually the movement as a whole became seen as
radical and socially undesirable.

> Although *ribu* is said to have died in 1975, it seems to live on as both an
> embodiment of the negative stereotypes about women's movements in Japan
> generally and as a basis from which to interpret the ongoing struggles in
> Japan over women's issues.
>
> (White 1999: 92)

Feminizumu or feminism since 1975

As briefly mentioned earlier, scholars of Japanese feminism usually distinguish
the early phase of second wave feminism, *ūman ribu* (women's liberation)
which began in 1970 and ended in 1975 from contemporary *feminizumu* (White
1999). Kazuko Tanaka (1995) explains the reasons behind the changes since
1975 as follows. Feminism in Japan attained a certain degree of legitimacy – the
International Women's Year in 1975 and the subsequent International Decade
for Women 1975–85 brought a large degree of support to Japanese women. The
Japanese government was forced to tackle women's problems seriously and
ended up ratifying the UN (United Nations) Convention to Eradicate all forms
of Discrimination Against Women (CEDAW). The government also spent huge
amounts of money during the International Decade for Women and consequently
there are today various kinds of women's centres, offering adult education
classes, conferences, and meetings of community groups, located in almost every
prefecture and major city (Mackie 2003). Furthermore, the UN international
conferences brought a higher degree of awareness to Japanese women about
their position in Asia, and *vis-à-vis* the Third World. Japan was seen by many
Asian women as a nation exploiting other Asian countries by using their cheap
labour. Furthermore, the 'sex-tours' by Japanese men to Thailand and Korea
prompted an angry reaction from local feminists, who sometimes showed their
anger by demonstrating at airports against such group tours. This view of the
contemporary Japanese 'economic and sexual imperialism' was reinforced by

memories of the earlier Japanese political and military imperialism, symbolized, at its worst, by the use of many Asian women as 'comfort women' to satisfy the lust of Japanese soldiers.

The composition of the feminist movement has also changed since 1975. The members of the various women's groups that emerged in the mid-1970s were likely to be professional women, trying to make discernible changes in women's lives rather than simply raising women's consciousness. For instance, the largest feminist organization today, the International Women's Year Action Group, initiated by Diet members Fusae Ichikawa and Sumiko Tanaka, was established in 1975. The organization focused on specific issues such as overcoming discrimination against women in employment, education, the mass media, government and administration. As the members of the International Women's Year Action Group and some of its affiliated groups had access to the political process, it became possible to influence government plans and policies (Tanaka, K. 1995). These developments, particularly since 1975, are important to this book as they have brought significant changes in the social and personal awareness of Japanese women as a whole – the year 1975 corresponds to the beginning of the recent delayed marriage trend in Japan.

The Equal Employment Opportunity Law

The Equal Employment Opportunity Law (EEO) was passed by the Diet in 1985 and was enacted in 1986. Women's groups, such as the Organization for the Formulation of Our Own Equal Opportunity Act, had skilfully applied pressure on the government which was afraid of losing face and being shamed by international opprobrium had it failed to meet its obligations. The law mandated equal opportunity and equal treatment at work and in the job market for both sexes. However, this new legislation consisting of 'prohibitions' and 'exhortations' had big loopholes and placed only limited legal obligations on employers. The law prohibited discriminatory treatment in vocational training, fringe benefits and mandatory retirement age. It also banned mandatory retirement or dismissal for reason of marriage, pregnancy or childbirth. The law, however, merely encouraged firms to 'make efforts' to treat women and men equally in the main areas of differential treatment such as in recruitment, job assignment and promotion. This illustrated a powerful desire on the part of Japanese firms to maintain the existing male-centred personnel management system.

In order to meet the requirements of the law, increasing numbers of large firms have introduced the 'dual-track career system' – a managerial career track and a clerical non-career track. However, in a society where women are mainly responsible for the private sphere of the household, it is unrealistic for many women to choose the career track, while others are unwilling to accept the rigid male norms firmly established in the firms, i.e. working many years without interruption, accepting transfers and working overtime. This new dual-track career system has resulted in creating a small number of elite career women and a large majority of non-elite women still restricted to mundane clerical work.

Critics demanding the reform of the EEO law, which provided only limited new rights for women, became more and more vocal. This led the Diet to make substantial revisions in the law in 1997, and these became effective in April 1999. The revisions prohibited discriminatory treatment in recruitment, hiring, placement and promotion. Furthermore, from around the time of the introduction of the EEO law, Japanese feminists also demanded the revision of the protection provisions of the Labour Standards Law which protected women from working overtime, from shift working, from working late at night, or from working in dangerous industries. They asserted that these protective clauses, directed at *all* working women, with an assumption that they are all potential mothers, in fact limited women's capacities to fully participate in the workforce. Mackie (2003: 181) notes,

> Protective provisions, then, are directed not at the physical reality of pregnancy for any individual woman but, rather, at an abstract potential. It was these provisions which caused most controversy in the context of the implementation of equal opportunity legislation.

Thus, the Labour Standards Law was also revised, abolishing all restrictions protecting female employees, with the exception of expectant and nursing mothers. These changes also became effective in April 1999. However, as Schoppa (2006) points out, this in fact makes it more difficult for women to combine work and childcare, as they can legally be forced to work overtime and so on, which reduces the flexibility required for working mothers.

The emergence of 'Academic Feminists' since the mid-1980s

The group of 'academic feminists' which emerged around 1985 has, right up to the present, played a major role in the debates about Japanese feminism. These included theoretical and political issues, as well as practical and personal: why women are oppressed, how to liberate them, how to improve their position at work and how to cope with domestic responsibilities, including motherhood. The debates by these academic feminists started with a discussion of ecofeminism in 1984.

This ecofeminism debate took place when Japan was establishing itself as an economic superpower. At the same time, this was also the period when the Japanese started to question the Western modernization model, leading some to call for 'Japanism', with its stress on indigenous tradition (Kanai 1996). In this nostalgic atmosphere, 'Motherhood and the fundamental value of women were taken up and praised against modern or industrialized society' (Kanai 1996: 10).

The two central figures of this debate were Yayoi Aoki, a freelance writer, and Chizuko Ueno, one of the best known academic feminists both within and beyond Japan. Aoki, a key promoter of ecofeminism, was severely criticized by Ueno and other feminists in the academic camp, primarily for her stress on the 'female principle' that (according to her critics) would push and lock women into their conventional nurturing role. In Ueno's words, Aoki's use of the concept could reinforce the idea 'that the maternal function is the only acceptable or worthwhile function for all women' (Ueno 1997: 281). This illustrates how *bosei* or motherhood has remained the pivotal issue for Japanese feminism.

Furthermore, Yoshiko Kanai (1996), another important academic feminist, asserted that the Japanese must seriously consider the fact that their affluent and highly consumerist lifestyle is closely related to the degradation of the environment and of people's lives in Asia and in the Third World. She noted that awareness of this issue would prevent ecofeminism from moving towards 'reactionary ideologies that celebrate motherhood and premodern communities, or to[wards] nationalist[ic] ideologies such as Japanism' (1996: 19).

Another controversy regarding *bosei* took place in the late 1980s. Once again widely taken up by the mass media, this was known as the Agnes debate. The debate started when Agnes Chan, a popular singer originally from Hong Kong, was criticized for bringing her infant into her workplace. People, including feminists, debated whether women with infants have the right to take their infants to work. This debate, sparked by criticism of one individual, led to a more general discussion about institutional problems, including the lack of childcare facilities, especially workplace-based childcare. The Agnes debate attracted wide attention among the public at the time when an increasing number of women were entering the workforce (Tanaka, K. 1995).

The sexual scandal concerning Prime Minister Sosuke Uno was also widely debated in the late 1980s. The newly chosen Prime Minister, leader of the Liberal Democratic Party (LDP), was discovered to be paying money to a *geisha* for sexual services. The media widely reported that Uno's sexual scandal led to a massive number of women suddenly turning against the perpetually ruling LDP, helping the Japanese Socialist Party to win the Upper House election of July 1989. However, feminists were very suspicious of this view and asserted instead that the defeat was primarily due to the recently introduced consumption tax (Buckley 1994). In other words, the feminists maintained that the election turned on a consumer and life-style issue, rather than a feminist one, and that the women who turned against the LDP were consumerist individualists not interested in the ultimate goal of women's emancipation.

This account of the historical background to feminism in Japan, including the recent debates by academic feminists, illustrates some of the limitations and characteristics of *feminizumu* in contemporary Japan. I will summarize some of the major points in the following section.

Feminism in Japan: characteristics and limitations

Motherhood

Motherhood is a key element in Japanese feminism just as it is in Japanese culture as a whole. It is considered one of the most, if not the single most, important of all vocations for women, who are expected to accept their roles as mothers with 'joy'. Ueno states

> . . . in Japan the mothering, nurturing function is the key concern of feminists and seen as something that must be protected. Our primary goal is not to be like men but to value what it means to be a woman. This aspect of Japanese feminism is deeply rooted in the history of the women's movement in Japan as well as the individual experience of women. It's a double-edged sword, I admit, but it is also fundamental to the identity of Japanese feminism. The emphasis on mothering over the individualism of American feminism is a characteristic shared by Eastern and some European women. (1997: 280)

Indeed, motherhood can be a double-edged sword because the combination of motherhood and career is an extremely heavy burden if you do not have enough legal backing to prevent discrimination. However, women should have the final say, as Ueno emphasizes in clarifying her position, 'What I am opposed to is any movement proposing that the maternal function is the only acceptable or worthwhile function for all women' (1997: 281). As motherhood is particularly problematic in the gender-biased society of Japan, the unprecedented decline in the birthrate during the past few decades, reaching the low of 1.26 in 2005 (Ministry of Health, Labour, and Welfare 2005b) can be seen as a rebellion of Japanese women against motherhood.

'Housewife feminism'

In 1982, Shigeo Saito, a freelance journalist, published his *Tsumatachi no Shishūki* (Autumnal Wives). This book not only became a bestseller but was also cited in the White Paper on Social Welfare, 1998 as a useful document of the way middle-class women lived in suburbia. The book showed how many dissatisfied women were closet drinkers or became mentally deranged. They were facing a situation similar to 'the problem that has no name' which surfaced among American women in earlier decades. In her well-known book of 1963, *The Feminine Mystique*, for example, Betty Friedan unmasked the myth of the 'happy housewife' and asserted that dissatisfaction with housewifery was caused to a large extent by financial and emotional dependence on husbands.

Under these circumstances, the second wave feminism of the 1970s and after questioned the myth of happy married life. Kanai notes that,

> The second wave of the feminist movement discovered that it was none other than 'the modern family' which constituted the apparatus dominating women in modernity. The 'modern family' seemed to ground gender hierarchy in a natural order between men and women, thus rendering its power relationship less visible. Consequently, patriarchal control in this private area emerged as something of deep significance for the feminist struggle.
>
> (Kanai 1996: 9)

However, in Japanese society,

> It has been difficult for 'housewife feminism' to look critically at the house-
> wives as a norm or at the social system which has institutionally supported
> the norm. As a result, feminist critiques of the sexual division of roles have
> not been able to confront the internal and subjective problems of sexual
> discrimination or to see the structural background of sexual discrimination
> as something shared by all women.
>
> (Kanai 1996: 9)

The limitations of 'housewife feminism' are causing many feminists to criticize
the current situation of the ecological movement in Japan. The movement is
run largely by housewives within the framework of their domestic responsibilities, i.e. their roles as wives and mothers in particular. Kanai (1996: 11) points
out that 'the elements of motherhood and eugenics coexist with the work many
women are doing in the anti-nuclear power, anti-nuclear weapons, safe food, and
anti-global warming movements.'

Since Japanese men are preoccupied with their work, they hardly have any
time or energy left to participate in citizen's movements. On the other hand,
because Japanese women are marginalized in Japanese society, they are, ironically enough, enabled to take part in these movements. Many feminists see this as
problematic not only because this phenomenon could simply enhance the existing
system based on gender, but also because they are extremely suspicious of the
extent to which these housewives would be willing to challenge their gender-segregated roles. Ueno (1997) notes that these housewives are definitely concerned
with women's issues but not in a feminist way: they lack the consciousness to
promote their independence or their rights as individuals. Buckley (1994: 182)
furthermore remarks that the material comfort achieved by middle-class housewives
is creating a new complacency. They are primarily concerned about 'quality-of-
life issues' such as housing, food quality, and leisure.

Under these circumstances, Japanese feminists today are trying to find a way to
motivate housewives to move beyond the so-called 'comfort zone'. It is exactly
this social context which has led some Japanese academic feminists, including
Yoshiko Kanai and Yumiko Ehara, to call for a revival of radical feminism. They
stress the need to understand that women's oppression cannot be simply a matter
of sexist ideas or an offshoot of class domination: neither liberal nor Marxian
feminism really understands the basis of women's oppression. The radical feminists argue that they have to re-examine the cultural and psychological oppression of women by linking these to the concepts of patriarchy, gender politics and
power relations – the primary concerns of radical feminists. In particular, Kanai
(1996) stresses the need for Japanese feminism to re-examine the concept of
patriarchy, one of the mainstays of the oppression of women in modern Japanese
society. She argues that this concept has unique connotations in Japan. This is
because until the Second World War, every aspect of Japanese life was closely
linked to the *ie* system and thus the concept of patriarchy is tied to the image of

'prewar, premodern oppression'. Under these circumstances, Kanai continues, it tends to be difficult for the Japanese to problematize the concept of patriarchy as the psychological and material foundation for the oppression of women in post-Second World War Japanese society (1996: 12–13).

The negative image attached to feminizumu in Japan

Chizuko Ueno (1996) dismisses the myths attached to *feminizumu* in Japan: that it is promoted by militant new left movements; that it is merely a direct import from the West; and that it denigrates motherhood. Unfortunately, the media's negative and distorted reporting of women's liberation in the early 1970s, has served to strengthen the negative image of *feminizumu* even today. To be sure, the shock tactics of groups like *Chūpiren* were far from the kind of behaviour expected in Japan, a society where conformity is stressed for the sake of the groups, whether it is a family, a workplace, or society itself. Their actions sharply contrasted with the image of a 'Japanese-ness' where conduct is regulated by the fear of shaming oneself in the eyes of the public.

More importantly, their behaviour was totally different from the concept of *onnarashisa* or femininity. Japanese women are expected to be 'repositories of "traditional" values' (Goldstein-Gidoni 1997: 105). White (1999: 50) amplifies this view, saying that

> Women are often charged with being the gate-keepers of the basic compo-nents of Japanese culture. Women are expected to be *nihonteki* (Japanese-like) as obedient daughters; subservient, if bold, wives; and finally, long-suffering mothers. Such images are challenged and complicated by the political activism of those involved in women's movements in Japan, providing a further rationale for calling any sort of 'women's activism' to change roles in society, outside the society.

Thus Japanese women who engage in activism risk the double stigma of being considered both 'unfeminine' and 'un-Japanese'.

The state and feminism

Basu argues that 'Women's movements tend to be weak where state control permeates civil society and strong where state control is or has been relaxed' (1995: 2). What about the case in Japan? I agree with some scholars who assert that feminism has been co-opted by the state or the system. This is closely asso-ciated with the government's role in promoting women's studies, both on the national and local level, since the UN conventions were adopted. As noted earlier, the government poured enormous amounts of money into establishing women's centres during the International Decade for Women. These women's centres may be found in every prefecture and large city: they offer various kinds of services, including adult education classes and conferences. One cannot ignore the fact that the government's 'support' for women has, ironically, contributed to the weakening of the radical aspects of feminism in Japan. Kanai calls it 'the crisis of feminism within administration'. She furthermore writes, 'While women's participation in society is being promoted by various government administrative bodies, I fear that these moves might lead to the restructuring of the patriarchal system into a new form' (1996: 9–10). Kanai is worried that Japanese society, together with the strong and immobile state, could further exploit women as a source of non-wage labour. This is of especial concern in Japan, where enormous amounts of help are already required to sustain an aging population.

Women's sexual autonomy

As mentioned above, women were given access to what essentially amounted to abortion-on-demand much earlier than western women. Abortion was effectively legalized in 1948, by allowing it where economic grounds indicated it was in the woman's interest. In practice, this covered nearly all requests for abortion.

At the beginning of the 1970s and during the 1980s, there were several attempts by conservative groups to restrict the right to have abortions by removing the 'economic grounds' clause. For instance, in 1982, Masakuni Murakami, Diet member and leader of the right-wing religious and political group *Seichō no Ie* (the name literally means something like 'The Home of Long Life'), tried to have the clause removed.

This conservative panic radicalized many women. The feminists were no longer satisfied by successfully blocking conservative moves; now they demanded complete control over their reproductive functions and the total removal of the ban on abortions from the Criminal Code (Mackie 2003: 166). Their demands reflected a radical critique of the philosophy behind the 1948 Eugenic Protection Law, which had allowed abortions on economic and eugenic grounds partly out of a concern for maintaining racial purity, and furthermore they challenged the whole idea that decisions about women's reproductive control are a matter of government policy (Mackie 2003: 166). A large number of disabled people were also extremely vocal against the Eugenic Protection Law, and in 1996 it was amended to remove its explicit eugenic philosophy: today it is called the *Botai Hogo Hō* or Law for the Protection of the Maternal Body. This law was a step forward for women because it shifted the emphasis from the needs of the state to the needs of women. It dispensed with listing conditions warranting an abortion, such as hereditary disease – mental or physical, malformations or leprosy, and concentrated instead on the paramount needs of women's health. The title, the Law for the Protection of the Maternal Body, however, shows quite clearly that the state's concern was specifically with the *maternal* body, not the female body in general. Although the movement against the removal of the economic grounds clause was successful, Kanai (1996) notes that in the 1980s and 1990s the demand for abortion did not lead to the discussion of wider issues. Women in Japan are still far from enjoying complete reproductive rights. Theoretically, at least, women still need their husbands' consent to have abortions and the cost of an abortion is not covered by the public health insurance system. Furthermore, abortion is still part of the criminal code, leaving it in a moral grey zone.

Despite the lingering limitations on the sexual autonomy of Japanese women, there is some evidence indicating that women's ideas about sexuality, as well as their behaviour, are changing in important ways. Inoue and Ehara (1999) report that since around the 1980s girls have started to become sexually active from an earlier age, and that the gap between the ages when girls and boys start having sex has been narrowing too. Moreover, prevalence of sexual experience has been increasing every year and for every age group. For instance, in 1974, only 5.5 per cent of female high school students and 11 per cent of female university students were reported to have had sex. These figures increased to 15.7 per cent and 43.3 per cent respectively in 1993. In fact, it was reported in 1993 that a larger share of high school girls (15.7 per cent) than boys (14.4 per cent) had experienced sex (Inoue and Ehara 1999). A later survey, conducted by the Ministry of Health and Social Welfare in 1999, showed that for both sexes, 79 per cent of those under the age of 24 had had their first sexual experience in their teens. The rise in promiscuity among young women was particularly notice-able. 37.9 per cent of women younger than 24 said that they had had at least five partners, while only 1.9 per cent of women aged 55 and older reported having had this many different partners (*Asahi Shinbun*, 13 March 2000). These sweeping changes in sexual behaviour among young people are of increasing concern for the wider public.

As will be discussed in detail in Chapter 6, in an increasing number of indus-trialized countries sex is becoming less associated with marriage. The widespread availability of birth control has broken the link between sex and marriage. In the view of Allen and Kalish (1984: 381) sex is no longer regarded as a 'reward' for marriage – 'willingness to participate in intimate personal and sexual relation-ships outside of marriage reduces the attractiveness of the marriage role.' Giddens (1992) even argues that in a non-repressive society sexual and emotional equality would lead to the disappearance of the 'traditional' marriage: the rise of what he calls 'plastic sexuality' would free sexuality from the need of reproduction.

This view is certainly not yet applicable to Japanese society, where at present gender roles are still highly segregated. Marriage and reproduction are still closely related, as indicated by the fact that Japan has an extremely low illegitimate birth rate compared with industrialized countries in the West.[2] Nonetheless, there can be no doubt that more permissive attitudes towards sexual activities and the weaken-ing of sexual mores are indeed influencing women in Japan, too.

One example can be seen in the 'ladies' comics' *(redīsu komikkusu)* analyzed by Jones (2002). Ladies' comics are sexually explicit comics produced and read, largely by women, which sell 2.5 million copies per month. Jones argues that the existence, and tremendous sales, of this type of comic 'indicate that their readers are demanding access to avenues of sexual expression that have been solely male until now' (2002: 25).

Jones, a scholar who is interested in image, sexuality, and feminism, admits that she finds the content of these comics very distressing: the heroines often undergo gang rape, sexual degradation and humiliation, even torture. She hypothesizes that social controls make it difficult for Japanese women to 'let go'. Therefore, she argues, 'a rape fantasy makes it possible to circumvent these social prescriptions without incurring psychological responsibility for doing so' (2002: 20).

She also explains that these comic stories are highly formulaic and designed to respond perfectly to the readers' fantasies and desires. The story of how a bored, lonely, and often sex-deprived middle-class housewife somehow manages to satisfy her sexual desires is a common theme. However, interestingly enough, not getting married, or leaving the marriage, are rarely options in most of these ladies comics. 'The implication is that there are other ways for the woman to find what she seeks: by reading magazines . . . purchasing sex toys, and even teaming up with another woman who may face a similar situation' (2002: 19).

Jones's article shows the way an increasing number of Japanese women are exploring their sexuality. These women are enjoying 'the fantasy of "a changed self through sexual orgasm"' (2002: 22). Thus sexuality has indeed influenced the identities of these women. However, their liberated sexuality does not appear to have affected their attitudes towards marriage, unlike in some countries in the West where sexual liberation has led to a rejection of the entire institution of marriage. While a tendency to delay marriages or remain unmarried is becoming more common in Japan and many western countries, the underlying reasons for those trends may be surprisingly diverse. As mentioned earlier, Japanese women do not, for the most part, reject marriage as an institution. They delay marriage or remain unmarried for a variety of socioeconomic reasons, discussed later, but their lingering approval of the institution results in some of the ambivalent feelings expressed by my informants.

Reproduction and rights

Japanese newspapers reported sensationally on the '1.57 shock' when the birth-rate in Japan dropped to 1.57 in 1989.[3] Ogino (1994) reports that some Japanese, in fact, criticized the 'selfishness' of women who would not bear children. Consequently, 1990 and the following two years saw nationwide pronatalist campaigns. 'Thus, Japanese women found themselves bombarded by both open and hidden calls to have more children for the future of Japan' (Ogino 1994: 89).

In response to these campaigns, Japanese feminists as well as housewives and working women in general protested. A letter in *Yomiuri Shinbun* said

> It is miserable for a grown-up woman to live without economic independence. So I decided that one child was enough for me. I don't want to spoil the life either of my child or myself . . . Why should women bear children for the aged and the state? Never, [not] for anything! . . . I want to say to the state, 'Stop exploiting women forever! We won't be duped any more!' and live my life free from regret.
>
> (*Yomiuri Shinbun*, 3 July 1990 cited in Ogino 1994)

The decline in the birthrate is a sign of women's struggle to take control of their reproductive rights and sexuality.

As noted earlier, despite the fact that marriage and reproduction are still closely connected, contraception and sex outside marriage is becoming more widespread in Japanese society. For young Japanese women delayed marriage has great rewards: they can enjoy their sexual freedom without worrying about motherhood, and a later marriage means fewer potential children, thus reducing the weight of the conventional burden placed upon women. Indeed, the fertility rate for married women (as opposed to the entire population of women) has been falling since the 1990s (National Institute of Population and Social Security Research, 2002).[4] Low fertility can be seen as a way of reconciling marriage and sexuality in a society where sex in marriage is treated as a means of reproduction, and where married women are expected to bear and raise children. This is not the conventional view among Japanese scholars who have researched this issue: they prefer to emphasize socioeconomic reasons, such as the high cost of education, that prevent couples from having as many children as they would wish. The truth of the matter will of course vary widely from one marriage to another.

The situation today: feminism and delayed marriage – is the *Hanako* generation as pathetic as it is believed to be?

In this section I will first analyze the debates about women's *atarashii ikikata* or new lifestyle and *ishiki* or consciousness through some Japanese women's magazines which emerged in the 1970s targeting young unmarried women. These magazines illustrate the way feminist ideals were disseminated in Japan during the 1970s and 1980s. I will then analyze new lifestyles among those young unmarried women who –since around the late 1980s – went, in large numbers, abroad to study, or to find jobs, or simply to travel.

The image attached to young Japanese women today portrays them as enjoying luxurious lifestyles as consumerist individualists, spending huge amounts of money on various kinds of leisure activities, anything from purchasing famous brand goods to travelling abroad. During the bubble years of the late 1980s, this perception was expressed in terms such as '*Hanakozoku*'. The *Hanakozoku* or Hanako Groupies were the readers of a consumer magazine called *Hanako*, targetting these 'single aristocrats'; *Hanako* is still published today, its contents mainly consisting of a plethora of advertisements for expensive designer goods. After the bubble economy burst, a perception started to spread that the *Hanakozoku* were sustaining their luxurious lifestyles by living with their parents, thus enabling themselves to spend almost their entire income on themselves. Gradually the term *Hanakozoku* gave way to a new label – that of '*parasaito shinguru*' or 'parasite singles'.

From some feminists' point of view in particular, the *Hanako* generation is regarded as uninterested in changing the sexist Japanese society, and, at its worst, supporting a gender-segregated society. Ueno (1997) also believes that one of the largest tasks that feminists face today is to overcome the generation gap. She finds it extremely difficult to raise the awareness of the *Hanakozoku*. Ueno (1997: 285) remarks that

The *Hanakozoku* believe in being open to their desires, being true to themselves, and doing whatever they want. These young women are usually perfectly happy, however, to be full-time wives. They enjoy the privileges of a good marriage and don't want to change anything . . . It is quite a challenge to find a way of getting a feminist message through to these women.

In the following section, through the analysis of the new lifestyle of many unmarried Japanese women, I will question the extent to which Ueno's view reflects the complexity of the struggles and frustrations of these young women today.

Japanese women's magazines

The Japanese women's magazines *An'an* and *Non'no* were launched in 1970 and 1971, respectively. These two magazines differed from previously available magazines in several respects. For instance, they did not gossip about celebrities or about the Japanese imperial family. These magazines aimed to show an inexperienced and vulnerable reader the way to establish a self-identity through themes like fashion, interior design, and travel that reflected her taste, her living space, and her joy of travelling on her own. In this way, by breaking their gender restrictions, the readers were able to discover new and different ways of living (Sakamoto 1999).

Another women's magazine, *Croissant,* emerged in 1977. Its popularity and impact became greatly increased when the editors changed its policy and designated it a 'women's newspaper' in 1978 (Ministry of Health and Welfare 1998). In fact, 450,000 copies were sold in 1980, double the number of the first issue (Matsubara 1988). It introduced a new, career-based way of life for women, focusing on 'women's independence'. The magazine's popularity even led journalist Junko Matsubara to publish a book, *Kurowassan Shōkōgun (The Croissant Syndrome)* in 1988. She remarks that the magazine *Croissant* introduced feminist ideals at the time when feminism started to permeate Japanese society. For instance, the magazine was quick to respond to best-selling books like Erica Jong's *Fear of Flying*. The term *'tonderu onna'* or 'flying-woman' became a catchphrase in Japan, identifying a career woman as an attractive woman. Many Japanese women's magazines got in on the act, with headlines such as 'Independent women are attractive women!'; 'Live more freely, women!'; 'Don't constrain yourselves in the framework of marriage!'; 'Intelligent women should never fear to fly!' etc.

In its 10 August 1978 issue, *Croissant* provided extensive coverage (six pages of feature articles) about '*kekkon shinai onna*' or 'women who do not marry'. These feature articles ended with editorial comments to the readers saying: 'whether you are currently satisfied with your marriage, or just about to get divorced, or determined to put your career first, or even if you are fond of children, we want you to confirm the following truth: women are able to lead their own lives without *marriage*.' The magazine introduced many Japanese female role models to drive home this point. These included Fusae Ichikawa, a member of the House of Councillors[5] (unmarried), Tomoko Inukai, a critic (divorced), Yoko Kirishima, a novelist (unmarried mother of three children), and so on. What these women had in common was that they were all *'kyaria ūman'* or career-oriented women, they were not young, and they did not live within a framework of ordinary married life. In Matsubara's view (1988), many Japanese women were inspired by feminist ideals in the magazine and this encouraged them to delay marriage.

In 1977 the women's magazine *More* was launched, targeting young unmarried women aged in their 20s and 30s. *More* dealt with themes including fashion, interior design, and travel but in more sophisticated ways than some other magazines like *An'an* and *Non'no*. In particular, travel was an extremely important theme for many women's magazines, but *More* stressed travelling abroad. The magazine introduced feminist ideals by emphasizing celebrity interviews which included foreign feminists such as Simone de Beauvoir, Jane Fonda, Gloria Steinem and Erica Jong. Drawing on feminist thinking, it also advocated new lifestyles to the readers, such as those of 'high-flying women', 'career women', and 'independent women', to show that women have the right to decide what they want from life (Sakamoto 1999).

In the January 1979 issue of *More*, for instance, there was an extensive 13 page article entitled 'The way to become a career woman: from isolation to participation in society.' The editors asked

> Why is it always women who are forced to lead a life within the 'framework' [of gender restrictions]? Increasing numbers of women have started to break this framework and are leading lives fulfilled by their careers; they are actively participating in society . . . They must be able to see the new future through this way of life . . . If you are craving to become a career-oriented woman, please break the framework of being a [conventional] woman and change your consciousness. We firmly believe this is the first step towards being a career woman.

The article analyses the situation surrounding working women, with points such as an increase in women's educational achievements and female workforce participation rates based on age cohort. The article then introduces four professional women to illustrate the problems they face as women and how they deal with them.

Sakamoto (1999: 185–6) notes that

> Many readers had a higher level of education than the previous generation, and had a job. They had already learned to organize their time and look after their own money without reference to their parents, under the guidance of *An'an* and *Non'no*. It is not difficult to understand that the traditional married lifestyle which demanded much sacrifice from women was no longer attractive . . . They were looking for a different lifestyle and identity and wanted to know how other women handled similar situations.

The magazine dealt extensively with issues related to work and marriage simply because women found it extremely difficult to combine these two roles.

However, Sakamoto (1999: 189) points out that even though both *More* and its readers shared liberal attitudes and thus supported feminism, the magazine did not agitate for social change. Rather, it was a vehicle for shaping the readers' changing identities. After the mid-1980s the magazine lost its critical angle: articles on feminism and new ways of life gradually disappeared and were replaced by earlier topics like fashion and cosmetics. Sakamoto explains that the reason was the growing conservative backlash against subversive lifestyles. Despite this setback, Sakamoto concludes that the new magazines advocating feminism did affect women in the 1970s and 1980s. In particular, these feminist ideas supported, encouraged and strengthened the belief that women have the right to make their own life choices. In short what is important here is the fact that the feminist ideals were disseminated because they met the needs of their readers during the 1970s and 1980s.

Going abroad: 'Travel broadens the mind'

As shown above, travelling – in order to find '*atarashii ikikata*' or new ways of life – has been one important theme in Japanese women's magazines since the 1970s. In fact, from the late 1980s onwards, a large number of young Japanese women did indeed go abroad to study, or to find a job, or simply to travel. In her book entitled, *Women on the Verge: Japanese Women, Western Dreams* (2001), Kelsky analyzes what she calls

> profound questioning of domestic Japanese expectations concerning the female life course, culminating in many cases in the assertion of a 'new self' (*atarashii jibun*) that is based on a broad and deep shift of allegiance from what women describe as insular and outdated Japanese values to what they characterize as an expansive, liberating international space of free and unfettered self-expression, personal discovery, and romantic freedom.
>
> (Kelsky 2001: 87)

She argues that Japanese women are placed on the 'margin' of the society because of gender discrimination, cultural marginality and professional exclusion. Thus, many women have gone abroad (particularly to the West) crafting 'new selves' by experiencing foreign societies and cultures.

Nonetheless, Kelsky basically sees the phenomenon as a means to *escape* the sexist and patriarchal Japanese society; a phenomenon which does not lead to social and political movements. In other words, she asserts that these oppressed unmarried Japanese women simply leave Japan in order to circumvent their 'personal' problems without changing society. She notes,

> What sets the current moment apart, however, is that the fantasy West has come to proliferate as a decontextualized mediated image, an empty signifier

that is infinitely manipulable but ultimately politically empty as a feminist emancipatory mechanism. Internationalist desires derived from this fantasy image give birth to no *social* movement.

(Kelsky 2001: 223–4)

At the same time, however, one cannot deny that, at least to some extent, the changes in the intellectual environment have increased the impact of feminism in Japan. Since the mid-1980s, feminism has been 'popularized' through the media and the debate which originally centred around academic feminists has entered the public arena. Several Japanese women's magazines in the 1970s and 1980s dealt extensively and seriously with feminist issues, and promoted new lifestyles for women. Although these magazines no longer advocate feminist ideals today, this does not simply mean that young Japanese women have given up on the pursuit of new ways of life. Instead, they are still struggling to find them, each in her own way, and 'going abroad' is one good example illustrating this phenomenon.

Generally speaking, Japanese women lack solidarity, but one should never underestimate their potential power as rebels. A large number of Japanese women are showing their frustration, struggle, confusion, anger, and stress about life as a woman in the patriarchal Japanese society by delaying marriage and childbearing, and by 'leaving' Japan: their behaviour as a whole could even shake the foundations of the existing system and structure. Young, highly-educated single women, in particular, are in the process of redefining the meaning of womanhood in a rapidly changing society.

Case studies

The fetters of the pre-war family system: Case studies

In Japan, the *ie* system has been a significant arena of feminist struggle. Many of my female informants also suggested that they felt the conventional ideas associated with the *ie* system acted against their autonomy and individuality as people. Junko (30), working in an electrical research institution as a temporary worker, said:

> You know, marriage is quite a different thing from *ren'ai* or romantic love. When you are in love, you only think about your partner but once you get married you become a '*yome*' or daughter-in-law and the sense of duty suddenly increases. The image I get from the word marriage is something that is *troublesome*. You have to go to a city hall to register your marriage and have your surname changed. Also if you want to combine your job and housework, then you usually end up as a part-time worker and think about the 1.03 million yen borderline [in order to circumvent paying tax]. And if you happen to get divorced, there will be more than enough troubles waiting for you!

Akemi (35), a care worker for severely disabled people for the past 10 years, put her hatred against the *ie* system in more concrete terms.

I have seen my mother suffering all her life as a *yome* who was only regarded as a 'labourer'. Her mother-in-law never acknowledged my mother's autonomy as a person. The worst thing was that my mother vented her pent-up feelings against me. She once said, 'If I had not given birth to you, I would have been able to get divorced from your father.' Today I understand that she could not get divorced primarily because she would not have been able to support herself financially. Nonetheless her words hurt my feelings and since then I have always asked myself why she brought me into this world.

The conventional notion of the *ie* system is certainly affecting women's views and attitudes concerning marriage. This issue will also be discussed in greater detail in other parts of this book.

Views on sexuality, marriage, and reproduction: Case studies

Another significant arena of struggle for Japanese feminists has been the fight for sexual freedom. Thanks to their efforts more Japanese women are expressing liberal attitudes towards sexuality, including some of my female informants. Masako (39), a career-oriented informant, said that she had been having an affair with her married boss (49) for the past 10 years. He once mentioned to her with deep regret that it was probably his fault that she had passed her *tekireiki* or marriageable age. As my long interview with Masako progressed, however, I learned that she had passed her marriageable age not because of this man but because of her career goals (which will be discussed in greater detail in Chapter 4). Masako explained that she had started the affair with the married boss because she needed someone to satisfy her psychological and sexual needs.

In fact, Masako is currently involved in another affair with a married man (43). She explained that when she started to have a sexual relationship with this man,

> We, in fact, made a kind of [informal and verbal] contract. At the very beginning of our relationship he said to me 'I have a wife and children. Are you sure you still want to start a relationship with me?' And I simply replied that I understood that.

She noted their relationship does not have a future, but with a combination of pride and resignation Masako said that 'I, nonetheless, do not wish to "snatch" someone else's husband.'[6]

The case of another career-oriented woman, Shiori (32), who is also having an affair with a married man (48) is quite a different story. Shiori had straightforwardly conveyed her feelings to him that she wanted to marry him. Then he said

> Shiori, you are attractive, financially independent, and still young, and so you can easily find a man who wants to marry you! My wife, who is a fulltime housewife, has no means to support herself and I cannot throw her away (*suteru*) because she is no longer young.

Shiori strongly wishes to get married quickly and have a child. She is now dating (*tsukiatteiru*) two other single men: a man aged 35 (a relationship that has continued for about 18 months), and another 32-year-old man that she recently started dating. In response to my question what she meant by *tsukiatteiru*, she replied that it meant someone you have a sexual relationship with; an example of a woman enjoying her premarital sexual freedom.

As mentioned earlier (the case studies in Chapter 1), Shiori is a successful career woman with an annual income of approximately around ¥ 20–30 million. It is not surprising that she is facing difficulties trying to find the man of her dreams. Shiori has no intention of marrying either of these two eligible bachelors and her high expectations about a prospective marital partner were only met by the married man of 48. Shiori, who is very concerned about her 'biological clock', is now involved in the dilemma of *furin* or an extra-marital affair.[7]

Some male informants touched on the issue of sexuality, too. Hideo (34) works in a Japanese securities firm. In regard to the issue of sexuality, Hideo said 'sexual desire for men is similar to women's desire to eat sushi.' What he probably meant was that, for men, to satisfy their sexual drive is similar to women satisfying an appetite for food – although his choice of 'sushi' – a raw and luxurious food item – may have some additional Freudian or Levi-Straussian significance. He talked about what is known as *shutchō sābisu* or 'delivery service' where a call-girl comes to visit your home. Hideo indicated that he uses this kind of 'service' and explained that the cost of these had been about ¥ 25,000 10 years ago but the price had fallen to somewhere between ¥ 17,000 and ¥ 20,000 these days. In this way, Hideo suggested how easy it is in Japanese society to satisfy men's sexual needs even if one is not involved in a relationship – the fall in the price of these services also suggests their widening availability.

As many as nine out of my 13 male informants,[8] including Hideo, did not have a girlfriend. One way of satisfying their sexual drive was to 'buy a woman' in the sex industry. However, these men often expressed their ambivalence about having sex without love; one informant said that he feels even lonelier after a visit to one of these shops. Not all informants enjoy these kinds of 'female services'; as one interviewee put it 'I cannot understand how one can have sex with someone you hardly know!'

Hiroshi (37), an editor, said that today premarital sex is also available not only with a '*kurōto*' or professional prostitute but also with a '*shirōto*' or non-professional one. And he claimed that the borderline between these two types of women is becoming blurred. This may also suggest the changing of the sexual mores, and the more casual attitude towards sex taken by Japanese women in general.

As I mentioned earlier, Allen and Kalish (1984: 381) note that sex is no longer regarded as a 'reward' for marriage, and willingness to participate in intimate personal and sexual relationships outside marriage reduces the attractiveness of marriage. My case studies also suggest that, given the more liberal attitudes towards premarital sex, Allen and Kalish are quite right to say that sex is no longer a 'reward' for marriage in Japan.

However, it is very questionable to what extent this affects Japanese people's propensity to marry. My interviewees' liberal attitudes towards premarital sexual behaviour did not seem to affect significantly their conservative attitudes towards the institution of marriage. In particular, they expressed the importance of having children within the institution of marriage. As mentioned in Chapter 1, ten out of 16 of my female informants were enthusiastic about getting married and six out of these ten women added that they would like to get married quickly because they wanted to have children. Since these six women seriously expressed their concern about their 'biological clock', the question about having extra-marital children naturally arose. However, these women (and my male informants in general) strongly believed that children should be born to a married couple. One female informant said that it would have been unrealistic to think about having an extra-marital child while she felt doubtful even about supporting herself. Indeed, women's salaries are still much lower than men's, not to mention the extremely insecure financial status of many single mothers in Japan. In addition to the difficulties they foresee without a husband as breadwinner, it is difficult to maintain the same level of childcare in a society where the demands of the workplace are very great. Moreover, most of my informants felt that the social stigma attached to illegitimate children was a very serious problem. As discussed in other parts of this book, illegitimate children in Japan have been discriminated against in various forms.[9]

These case studies illustrate the changing attitudes towards sex – women in particular seem to enjoy more premarital sexual freedom than ever before in the modern period. However, it is important not to overestimate its impact on their actual marriage behaviour. Relatively conservative norms surrounding marriage still operate in Japan, influencing the minds and actions of many.

Conclusion

There are profound limitations to be found in *feminizumu* in Japan. As I discussed in this chapter, some of the major causes of these limitations include the protection of the idea of motherhood, 'housewife feminism', the negative image of feminism brought about by *ūman ribu* (woman's liberation) in the early 1970s, social pressure for women to be 'feminine' and therefore obedient, and the co-opting of feminism into the system.

Given all these factors, it is not surprising that young Japanese women today show little appetite for participating in any social movement. Their psychological hesitation to be labelled as feminists is perfectly understandable. However, this does not mean that young Japanese women today are willing to conform to the conventional norms. As discussed earlier, more Japanese women are enjoying premarital sexual freedom than ever before. These young women are experimenting with and exploring their sexuality and their changing behaviour is indeed affecting their gender identity. The considerable change in their sexual behaviour is causing great concern and lascivious curiosity among sections of the public.

The conflict of ideas about what is, and what is not, permissible for women is getting more noticeable. One can look at this phenomenon as a manifestation of young women resisting social pressure and conventional norms.

The recent phenomenon of delayed marriage is another good example illustrating their new attitudes. Young Japanese women are quietly undermining the foundations of Japanese patriarchal society and could even be seen as crypto-feminists. 'Listening carefully to the voices of the younger generation, . . . I think they are speaking not of "the end of feminism" but rather "one end of feminism", . . . they are fighting to push feminist discourse to a new stage' (Kanai 1996: 6). What is significant from the feminist perspective is the fact that young Japanese women today are not only redefining the meaning of motherhood through delayed marriage and childbearing, but, by doing so, are also redefining the meaning of womanhood, or in other words, gender identity.

In this chapter, I have discussed in some detail the impact feminism has had on understandings, and constructions of, gender identity in Japan. My major arguments dealt with the way young women resist their typical gender roles as wives and mothers. The underlying argument is that women today find it extremely difficult to develop their own individual identities within marriage or rather that the institution of marriage works unfavourably for women trying to express their 'selves', their authentic individual identities.

In particular, to illustrate this point, I discussed the large numbers of Japanese women who have gone abroad crafting 'new selves' (*atarashii jibun*). Kelsky (2001: 90) notes that

> the question is a gendered one: What is a good life for a woman, a life that is not limited to marriage and family? . . . it is toward an intensifying 'individualism' (*ko toshite no ikikata*) that women are groping, an individualism that has led them to refuse the demands of family and company in favor of independence and self-sufficiency.

Another important issue related to the construction of gender identity is the argument specifically dealing with the 'female principle'. As mentioned earlier on page 36–7, Aoki was severely criticized by feminists 'for her stress on the "female principle"' that would push and lock women into their conventional nurturing role'. In a society where people give great weight to the mother-child bond as the essential element for the child's physical and psychological well-being, marriage is considered very important for providing a stable environment to bring up dependent children. One of the most, if not the most, important function of contemporary marriage in Japan is to provide this socially sanctioned environment – the only one available, so far. However, I have argued that the recent trend in delayed marriage and childrearing, and the resulting low fertility rate, can be seen as manifestations of women's revolt against the 'female principle'. In part this is because the government has inadvertently supported the existence of the glass ceiling in almost all positions of power and authority by failing to provide adequate public infant and child care services (Yorburg 1974).

Japanese women's rebellion against motherhood can also be interpreted as a way to negotiate, and experiment with their new identities in a rapidly changing society because conventional gender identities no longer fulfil their individual needs. Yorburg (1974: 3) notes that

> Social conditions change, but values and ideals often lag behind . . . Identities become fragmented as individuals experience ambiguities and contradictions in their roles. Roles become less rigid and identities more flexible as alternative lifestyles multiply. Roles do not disappear in modern societies, but they tend to become more negotiable. Power and ethics become increasingly situational and less predetermined by culture. Roles, more often, are worked out on the basis of individual preference rather than societal dictate.

This chapter has explored how the impact of feminism makes itself felt through the actions of millions of women who are not organized in a conscious or coherent movement, but whose actions are nonetheless extremely significant: they are the embodiment of social change.

The discussion in this chapter leads us to question the situation of Japanese men. Smith (1987) notes 'to describe the situation only of one sex is to imply something about the other' (1987: 1). Based on the assumption that gender is indeed a relational concept, it is essential to examine closely the way Japanese men define the meaning of manhood. Chapter 3 will discuss the attitudes of Japanese men towards their gender roles and masculinity.

3 Male gender roles and masculinity

Introduction

Researchers in the West began to pay attention to the study of gender roles as a result of the women's movement in the early 1970s. Initially, attention was focused mainly on re-examining women's conventional gender roles, but later, inquiries started to include men and especially their roles within the family. The delay in the study of male gender roles was caused partly by the fact that researchers and the public were blinded by gender-stereotypes and took it for granted that the man's role within the family was that of a provider. For instance, this is clear from the fact that while a large number of people show their concern about the ability of working mothers to care for children, only a few express a similar concern about working fathers (Strong and DeVault 1992).

According to Carol Ember (1979), cultural research suggests that few differences are apparent between the sexes before puberty and that much learning of gender roles, in fact, takes place in adolescence and adulthood. However, other studies indicate that groups of children under the age of 10 already show gender differences, and awareness of social status is already in place (Tannen 1994). In adult lives, marriage obviously functions as an extremely important agent in the implementation of gender roles. Married couples influence each other to shape what they think of as appropriate roles of husbands and wives. In conventional gender-role stereotypes, instrumental character traits such as nonemotionality, self-confidence, logic, and competitiveness are believed to be the inbuilt traits of men, helping them to provide for their families. Meanwhile, femininity is perceived to be suited to housewives and mothers, because it is assumed that it entails expressive traits such as sensitivity to the needs of others, warmth, and the ability to express tender feelings. However, the dichotomy between instrumentality and expressiveness seems to be breaking down. This is because in reality instrumental and expressive traits coexist in both men and women (Spence *et al*. 1985) and thus the dichotomy itself is meaningless (Strong and DeVault 1992).

People's perceptions of gender roles may differ according to class, race/ethnicity, or historical context. Cultural conditioning also has significant impact on gender roles. Margaret Mead (1935) conducted research among three tribes in New Guinea in the 1930s, and this research is often cited to explain how men and women behave differently according to the norms of their own culture. Among the Arapesh, both males and females demonstrated what Americans see as feminine traits of nurturance and compliance. Men and women of the Mundugumor, on the other hand, displayed characteristics that Americans would assume to be masculine, such as competitiveness, strong independence, and even violence. Furthermore, the Tchumbuli exhibited reversed gender roles from the point of view of Americans (Mead 1935). Although we understand today that gender roles vary in a much narrower band than that which Mead first suggested,[1] 'her message that gender constitutes an arena of great variability in human experience has borne out under empirical evidence' (LeVine 1990: 5). Masculinity and femininity, in any given society, is not something that is fixed or concrete in its nature, but rather depends on socio-economic, cultural, political, and historical determinants in a given period. Based on this recognition, the issue of masculinity in this chapter is approached from the position of *constructionism* theory, which proposes that gender is learned or created, as opposed to *essentialism*, which asserts that gender is an inbuilt trait. With these in mind, the following section will focus on Japanese male gender roles, male identity, and masculinities.

Male gender roles and masculinity in Japan

This section is composed of two main analyses. First, I have tried to encapsulate the ambiguities or even the ambivalence that many Japanese men feel about their masculine identity mainly through the analyses of the hegemonic masculine role model in Japan. Second, the *nagare-mono* (drifters) and *bōsōzoku* (motorcycle gangs),[2] two examples of non-mainstream discourses, are analyzed in order to highlight the fact that a 'man' varies not only between cultures but also within a culture underscored by age, class, sexuality, and so on. My analysis mainly focuses on class or status determined by educational achievement that shapes the individual masculine identity. This analysis of the 'outsiders' casts questions on the validity of notions of Japanese social and cultural homogeneity – notions that remain influential in Japanese society despite having been criticized for many years in the academic literature (Befu 2001; Sugimoto 2003).

Regarding the issue of masculinity and femininity, Buchbinder states that, 'there are norms, standards or models to which men and women in the culture are expected to conform if they wish to interact appropriately and acceptably with others' (1994: 4). Although there is more than one way of 'being a man' within society, one cannot ignore the existence of hegemonic masculinities (Cornwall and Lindisfarne 1994). There are always some discourses that are more powerful than others, and represent the stereotypical example of masculinity. Within the framework of Japanese society, it is widely accepted that the salaryman (*sararīman*), often referred to as a 'corporate warrior' (*kigyō senshi*) represents the hegemonic masculine role-model. Hard-working Japanese men are often described as playing the leading role in the economic miracle after the war. This image is created around white-collar elite employees in institutions sustained by a system of life-time assured employment, seniority-based pay and promotions, and corporate paternalism. In reality, only a small number of people fit into these categories, but it is precisely these types of men who constitute the hegemonic discourse of masculinity in patriarchal industrial-capitalism in Japan (Dasgupta 2000).

Vogel notes that '[t]he roots of the salary man can be traced at least as far back as the Tokugawa period' (1963: 5). Dasgupta concurs, arguing that many traits found in *bushido* (or the code of the samurai),[3] such as loyalty, diligence, dedication, self-sacrifice, and hard work constitute some of the most important elements of being an ideal salaryman (Dasgupta 2000: 193). Henshall also states that:

> One widely held image in postwar times – though it is weakening of late – has been that of the corporate warrior or latter day samurai, committed to serving his company and his country. Until quite recently, a true man was expected as a matter of course to sacrifice his family life and any personal wishes in order to concentrate on the all-important duty of selflessly serving his master ... This ideal was based largely on the *kōha* ('hard school') male, supposedly represented by the samurai of old. (1999: 2)

Bushi or samurai belonged to a privileged feudal class,[4] whose history goes back as far as the late twelfth century. One highly acclaimed 'classic' book *Bushido* by Inazo Nitobe (1998 [1900]) was, and to some extent still is, extremely influential in explaining the code of the samurai, and became an international best seller. Nitobe stated that this class was recruited from the most adventurous, aggressive masculine types who survived a long harsh period of warfare. Possessing great privileges, honours and also responsibilities, they soon felt the need to form a common standard of behaviour which became the code of the samurai. He furthermore emphasized the importance of loyalty for the samurai and notes that: 'it is only in the code of chivalrous honour that loyalty assumes paramount importance' (1998: 145).

Some scholars like Hurst (1990), however, criticize Nitobe for lacking historical support in asserting that there was a normative system of ethical thought or one school called '*Bushido*' among the samurai. Hurst analyzed the often linked concepts of *bushido*, loyalty, honour, and death in mediaeval and early modern Japan to see if there is any consistent view of them. For instance, the loyalty of a samurai to his lord, as well as the loyalty of the contemporary Japanese worker to his company, is examined. He argues that even in mediaeval times there were differences in house laws and codes pertaining to samurai so that in fact there were no standard codes of practice. And this possibly led to the numerous incidents of disloyalty which were prevalent in ancient Japanese warrior life. He then states that the emotional nature of the bond of loyalty was very weak for many warriors. 'Loyalty was thus purchased, and exhortations to loyalty to the contrary, samurai frequently changed masters to improve their immediate and future circumstances' (1990: 518).

In theory samurai may have been supposed to be faithful to their lords, as Nitobe described in his book, but in reality as argued by Hurst, many samurai were famous for being rebels. In this regard, Hurst argues,

> we have simply misinterpreted the data. That is, we often read both premodern and modern exhortations to loyalty as representations of what *is* rather than what *ought to be*. This is a classic mistake of assuming that a system of normative ethics describes an actual field of behaviour. (1990: 517)

Furthermore he states that, while some people (like his students in the West) are inclined to believe that Japanese workers today are somehow 'genetically' loyal to their company, they are unaware that the Japanese company system came into existence in the late 1910s to deal with the problems caused by Japanese workers changing employers to enhance their own interests. In this regard, the samurai ideal, as well as the mainstream salaryman ideal, are not simple or monolithic ideals but rather indefinite notions containing contradictory elements. Nonetheless, whatever the reality of samurai behaviour may be, to a large extent what matters in the modern world is the popular *perception* of the samurai, i.e. a myth of loyalty and an ideology of loyalty that has been built up among company employees,[5] partly reinforced by perceptions of the 'samurai ideal'. Works such as Nitobe's undoubtedly contributed to fostering or even reinforce these perceptions.

While the samurai ideal represents one side of the masculine image, Anne Allison, in her book, *Nightwork: Sexuality, Pleasure, and Corporate Masculinity in a Tokyo Hostess Club* (1994) deals with another side of being an elite salaryman. The book presents an in-depth analysis of how these high-ranked white-collar employees actually perform their image of masculinity in one of the expensive hostess bars in Tokyo. According to Allison, the costs incurred at these expensive bars are paid by company funds, meaning that only elite salarymen are able to come as regular customers, fostering their sense of superiority over other 'ordinary men'. At the hostess club, men act as lechers (*sukebe*) by making comments about the personal and physical attributes of the hostess. They act in this manner partly because they are expected to play the role of the 'lechers' which constitutes part of the image of masculinity. However, Allison clearly indicates that the work of hostesses does not normally involve sex and in fact it rarely happens. She states, 'though hostess clubs are sexually charged, the rituals of hostess club sexuality are, as a practice that is supported and endorsed by corporations, much more about gender than they are about sex' (1994: 202). This means that the most important job allocated to the hostesses is to bolster the male ego or masculinity by letting themselves be degraded. Constant attention and flattery make their male customers feel superior, while at the same time, the hostesses cosset their clients by acting maternally. They bolster the salaryman's self-image 'of being a male who can pay a female to serve him' (Allison 1994: 204). It can be argued that these performances reinforce the idea that women are meant to serve men in various ways, especially by emotional nurturance.

These performances would not work if there were not a strong expectation of female emotional nurturance. Nor would it work if there were not a strong tradition of seeing sexual prowess as central to masculinity, as in many societies. On the other hand, at least during prosperous times, companies have often paid the expenses incurred at hostess clubs in order to compensate male workers for long hours of heavy work and the loss of human relationships outside of work. At the same time, companies have generated the image of a masculine man who is entitled to have such 'luxurious' services. Allison also points out that ironically these men are in fact living out powerlessness and they have to go to the bars whether they like it or not. 'Business' outings are arranged to develop human relationships, especially to strengthen male bonding. Thus, Allison concludes that the explanation for why men go to clubs on company expenses cannot be found in factors of nature or even in culture but rather in the fact that 'mothers who stay at home with children and men who stay at work in clubs, away from home, are rewarded in these patterns by major Japanese institutions' (1994: 204). Allison defines the stereotypical company worker as a man:

> who, by the constructions of maleness, works hard, doesn't leave the office before his boss, rises in rank, brings a good paycheck home to his family and wife, goes out to drink with men he works with, plays golf on weekends with coworkers and clients, minimizes family vacations and doesn't take all the vacation time allocated him, doesn't spend much time at home or with his children, leaves the management of the family to his wife, and considers himself first and foremost a worker whose commitments are first and foremost to his job. (1994: 200–1)

Increasing numbers of people, of course, perceive this strict division of labour between the sexes as problematic because of its social and personal costs. Nonetheless, the salaryman is still the hegemonic model of masculinity in Japan (Roberson and Suzuki 2003).

Non-mainstream discourses – the bōsōzoku sub-culture

The hegemonic model is always under threat from other non-mainstream discourses. This is a matter of course as all hegemonic masculine identities are crafted out of countless discourses and, 'appear[s] to be an ongoing, never-ending project that is frequently characterised by ambiguity, tension, and uncertainty' (Collinson and Hearn 1996: 65). The dominant role model of the masculinity of the salaryman is no exception, and Standish, for example, argues that the sub-culture of bōsōzoku (motorcycle gangs) challenges the mainstream white-collar, high status salaryman and asserts that 'a new generational consciousness poses a direct challenge to the traditional "work ethic" and achievement-oriented ideology of the previous generation' (1998: 58).

Sato (1991), in his book *Kamikaze Biker: Parody and Anomy in Affluent Japan* provides a solid ethnographic description of the bōsōzoku and describes how the *bōsōzoku* present their masculinity. The terms *kōha* (hard-type) and *nanpa* (soft-type) are used in explaining two major types of masculinity. According to Sato, *kōha* is 'a traditional image of (adolescent) masculinity which combines violence, valor, and bravado with stoicism and chivalry' (1991: 86). The ideal image is based largely on that of a samurai with self-control and discipline, who is a man of few words and possesses an aura of intimidation that makes it difficult for women even to approach. The *kōha* type is in contrast to the *nanpa* type of masculinity who is 'a skirt-chaser or ladies' man' (1991: 86). Sato asserts that although the *bōsōzoku* would like to be perceived or portrayed as *kōha* and 'pose' accordingly, in reality they are all *nanpa* as his informants admitted their behaviour is perverted and only for showing off (1991: 92). There is a discrepancy between the ideal image of masculinity and their actual behaviour and thus one can argue that in fact they are performing conflicting ideas of masculinity. This is another good example of the ambivalence that Japanese men feel today about their masculine identity. Furthermore, Sato provides us with a useful description of how they transform from youth to adulthood. The *bōsōzoku* define the action-oriented life-style as 'childish' behaviour and therefore they 'graduate' around the age of 20 to become 'ordinary' citizens. This means they have their own definition of age-appropriate behaviour and thus after quitting at the approved age, they move on to the next stage to 'settle down' in order to pursue an 'ordinary life' based on a stable job, marriage, and family. This illustrates how the perception of masculinity takes on different meanings at different ages; the idea can shift as young men grow older, and it can also be seen that they are satisfying conflicting masculine ideals by 'staging' them one after the other.

The main theme of Sato's book is to find and explain the reason behind the *bōsōzoku*'s delinquent behaviour. Sato uses attraction theory and explains such delinquent activity in the context of play – it quite simply makes their lives less boring and more fun. At the same time, Sato asserts that the three major conventional theories of delinquency, namely the strain theory, the cultural deviance theory, and the social control theory, are insufficient to explain their delinquent acts. He notes that:

> Needless to say, most of the scholars who hold the strain theory or cultural deviance theory discount the playlike quality of delinquency. They treat delinquency either as the behavioral expression of frustrated wants and needs or as an almost automatic response to subcultural imperatives. Even the social control theory, especially its recent versions, cannot fully appreciate 'fun' in doing evil (1991: 211).

However, as Creighton (1993) argues, Sato discards these theories as contributory factors too easily. For instance, Sato states: 'My informants are clearly aware that they are in a minority with regard to "academic pedigree," or *gakureki*, and did have an inferiority complex about their failure to attain the common level of schooling' (1991: 135). The strain theory that explains deviant behaviour as a 'behavioral expression of frustrated wants and needs', would help to unravel their behaviour based on discontent with a sense of inferiority. Their low-status and low-paid work provide little ground for self-esteem and this, at least to some extent, will influence their expressions of being male. Sato continues that 'while many motorcycle gangs may be categorized as working-class or blue-collar in terms of their occupations and tastes, class-consciousness or psychological strain play little, if any, part in forming their deviant behavior' (1991: 138). However, social class itself is an indefinite concept and therefore it is difficult to determine any of its consequences. Yet, with or without one's own intention, people's tastes would invariably adopt to their social surroundings after many years of exposure, as Okano points out:

> Can one's taste be independent of one's class location which provides shared material conditions and affects the kind and range of one's past experience? In the same way, can one's stake in conformity (to whatever) be independent of one's class location? (1999: 516)

These arguments are important because they explain how one's social class can, in fact, shape the construction of masculinity even in cases like Sato's where it may not be immediately obvious. At the same time, the idea of masculinity shaped by class provides an antithesis to the prevailing views of the sameness and classlessness of Japanese society. In this regard, I agree with Standish (1998), who disputes the notion of social and cultural homogeneity in Japan and asserts that there is a polarization based on occupational status. There is a clear boundary between low-status workers and high-status workers, determined by education. This creates status problems for those who fail to do well in a competitive education and employment system because, as Standish argues, social standards and norms are determined by a dominant elite. The following analyses of *nagare-mono* sub-culture should further elucidate this point.

Non-mainstream discourses – nagare-mono sub-culture

Nagare-mono or drifter sub-culture is another alternative masculine identity that exists on the fringes of society. The film series *Otoko wa Tsuraiyo* ('It's Tough to be a Man') challenges the dominant discourse of the salaryman mainly through the leading character, Tora-san, a middle-aged unmarried man who is a sort of *nagare-mono*, travelling around the country as a *tekiya* or peddler.

Tora-san featured in a series of 48 films, directed by Yoji Yamada and starring Kiyoshi Atsumi, that were released during the period 1969–1995, which have been extremely successful in attracting large audiences. Yamada states that it first appeared as a television drama and was especially popular among male viewers (1979–80). Probably the key factor behind Tora-san's continued success in attracting male audiences is that these men are deeply embedded in the hegemonic discourse of 'company society', and are placed under intense social constraints to conform to or even 'perform' the mainstream masculine identity. Thus they gain momentary relief by watching a man roaming around the country, free of the restraints of the roles of father and breadwinner. In other words, these films provide male viewers with an emotional release whereby they can briefly escape from their daily oppressive pressure of conforming to the stereotype of a 'real man'. In 1969, when the first Tora-san film was made, Japan was nearing the end of her high-growth period. It was a time when various social problems became apparent as outcomes of a regulated and controlled society that prioritized economic growth above all things. In the films, white-collar elite employees living in a rigid 'company society' often appear in contrast with the *nagare-mono*. Blue-collar workers also appear and further highlight the contrast with the white-collar workers. One typical case is the relationship between Hiroshi (Tora-san's brother-in-law) and his family. Hiroshi was born into an 'upper-class' family, his father was a university professor and his two brothers 'elite salarymen'. Hiroshi rebelled against the self-centred utilitarian course of his father's and brothers' lives, and ran away from home after graduating from high school. He became a worker in a small printing factory in an old working-class (*shitamachi*) section of Tokyo. His brothers regarded Hiroshi as a dropout and they became estranged from each other (Film #1).

In another Tora-san movies (Film #8, 'Love Song of Torajiro' 1971), Hiroshi meets his family after a long time at his mother's funeral. Hiroshi expresses great emotional anguish at the death of his mother, whereas his father and brothers appear unmoved. Although his father finds it extremely hard to accept the death of his dedicated wife, he is a conventional type of man and acts in a restrained manner, remaining unruffled and cool.[6] Observing their behaviour, Hiroshi finds it difficult to control his contempt for their lack of emotion. At this point, Hiroshi's father expresses his personal recollections of his deceased wife saying, 'What shall I say . . . but that she was the kind of woman who had few desires,' his brothers agreeing with the father. Hiroshi then turns to his father and brothers and angrily says,

> It is not true that my mother did not have desires as other women do. When I was small, she sometimes took me to the harbour to watch the ships sail out to sea. She told me of a dream she had in her youth, that she sailed away on one of these ships to foreign lands. She dreamt of dancing the night away wearing low-cut dresses. But all of these dreams she gave up when she married you, father . . . She also dreamt of falling passionately in love with someone and living an exciting life in the city. But all of these dreams she gave up . . . and lived a life of misery as if she were your maid.

Hiroshi is exasperated by his father who is too concerned about his own personal honour as a man and insists on maintaining 'appropriate' behaviour even at the death of the most intimate person in his life, his wife. In this manner, the films cast questions on the issue of the true meaning of a 'real' man. Furthermore, although Hiroshi's father played his role perfectly as a provider, his wife was never satisfied with her life, which was firmly built upon the conventional role of a woman. In this way, the film becomes a critique of the hegemonic masculinity of the corporate warrior role, which always prioritizes work over family life (Film #8).

Basically the series' formula always remains the same. Tora-san meets a beautiful woman or 'madonna',[7] who is depicted as an attractive and idealized object of desire. Tora-san immediately falls in love with the 'madonna' and pursues her, but in the end they separate and go their own ways. In some cases, the 'madonna' may be attracted by his honest and sincere manner; but when they become too intimate, Tora-san intentionally breaks up their relationship. Why does he never get married? He sacrifices his own desires because he knows that it will not be in the interests of the beautiful young 'madonna' to marry an elderly drifter like himself. Tora-san always carries an old suitcase, which symbolizes his lifestyle of 'living out of a suitcase'. Certainly, being a peddler who travels around the country as a *nagare-mono* contradicts the tradtitional idea of marriage. It seems to be more complex than that, however. His lifestyle challenges that of the 'ordinary' salaryman who lives in a rigid institutionalized framework of marriage and company. This is far removed from Tora-san's lifestyle, as is made clear in one of his commonly used stock phrases: 'I come and go as the wind blows.' His idea of being 'manly' or rather 'human' is to be non-conformist, the little guy who bucks the system. His non-conformity even extends to his asocial personality. If he settles down and leads a life just like an 'average man', his aesthetic value as an ideal of humanness would undoubtedly be destroyed.

Social stigmas placed upon non-mainstream masculinities

Tora-san's free-wheeling solitary lifestyle does not merely challenge mainstream masculinities. In describing Tora-san's freedom, director Yamada, does not forget to point out that there is also another side of the coin, namely the social stigmatization of Tora-san from the *seken* (the general public), who resent him because of his 'extraordinary' lifestyle.

Tora-san is a dropout from junior high-school and his status, determined by his occupation as street-stall peddler, is far from 'respected' by the general public. In his hometown of Shibamata, a working-class district of Tokyo, everyone knows Tora-san as a man who has an 'extraordinary lifestyle'. Thus, for instance, when the mothers in the neighbourhood scold their children for their misbehaviour, they often say, 'You'll end up like Tora-san!' In another example, a close acquaintance in Shibamata, Tako-shachō (Boss Octopus), who runs a very small printing firm, tries to arrange an *miai* for Tora-san and goes to one of his customers who has a daughter who has passed her 'marriageable age'. When her father learns that the prospective marriage partner is Tora-san, he is furious, feeling that his family has been disgraced, as the *miai* is supposed to match couples of 'similar backgrounds'. The daughter, on hearing this marriage proposal, also feels offended and bursts into tears. Tako-shachō ends up losing an important customer. Although Yamada depicts the scenes in a humorous manner, these incidents reveal the public consensual view of Tora-san, showing the social stigma placed on a man without education, qualifications or a steady job (Film #10).

This again brings us back to the issue of the existence of the educationally determined boundaries between low- and high-status workers. The dropouts in a competitive educational and employment system are confronted with status problems.

In a society where marriage is highly valued and a man is recognized as being fully-fledged only once married, leading an unmarried life can also be a trial. The general public can be very critical towards those who do not get married, and Tora-san is no exception. In this manner, the films challenge social norms that intervene in the way people live rather than allowing them to choose individual lifestyles. They also criticize the bias against males who do not conform to the mainstream discourse of 'accepted' masculinities. Yoji Yamada once mentioned in the press that the Tora-san films describe in a humorous manner the difficulties of living honestly as a man and as a human being, in the sense of living as an individual rather than in the way society dictates.

To summarize, the *nagare-mono* sub-culture embodied in Tora-san, and the mainstream masculinities of the corporate warrior, 'mutually reinforce each other' (Connell 1995). While on the one hand the films challenge the mainstream masculinities of salarymen who sacrifice everything for work, they also reinforce mainstream masculinities by showing how the general public places social stigmas upon people who do not conform to these hegemonic masculinities.

Hanamuko Gakkō (Bridegroom School)

The following section analyzes a school known as the Tokyo 21st Century College (formerly *Hanamuko Gakkō* or Bridegroom School), an experimental programme which lasted from 1989 to 2000, attempting to change and modify the hegemonic ideas of masculinity through education. Before describing the work of the school, however, let us take a look at the social and intellectual trends that led to its creation.

Changing views of gender in the 1980s

The founders of the *Hanamuko Gakkō* were driven by a perception that the masculine role-model of the salaryman placed too much emphasis on the dominant heterosexual/father/husband/provider role (Dasgupta 2000). This led many Japanese people, including the school organizers, to view the hegemonic masculine role model as problematic because of the social and personal price extracted by confining gender roles. Gordon Matthews says that work still serves as *ikigai* or 'that which most makes life worth living' (2003: 109) for Japanese men and notes that:

> *Ikigai* as work for one's company or organization has been the taken-for-granted masculine *ikigai* for older Japanese men, but younger Japanese men no longer profess such an *ikigai*. Yet, because work continues to demand so much of men's time and energy, it continues to be, in effect, the *de facto*

ikigai for many men today. *Ikigai* as family meant, for some older Japanese men, that they economically supported their families while being emotionally devoted to work; but many younger Japanese women have sought more – that their husbands be emotionally committed to their families (2003: 121).

This gender gap in attitudes to the roles of the sexes in work and marriage identified by Matthews is undoubtedly one of the factors contributing to the recent delay or avoidance of marriage (see also Iwao 1993; Jolivet 1997; Ohashi 2000; Tsuya and Mason 1995). Many scholars assert that women's ideas and attitudes about their role in the family are changing more rapidly than those of men. Tsuya and Mason (1995) argue that women who enjoy increased educational and career opportunities are reluctant to conform to the role of the Japanese wife, which remains oppressive. They quote a series of national opinion surveys by the Prime Minister's Office to illustrate their point. The surveys find that both sexes supported the notion of men as breadwinners and women as homemakers in the early 1970s: for instance 83 per cent of women and 84 per cent of men agreed with this notion in 1972. These figures have decreased during the past three decades for both sexes, but more rapidly for women: by 1997, only 52 per cent of women agreed with this idea, against 65 per cent of men. The perception gap between the sexes had widened from 1 per cent in 1972 to 13 per cent in 1997 (see also Ministry of Health and Welfare 1998).

The *Hanamuko Gakkō* (Bridegroom School) was founded in 1989 in order to offset this growing gender gap. It was originally designed exclusively for men and was based on the school organizers' belief that men need to realize how women today have changed, particularly in their views on marriage and gender roles.

The birth of men's studies

It was psychologist Tsuneo Watanabe who initiated men's studies and advocated 'men's liberation' in Japan. In his book *Datsu Dansei no Jidai: Andorojinasu o Mezasu Bunmeigaku* (The Age of Escape of Masculinity: Studies Towards an Androgynous Civilization) (1986), he conducted research on Japanese men who indulged in transvestism and reached the conclusion that in the same manner that women have been oppressed by *onnarashisa* or ideas of femininity, men were oppressed by *otokorashisa* or ideas of masculinity. In 1993, Kimio Ito published a book *'Otokorashisa' no Yukue* (The Future of Masculinity) which outlined the general idea of men's studies. Ito suggested in the book that 1989 (the year of the foundation of the *Hanamuko Gakkō*) was a year when a number of incidents occurred that symbolically indicated the collapse of the 'men's era'. There were many cases that were linked closely to men's problems. Ito cited a murder case where a female high-school student was buried in concrete [by four male teenagers] and another case where young girls were kidnapped and murdered in the

Tokyo and Saitama areas [by a 27-year old man]. He asserts that what these cases had in common was that they both involved one of the most important elements of masculinity, i.e. 'the myth of strength', and that both incidents targeted 'the weak' through sexual violence. He states that these incidents were created by situations where a man had failed to overcome a series of frustrations to become fully mature, leaving a man who was a threat to society as he could only prove his own existence through physical domination. In his view, these cases revealed a crisis of masculinity. Under these circumstances, Ito predicted in the *Asahi Shinbun* on 16 December 1989 that the 1990s would become the era of men's problems (Ito 1993). In fact, in 1992, Ito started a series of lectures on men's studies at Kyoto University, the first such series at a Japanese national university. The number of students who attended Ito's lectures amounted to 1,700 by 1993, which reflects the popularity of this subject. Ueno states that 'in this manner, men's studies became one of the most pressing problems for men themselves' (Inoue *et al.* 1995: 76).

The era of 'dansei kekkon nan' or 'marriage difficulties for men'

As noted earlier, a documentary writer, Yumiko Suzuki stated (1995) that although the phenomenon of farmers facing difficulties in finding a bride had existed since the 1960s, the issue was not widely taken up by the mass media until young men living in urban areas began to face similar difficulties. It was then referred to as *dansei kekkon nan jidai* or 'the era of marriage difficulties for men' in the early 1980s. Many articles about the *Hanamuko Gakkō* in 1989 reported the establishment of the school in relation to this social problem. For instance, the *Nihon Keizai Shinbun* (10 May 1989) reported the results of a population census in 1985 indicating that there were 2.2 times more never-married men (3.67 million) than never-married women (1.66 million) aged 25–35.[8] The article continued with comments by the school organizers to the effect that men faced difficulties in getting married not only because of the imbalance in the sex ratio between unmarried men and women, but also because women's ways of thinking had changed with the times while men did not seem to have kept up, and furthermore some men seemed to have difficulties in building stable relationships with other people.

In short, the late 1980s was a period when men themselves started to take men's studies seriously and when the media also began to report on the social problems of men finding difficulties in getting married in urban areas. Against this historical background, the *Hanamuko Gakkō* was established as an apparent pioneer in reacting promptly to the demands from society.

The organizers and their aims

The school principal, Keiko Higuchi (Professor at Tokyo Kasei University and a prominent feminist intellectual) specializes in women's issues, aging problems, and education. Higuchi asserts that it is essential to educate men in order to build a society which provides equality for men and women. At the time of the school's founding, she stated:

> There is a growing gender gap between the sexes because women have rapidly changed their way of life while men remain unchanged. Thus there are many difficulties in establishing a relationship between the sexes in the early stages of courtship. Even those who are married are facing difficulties in maintaining their marital relationships. The objective of the school is, therefore, to teach the true meaning of the word '*katei jin*' (a family-oriented person) and provide an opportunity to understand about women today.
>
> (*Jōyō Shinbun*,[9] 29 September 1989)

Yoko Itamoto (General Director of the marriage consultation office of Japan Youth Foundation) was another organizer of the school. Itamoto's long experience in working at the marriage consultation office made her fully aware of the issue of the emergent problems involved in marriage formation. In an interview with the author, she said she saw a huge gap in the way men and women perceived their future marriages. For instance, women seemed to be stressing the importance of sharing common interests while men seemed to see this as less important. Itamoto was convinced that it was essential for men to become more conscious of the discrepancies between the sexes.

Another organizer, Shigeo Saito (a freelance journalist) stated that the purpose of the school was to reconsider 'traditional' Japanese views and attitudes towards marriage and the family and to discover different ways of life based on a new sense of values.[10] He was particularly sceptical about conventional Japanese gender thinking with its strict division of roles between the sexes. This is clear from his best-selling investigative book *Tsumatachi no Shishōki* ('Autumnal Wives') (1982). This book deals with the life experiences of frustrated 'middle-class' housewives living in the suburbs. When he started to write the book, it was focused on men as corporate warriors contributing towards building a major economic power. As he progressed in collecting data through interviews with psychiatrists and counsellors, however, he became aware of the fact that although men were under extreme stress, the lives of their wives were equally stressful. He then became more and more interested in the way these housewives lived, which resulted in his publishing the book.

Saito stated that men should involve themselves more in family matters and the local community, while women should participate and advance more into the workplace to lead a life that was truly independent (Higuchi *et al.* 1990). Based on this, Higuchi commented in the magazine '*W*' that she was convinced that Saito was 'one of the few men who can actually understand that women are placed in a weak position',[11] and this was why she invited him to join her in establishing the school (10 August 1999: 2).

Although Higuchi, Itamoto, and Saito came from different backgrounds, they possessed a common belief that the establishment of the school was essential as a place where men could focus on reassessing their ideas and values to create a society built upon equality rather than conventional male dominance.

Development of the Hanamuko Gakkō

The school programme underwent many changes after its establishment in 1989, and the following three are the most significant (see Appendix 3). First, the organizers believed (at least for the first few years) that men should first understand the issues surrounding men and women 'theoretically', and thus they provided a lecture-based curriculum. Yet, although the students were able to understand these issues theoretically, they were unable to put them into practice. In order to solve these problems, the school introduced some new measures allowing more active participation by students from around 1994. Courses were then based on a wide range of group activities and workshops such as conducting interviews or questionnaire surveys.

Second, the school became co-educational in 1993. This meant a change in its target markets but also implied a modification in its original objectives, which saw it as 'designed exclusively for men'. Itamoto explained that the decision to go co-educational was made in response to requests from women that revealed their desire to learn more about men (*Nihon Keizai Shinbun*, 18 October 1995). However, as shown later in this chapter, it is possible that the school had some difficulties in attracting men and therefore had to include women in order for the school to continue. For instance, there were 40 participants in the 1999 programme and the sex ratio was 2 women to 1 man, showing its popularity among women rather than men.

There is a tradition of bride training or *hanayome shugyō* in Japan where an unmarried woman is trained to become a good, desirable wife, mastering manners and etiquette and so on – but there has never been any comparable *hanamuko shugyō* or bridegroom training. There seems to be an underlying assumption that women need training in order to become a qualified wife whereas men do not. The emergence of the *Hanamuko Gakkō* was ground-breaking in this regard. In fact, the organizers had disputes at the time they first considered the name, *Hanamuko Gakkō*. They thought that the participants might find it embarrassing to attend a school named *Hanamuko Gakkō*, and in fact, had some alternative names such as 'lectures in order to become a nice guy' ('*ii otoko ni naru tame no kōza*'). However, as they believed that men lacked the right attitudes to build a rich and fulfilling life as a family oriented person or *katei jin*, they persisted in using the name although aware of the risk involved. Their concern became a reality from the very first year: the *Mainichi Shinbun* quoted Itamoto as stating that there were many school participants who were hesitant about the school's name, and thus the organizers might consider changing it in the future (28 December 1989). In other words, the school's name gave the impression that it was designed for certain types of men who have difficulties in getting married and thus require training to become a groom. This was probably the most important reason why it was renamed the Tokyo 21st Century College in 1998. A secondary factor was the need to present the school as a 'new project' to meet the terms of the government grant received that year – the management having found it financially impossible to run the school with just enrolment fees (Yoko Itamoto, personal communication, 24 September 2008). The new name, however, had problems of its own – it was very bland and told nothing about the school's objectives. As it turned out, the name-change failed to stem the decline in student numbers – especially among men, who were the original target – and the school finally closed in February 2000, at the end of its tenth academic year.

Visiting the programme in 1999

In 1999, I had an opportunity to visit and attend some of the lectures held at the school at the Japan Youth Foundation. The programme for this year primarily aimed to elucidate the pressures of being male and female in Japanese society. Participants formed groups of people possessing similar interests in gender-related topics, and collected data, mainly through interviews. After that, each group discussed and submitted their research reports in a magazine-like format entitled *Gender Free Magazine*.

There were 40 participants, of whom 27 were women while 13 were men. 16 participants were in their 20s, eight were in their 30s, and 16 were 40 or older. The motives for joining the programme seemed to differ greatly among students. Some wanted to deepen their understanding of gender issues, whereas a few admitted they had heard about the main theme of the programme, gender, for the first time there. Another group of people came simply because they admired the work of current or previous lecturers. Others showed interests in journalistic work because the goal of the 1999 programme was to publish a *Gender Free Magazine*, while the rest said that they wanted to experience something different from their routine lifestyle.

The programme was divided into four stages, which started in mid-September 1999 and ended in early February 2000. I was able to participate in the first and second stages of the course. The first stage of the programme consisted of two days of lectures which provided a basic understanding of gender issues as well as knowledge of the school history and its objectives. The second stage was also held for two days and was programmed to give some rudimentary journalistic skills. The third stage contained the main activities; it started in October and ended in January. The participants were actually in the 'field', conducting their interviews. After this, there was a session where each group discussed how to write and edit their papers which were then sent for printing. A graduation party was held at the final stage in early February 2000. Yumiko Ehara, then Assistant Professor of Tokyo Metropolitan University (currently full professor), gave a speech entitled *How Should Men and Women Lead Their Lives in the 21st Century?* and a discussion was held amongst the participants.

Gender Free Magazine was composed of six main themes. Group One focused on gender bias found in newspapers through interviews with journalists to find out how the journalists dealt with these issues. Group Two dealt with the generation gap and focused on the various views towards gender among young people by conducting interviews with some male and female high-school students. Group Three interviewed married working couples and mainly asked questions regarding maternity leave. Group Four analyzed gender through people who specialized in music, sports, and arts. Group Five focused on sexuality by interviewing lesbian and homosexual couples. Group Six asked questions to some married couples about the communication gap and focused on quarrels they had had in the past.

The programme in 1999 was significant in three aspects. One striking feature was that the participants came from totally different backgrounds in terms of age, sex, marital status, and occupation. Thus the participants first learned from each other, as each possessed different points of view, especially on topics related to gender. The students were also given a chance to acquire knowledge by conducting interviews on their own with people working in different fields. In this particular year, participants also had a chance to review what they had learnt through the process of writing and editing the articles. These activities reflected the school's belief in the merits of a self-guided seminar style. Although the school organizers and supporters assisted the participants during the process of writing their articles by giving them advice, such as tips on writing and editing skills, the basic concept underlying the course was to encourage participants to get actively involved in each process and let them learn from their own experiences. This interesting and innovative approach did, however, have some disadvantages. The quality of the articles differed greatly, revealing widely differing levels of knowledge regarding the issue. Since the seminar was not primarily lecture-based, the programme, at least to some extent, had to rely on the participants' own knowledge before coming to the school. This raises the question of the effectiveness of the method for some participants in acquiring knowledge about the main subject despite relatively long hours spent for the programme; this may be seen as a weakness of a student-initiated course or self-guided seminar.

An analysis of the school's rise and fall

The school was successful, especially in the first few years, and generated wide publicity. The extensive media coverage reflected the interest and concern about marriage among Japanese people. The government, probably out of concern about the falling birthrate, accepted the school's application for financial support, as it became apparent that the decrease in the birthrate was caused at least in part by the delay or avoidance of marriage. Thus, from 1998, the school's programmes became part of a contract project called the 'Gender-Equal Seminar for Youth' (*Seinen Danjo Kyōdō Sankaku Seminā*) carried out by the Ministry of Education (subsequently renamed the Ministry of Education, Culture, Sports, Science and Technology). After that students were able to attend the school basically free of charge, only paying for accommodation and food. Previously the participants had had to pay fees of between ¥ 34,000 and ¥ 70,000. In these respects, as I mentioned earlier, the establishment of the school clearly responded in a timely way to the needs of society.

Yet, as one organizer explained, the school gradually started to find it more difficult to recruit male students. Possibly the decision to admit women in 1993, and the increasing numbers of female students, made it hard for men to participate as freely as before. The school mainly recruited students through an advertising brochure distributed in various places such as libraries, or through their web pages. However, the school received much less attention from the media in its later years. The media obviously helped the school to attract more students during the first few years. For instance, in 1989, although the school advertised for 50 male students, there were far more applicants than that. Of a total of 83 male students there were 58 who attended all the lectures. In the 1999 programme, however, there were only 40 students, including 27 women and a mere 13 men. Despite the fact that the students were no longer required to pay fees, the college was facing difficulties in attracting male students – difficulties that would shortly lead to its closure. Moreover, many of the men who were still attending the school were 'repeaters' – they had attended for several years and seemed to be treating the school as a psychological refuge, or in Itamoto's words, 'bridegroom's hospital' (Yoko Itamoto, personal communication, 24 September 2008).

Students expressed various opinions after attending the lectures in the school's first year (Higuchi *et al.* 1990). Some said that the lectures were simply 'interesting' while others stated that 'they could not bear to hear any more about it' (*mō kikitakunai*). One student commented, 'I was shocked to learn the reality of how women have been discriminated against' (Higuchi *et al.* 1990: 226). In 1999, the final year of the school, one female participant in her late 20s stated that she had decided to quit the school halfway through, since she felt that the school took a feminist standpoint, which she could not totally accept. It is perhaps not surprising to find that male students were reluctant to enrol in the school's programmes because of its ideological position. Many lecturers spoke from a feminist point of view, as is clear from their programme titles: 'Woman changes as the world changes – the demand for the *Hanamuko Gakkō*'; 'Men don't understand the oppressive structure towards women'; and 'What is a "nice guy" from women's point of view?' The organizer, Itamoto, also mentioned in the *Nihon Keizai Shinbun* (18 October 1995) that there had been disagreement between participants and organizers. The school received criticism from some male participants who thought that they were being forced to accept feminist ideology.

There was also the practical problem that many male participants were unable to attend the school programmes after work. For instance, in 1989 lectures were provided from 7pm to 9 pm every Thursday night from September 1 to November 26. There were students who actually had to take a day off to attend the school and others only managed to come to the school just before the end of the lecture at around 9 pm (Higuchi *et al.* 1990). Ironically, this was the reality for the male participants or 'corporate warriors,' whose work was eating up all their time.

Another problem in attracting male students was, as briefly mentioned above, the bias against men who attended the school. Higuchi said that in 1989, reporters asked the organizers such questions as 'What kind of people attend the class?' and 'Are they having difficulty in finding wives or are they just odd fellows?'

(*Weekly ST Report*, 5 November 1993: 6). Even a female school participant, Miyuki Suzuki (29) reported biased preconceptions about the male participants:

> To be honest, I used to think that men who attended a school like this were unable to find partners because they themselves had problems. But now that I've talked to them face to face, I find that I was wrong. They are very interesting and only wish to transform themselves. The only problem is that they feel shy in the presence of others or are poor at talking to them.
>
> (*Weekly ST Report*, 5 November 1993: 6)

The school seems to have had an image of being for men who were unable to find a partner and thus had to be 'educated' in order to transform themselves into a 'desirable guy'. Under these circumstances, the school undoubtedly faced tremendous difficulties in attracting male participants.

Why is it so difficult to close the gender gap?

Men attending the school had many different motivations. Some simply wished to learn more about women, while others wanted to be free from conventional masculinity. However, once they joined the school, many participants probably felt that they were being put in the dock by feminist ideals. In this regard, the school revealed the difficulties in bridging the gap between the sexes in their views of family and gender roles. The organizers touched on their difficulties as follows. Itamoto notes that, 'When they (male students) were taught by female lecturers, they felt that they were being accused by them and these feelings came back as a rebound against feminist ideals.' According to Saito, 'I think these issues are strongly embedded in our culture and thus they believe that they have to be strong or be an excellent corporate warrior and they cannot show their weakness' (Higuchi *et al.* 1990: 227–8).

The problems that the school faced reveal how difficult it is to change gender roles. As noted by Strong and DeVault (1992), gender roles are closely linked to people's self-evaluation and their understanding of gender identity. There is a close link between gender role and gender identity because they are both internalized within one's self. People tend to understand society as a whole in terms of gender-based concepts. Thus, the male students, who were taught that they belonged to the oppressing gender, felt that they were being accused in terms of their personal identity. In this regard, Strong and DeVault state that:

> Our sense of adequacy depends on gender-role performance as defined by parents and peers in childhood . . . Because gender roles often seem to be an intrinsic part of our personality and temperament, we may defend these roles as being natural even if they are destructive to a relationship or to ourselves. To threaten an individual's gender role is to threaten his or her gender identity as male or female, because people do not generally make the distinction between the gender role and gender identity. (1992: 109)

Conclusion

In the first part of this chapter, I outlined several important ideas or discourses of masculinity in Japan. I tried to show that many different forms of masculinity exist within Japanese society and each particular form may be either dominant or subordinate in terms of power, depending on one's age, class and other social circumstances. By doing so, I have challenged the popular image of Japan as a homogeneous society. At the personal level, masculinity means different things to different people; it is far from being a stable and constant factor. It even varies according to the point of time in one's life-course, shifting with the change from child to adolescent and from adolescent to 'full-fledged' adult. Thus, as shown in my analysis of the *Bōsōzoku* sub-culture, what is acceptable in the early teens may become totally unacceptable in the early 20s. These changes come from a number of contributing factors including social class, status, education, and employment which influence ideals and ideas of what constitutes being a 'real man'. This again is an issue of gender identity and what is permissible for a man – an issue of legitimacy.

In the latter half of this chapter, I examined the innovative programmes offered by the 21st Century College, formerly the *Hanamuko Gakkō* (Bridegroom School). I focused on the historical background of the school in order to elucidate some changes which have taken place during the past decade and showed the organizers' efforts to change the hegemonic ideas of masculinity through education. The school was successful and attracted attention from a wide range of people, especially during the first few years of its existence. The state funding which started in 1998 also showed an awareness on the part of government of the significance of programmes that attempt to solve some social and personal problems caused by the strict division of labour between the sexes. Yet I also demonstrated some of the difficulties which the school organizers faced and which show the underlying complexities involved in closing the gap between the sexes. Ultimately the school was unable to overcome those difficulties and was forced into closure.

The question arises, how and in what kind of social context did this strict division of labour between the sexes become firmly established in Japanese society? Chapter 4 focusing on the roles of wife and mother, dominant themes in defining the identities of Japanese women, will further help in the understanding of gender relations in Japan.

4 Gender roles

The roles of wife and mother

Introduction

This chapter focuses on female gender roles, particularly the roles of wife and mother. There are two main reasons for this. First, the role of mother is the one that determines gender role most decisively in Japan and at the same time heavily restricts women's behaviour (Ehara 2000; Okamoto 2000). Despite rapid technological improvements, which have reduced women's housework hours (Ministry of Health and Welfare 1996), child-rearing still remains overwhelmingly in the hands of mothers (Jolivet 1997; Funabashi 2000; Ministry of Health and Welfare 1998). Not only men but also women strongly adhere to, or are pressured into, the idea that mothers should be the ones to raise their children, and this limits their behaviour. Second, we are inclined to believe that more Japanese women advanced into the labour force after the war. However, this is a fallacy. As Ochiai (1997: 14) points out, the female labour participation rate, in fact, decreased for three decades after the war. The idea of a strict household division of 'men as breadwinners and women as homemakers' actually became more popular and acceptable in the era of rapid economic growth – the late 1950s to 1973. One of the main contributing factors to this could be the break-up of the household as a production unit, which restricted the role of the female to either worker or housewife, whereas before they could perform both duties within the household unit (Ochiai 1997). I would argue that the nature of the productive labour that women engage in has changed, and that this has forced them to select between the mutually exclusive roles of worker and housewife.[1] This may suggest another reason for the increase in delay or avoidance of marriage because women foresee difficulties in carrying out both productive and reproductive labour. At the same time, the high rate of economic growth enjoyed by Japan from the late 1950s to the early 1970s made it more feasible for married women to stay at home and focus on reproductive work because it was easier to support a family with a single wage.

Historical background

Before attempting to explore the current situation surrounding women's gender roles in Japan, I will first look into the historical background of the way women participated in the workforce (household-based versus company-based work). This should illustrate how family roles have been affected by the separation of workplace and home, particularly after the war.

Dichotomy between productive labour and reproductive labour

As Figure 4.1 demonstrates, the female labour participation rate decreased for three decades after the Second World War. The Statistics Bureau of the Ministry of Internal Affairs and Communications reports the following decline in the female labour force participation rate: 56.7 per cent in 1955, 54.5 per cent in 1960, 50.6 per cent in 1965, 49.9 per cent in 1970, and 45.7 per cent in 1975 (Labour Force Survey).

Figure 4.2 also shows that the M-shaped curve depicting women's participation in the labour force by age deepened in four particular periods, that is, 1930–34, 1935–39, 1940–44, and 1945–49, with 1945–49 showing the greatest depth. Thus more people in the birth cohort 1945–49 stayed at home than any other group at the time of marriage and child-rearing. This group (1945–49) represents what is known as '*dankai no sedai*' or the baby-boom generation (Ochiai 1997). They reached the time of marriage and child-rearing around the end of the rapid economic growth period in 1973. In other words, it also shows that it was at the end of the rapid economic growth period that the gender roles of 'men as bread-winners and women as homemakers' became most firmly established (Ochiai 1997; Ministry of Health and Welfare 1998).

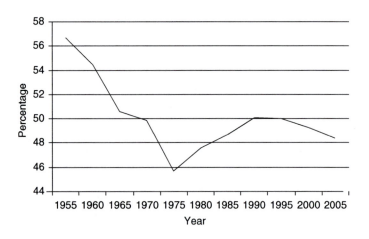

Figure 4.1 Trends in female labour force participation rates.
Note: This is the proportion of the female labour force to the total female population aged 15 or over.
Source: Statistics Bureau, Ministry of Internal Affairs and Communications, *Rōdōryoku chōsa* (Labour Force Survey (Time Series)).

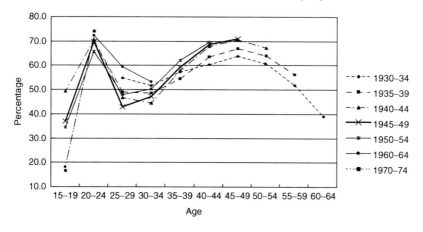

Figure 4.2 Age-specific female labour force participation rates in Japan by birth cohort.
Source: Statistics Bureau, Ministry of Internal Affairs and Communications Agency, *Rōdōryoku chōsa* (Labour Force Survey (Time Series)).

The trend showing the decrease in the female labour participation rate needs further explanation. The timing of the decline corresponds to the era of rapid economic growth (the late 1950s to 1973) which caused a structural transformation of the economy. In 1955, the majority of people were engaged in primary industries, which accounted for 41.1 per cent of the workforce, whereas 23.4 per cent were engaged in secondary industries and 35.5 per cent in tertiary industries. However, these numbers were completely altered by the end of the rapid economic growth period. The tertiary industries became the chief employers, accounting for 51.8 per cent of the total labour force. An all-time low of 13.8 per cent was engaged in primary industries and 34.1 per cent in secondary industries in 1975 (Ministry of Health and Welfare 1998).[2]

The structural transformation of the economy also changed the functions of the family. Before the era of rapid economic growth, the majority of families functioned as production units (Lockwood 1968). It was common for women to participate in the family business as well as being responsible for the housework and rearing children. For instance, Ochiai (1997) reports that women born in the 1920s typically married farmers, small shopkeepers and factory owners, and states: 'Although female labor in the past had a different structure, we should not allow this to obscure the fact that Japanese women have always worked at other jobs in addition to their household duties' (1997: 17). In other words, women could more easily participate in productive labour as an extension of their household roles (Roberts 1994; Kondo 1990; Uno 1991). Rapid economic growth, however, changed Japan's social structure completely and the majority of workers became company employees. This meant the widespread separation of the household from the economy. Workplaces outside the home made it difficult for women to carry out both responsibilities of productive labour and housework. Also, there was less support from other family members due to the increased number of people living in nuclear families, and also support from the local community decreased as relatives moved apart due to the rapid growth of the suburbs (Ministry of Health and Welfare 1998). Therefore, nuclear families based on 'women within the domestic realm and men in the public realm' became firmly established, increasing the actual number of full-time housewives after the war for three decades until 1975 (Ochiai 1997; Iwao and Kato 1997; Inoue and Ehara 1999; Mackie 1997).

This trend was accompanied by an ideological discourse that viewed the stay-at-home housewife with an interesting mixture of awe and envy. Women were described as having changed from 'slaves of housework' (*kaji no dorei*) to 'queens of consumption' (*shōhi no joōsama*) (Saito 2003: 246), and the benefits of the housewife's position were described as 'three meals with siesta included' (*sanshoku hirune-tsuki*) (Saito 2003: 250). Ochiai puts it even more strongly, saying that 'the value system now in the ascendant said that it was better to "do nothing" during the day – better, that is, to devote oneself to housework and child rearing' (Ochiai 1997: 35). Underlying these discourses was a class-based assumption that a wife who stayed at home was an important status symbol representing the attainment of consumer affluence.

These analyses show how economic, social and cultural factors combine in defining women's roles. These factors emerge in a prescriptive ideology that defines married women's gender roles. The following section analyzes some important ideological factors influential even today in Japan, such as the motherhood ideology, the ideology of '*ryōsai kenbo*' or 'good wives and wise mothers', and the 'myth of the first three years'.

The ideological perspective – influence of motherhood ideology

'Motherhood could refer to physical reproduction, a social role, or to abstract qualities of nurturance and compassion' (Mackie 1997: 70). However, it is never clear what kind of social roles or qualities exactly constitute motherhood. Without any clear definitions, the idea of motherhood is however disseminated in Japanese society through various phrases such as *bosei ai* (maternal love), *bosei honnō* (maternal instincts), *bosei shinkō* (belief in motherhood), *bosei shugi* ('maternalism') and *bosei genri* (the principles of motherhood). These are justified by regarding them as natural inbuilt traits. But are these maternal instincts really a universal phenomenon? To what extent are they socially and culturally constructed in Japan? In order to understand the influence of motherhood ideology, it is necessary to analyze how the ideology was first created and disseminated in Japanese society, and for what purpose.

The word 'motherhood' was first introduced into Japan in the latter half of the 1910s and was a translation of the Swedish word 'moderskap' (Ohinata 1995). Kano reported in 1991 that the word '*bosei*' or motherhood had only been used in Japan for about 70 years (Kano 1991). However, before the word was imported to Japan, there existed the ideology of '*ryōsai kenbo*' or 'good wives and wise mothers', which stressed the role of mothers as educators who manage domestic affairs within the family. The woman's role model based on this ideology was greatly influenced by the idea, then current in Europe and America during the nineteenth century, 'that women should provide the moral foundation of the home, educating the children and acting as "better half" to their husbands' (Rodd 1991: 176). The ideology was also promoted and encouraged by the Meiji government's Ministry of Education. This took the form of persuading women to concentrate only on the responsibilities of childbearing and child-rearing within the patriarchal system rather than taking control of the household (Rodd 1991). The Meiji government also actively propagated the ideal of feminine virtues based on motherhood ideology, such as mildness (*yasashisa*), stoicism (*gaman*), and consideration of others (*omoiyari*) from the 1880s (Refsing 1998).

The state policy towards women, especially for the two decades between 1890 and 1910, differed from that which had been dominant earlier (Nolte and Hastings 1991). Certainly, prior to 1868 in the Edo period (1603–1868), the definition of womanhood did not primarily consist of the idea of motherhood. Niwa (1993) even suggests that women were only valued as 'vehicles of procreation' illustrating this from a popular moral tract, 'Greater Learning for women' (*Onna Daigaku*, 1716). The tract, based on Confucian ethics, stated that: 'They (women) are not fit to raise children since they tend to be carried away by their love. Since women are ignorant, they should remain humble, obeying their husbands' orders at all times' (cited from Niwa 1993: 72). Uno (1991) also agrees that motherhood was not emphasized in Tokugawa Japan. She reports that the unity of production and reproduction within the household unit enabled both men and women to participate in childrearing and states that; 'the evidence presented concerning the division of reproductive labour in Tokugawa and early Meiji households implies that to view mothering as woman's universal and natural destiny is to deny history' (1991: 40). Considering the fact that there is no society that is static or free from class and regional differences, it is always difficult to define women's role in any given society at any specific time in history. Nonetheless historians have indicated that, in Tokugawa Japan, the importance of women's role as mothers was not emphasized as much as their roles as wives and daughters-in-law.

The Meiji government's policy towards women – female textile workers

The Meiji government, especially for the two decades between 1890 and 1910, actively exhorted women to contribute both productive and reproductive labour to the state in the interest of industrializing the country. One measure the government took was to encourage women to work in newly-established factories, especially in cotton and silk textile mills (Kondo 1990). Before I continue the discussion about the ideological aspect of motherhood, I will briefly describe the female industrial-workers of the Meiji period. One of the most important features of the cotton and silk factories was the composition of their workforce.

To illustrate, in 1889–1923 nearly 80 per cent of the cotton-factory workforce was female (Kidd 1978). Many of the workers were daughters from poor rural farming villages whose families were in desperate financial need. Tsurumi (1990) reports that these girls not only contributed to their families by providing financial assistance but also reduced the number of mouths that their parents had to feed, as most of the girls lived in dormitories. These country girls were recruited because they supplied cheap labour. Also from the mill owners' point of view, women were easier to control compared to men 'under the outwardly paternalistic nature of the dormitory system' (Kidd 1978: 3). Just like the image captured by the well-known book *Jokō aishi*,[3] many women endured exploitation, working under an extremely harsh environment with very low pay.

The stories of the textile factories are significant in my study not only because they speak to the contribution made by working women to the success of the first stage of Japan's industrialization process,[4] but also because they elucidate women's status within the family system. As Tsurumi puts it,

> By helping desperate families to pay the tax collector and the landlord, girls and women in the textile plants helped perpetuate the hierarchical and exploitive [exploitative] relationships of the pre-Meiji countryside. Their labor in the factories also supported the general expectation that women would work long and hard for the families.
>
> (Tsurumi 1990: 192)

No matter how significant their contribution was to the success of Japan's industrialization, their status nonetheless remained defined within the private sphere. Thus the pattern sometimes seen in industrialization, where increasing work by women outside the home leads to higher social status or empowerment, was not to be found in Meiji Japan.

Ryōsai Kenbo ('good wives and wise mothers')

Another important policy of the Meiji government was focused on women's reproductive roles. It included the propagation of the idea of 'good wives and wise mothers' to advertise women's importance within the domestic sphere. It was based on two assumptions by the government; 'that the family was an essential building block of the national structure and that the management of the household was increasingly in women's hands' (Nolte and Hastings 1991: 171). Furthermore, the educators thought that it was advisable to educate women in order to stabilize the home front after the Sino-Japanese War of 1894–95 (Sechiyama 1996), which led to the state reconsidering and re-evaluating women's roles, nature, and abilities (Uno 1999). In fact, in 1899, the idea of 'good wives and wise mothers', became the basis of the curricula of the girls' higher schools attended by daughters of the elite. In 1911, it was introduced into the curricula of elementary schools with the revision of the ethics textbooks (Uno 1999).

Sechiyama (1996) argues that the emphasis on the role of mother granted women a clear role and responsibilities and that in a way this was a benefit under the patriarchal system. He states that the *'ie'* system placed women under strong pressure to bear children in order to secure the family line. In other words, women were unable to establish their position within the family unless they bore children, especially sons. Furthermore, he stressed that, among the upper classes, the bond based on love between husbands and wives was never considered important and arranged marriages were practised in selecting a prospective partner. Thus, for instance, Sechiyama argues that communication between husbands and wives was poor and the stereotypically taciturn husbands or fathers saying nothing more than *'meshi, furo, neru'* or 'food, bath, bed' were quite apparent until recent years. The weak bonds between couples led married women to bond with their children to express their feelings. For women who married into the new family as *'yome'* or 'young wife' in a patrilineal family, children were their only defence against a lonely and insecure future. These factors contributed to women's readiness to affirm that their roles of mother and sole child-raiser were in fact the norm. Sechiyama's analysis explains how and why the slogan was disseminated according to the socio-economic and political environment of that time. It was culturally and socially accepted by women in Japanese society, especially as a result of the demands of the society itself and the needs of the women themselves.

Today motherhood ideology is often seen as restrictive in confining women to the roles of wives and mothers. However, the education associated with the idea of 'good wives and wise mothers' during the Meiji period could be regarded as a sort of 'modern education' for Japanese women as the definition of womanhood as motherhood gained legitimacy for the first time (Bernstein 1991). Thus, some feminists in the Taisho period (1912–1926), notably Raicho Hiratsuka, saw the motherhood ideology as a way of enhancing women's status and roles. Hiratsuka highly valued women's role as mothers and believed that, in Rodd's words, 'educational and political equality for women was desirable precisely because they would better prepare women for their roles as mothers' (Rodd 1991: 190). It was in the Taisho period that the first calls were heard for the protection of motherhood. This was commonly known as *bosei hogo ronsō* (the debate over the protection and support of motherhood) and was debated in several publications on the 'new women', including the literary magazine *Seitō* (Bluestockings), founded by Hiratsuka in 1911 (Rodd 1991). Yet Hiratsuka, who stressed the importance of the state as a protector of mothers, did not escape criticism. Another feminist, the prominent poet and writer Akiko Yosano, argued that, irrespective of sex, people should be allowed to take on as many roles as they could manage (Rodd 1991). In any case, the discussion over 'new women' in the Taisho period revealed for the first time that women themselves could contribute to redefining their own gender roles. This at the same time meant, as Rodd puts it, that 'the state lost its monopoly over gender construction in Japan' (1991: 176).

The myth of the first three years

This, however, did not mean the end of control over women by the state. For example, Kondo holds that the idea of 'good wives and wise mothers' continued to define women in the interwar and post-war periods sponsored by the state (Kondo 1990: 280). Indeed, the state reinforced the motherhood ideology when needed, including during the period of rapid economic growth (the late 1950s to 1973). The government, which made economic growth a national goal, thought that it was an absolute necessity for women to play their roles as homemakers, in order for men to devote themselves entirely to the workforce, thus allowing women to reproduce and raise the future labour force of the country (Ohinata 1995). The propagation of motherhood became conspicuous especially during the 1960s through the myth known as the '*san-sai ji shinwa*' or 'the myth of the first three years'.

The myth of the first three years was strongly influenced by Western research which had its basis within attachment theory, as formulated by John Bowlby. Bowlby had been a British army psychiatrist during the war, before becoming a director of the Child Guidance Department of the Tavistock Clinic in London. It was here that he studied young children's reactions when separated from their mothers (Eyer 1992). The World Health Organization (WHO) commissioned him to conduct research on the mental health aspects of the problem of orphans, as a result of which he presented a report entitled 'Maternal Care and Mental Health' in 1951 (Bowlby 1951). His attachment theory tries to explain how the presence of responsive loving attachment figures during infancy is essential for achieving lifelong mental good health (Bruer 1999). The research helped to improve significantly the conditions of institutional care for children. Bowlby concluded in his report that there was 'a lack of conviction on the part of government, social agencies, and the public that mother-love in infancy and childhood is as important for mental health as are vitamins and proteins for physical health' (1951: 158). The theory, however, has been criticized by many other researchers. Michael Rutter in his book, *Maternal Deprivation Reassessed* (1972) criticized Bowlby for placing too much emphasis on the role of the mother. He argues that Bowlby lacks evidence in asserting that the bond with the mother is fundamentally different from the bond with others. Rutter writes 'The father, the mother, brothers and sisters, friends, school-teachers and others all have an impact on development, but their influence and importance differs for different aspects of development. A less exclusive focus on the mother is required. Children also have fathers!' (1972: 124–5).

All children need someone to take care of and love them, of course, but it is extremely debatable whether the caregiver must necessarily be the biological mother. In fact, in early modern Japan, the separation between the biological mother and child was accepted in that the child was taken care of by many people including fathers, grandparents, servants, siblings, and apprentices (Uno 1991). The majority of specialists in the field of child care study today agree that what should be emphasized more is not whether or not the child is taken care of by the biological mother, but rather how he or she is treated or cared for by the caregiver or caregivers, i.e. the quality of care should always take precedence.

The myth, however, is still very influential in Japanese society and a large number of women are still bound to this belief. For example, according to a survey carried out by the Institute of Population Problems in 1992, almost 90 per cent of married women in Japan agreed that it was better for mothers to stay home without a job, at least while the child is young (Ministry of Health and Welfare 1998). Jolivet also notes that 'The option of outside assistance is only ever considered once the child has reached the age of 3 which shows the extent of the impact of the slogan: *Sansai made, haha no tede*! ("In mother's hands up to the age of three!")' (1997: 55). Looking at the Japanese female labour pattern today provides further support for this analysis, as discussed in the next section.

Current situation

Female labour pattern

The M-shaped curve

Figure 4.3 shows the Japanese female labour pattern. It resembles the letter M and thus is known as an 'M-shaped curve' (Ochiai 1997:11). The M-shaped curve peaks twice, in the age groups 20–24 and 45–49, and drops in the age group 30–35. This means that many women leave their careers for marriage or child-rearing, which reflects the reality that Japanese women still strongly

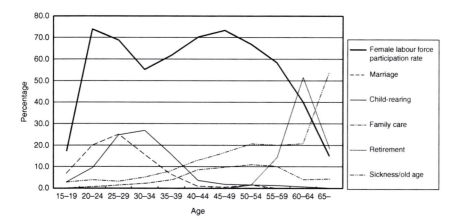

Figure 4.3 Age-specific female labour force participation rates and reasons for female employees to quit their jobs

Notes: Data on female labour participation rates were obtained in 1998. Data on reasons for people leaving their jobs were obtained in 1997 and they were limited to employees only.

Source: Statistics Bureau, Management and Coordination Agency, *Rōdōryoku chōsa* (Labour Force Survey), 1998 and *Shōgyō kōzō kihon chōsa kekka no gaiyō* (Summary Results and Analyses of Employment Status Survey), 1997.

conform to the conventional gender roles of women as homemakers and child raisers. However, as Ochiai points out (1997: 11), this pattern is not universal, and some countries in the West, such as the United States and Sweden, display the 'reversed U-shaped curve' which resembles the male labour force pattern.

The question then arises, how about other regions in Asia with a similar cultural heritage to Japan's? Do we find a similar pattern there? Sechiyama (1996) investigated the female workforce pattern in Taiwan and reported that women in Taiwan do not quit their jobs in the 25–34 age group. In fact, according to a Man-Power Management Report in Taiwan in 1992, approximately 40 per cent of women with children under the age of three were engaged in productive labour, and this share increased to 80 per cent among college graduates. In Japan, less than 30 per cent of women with children under the age of three are engaged in the workforce (Sechiyama 1996). These findings suggest significantly different views about child-rearing in Japan and Taiwan. It is easy to presume that similar social phenomena should be found in Asian countries because they possess a similar cultural heritage. Yet the above discussion suggests that similar broad traditions of thought are not necessarily enough to explain specific patterns of behaviour in contemporary society. The comparison demonstrates that the motherhood ideology found in Japan is far from universal even in East Asia, and again displays that it was constructed both socially and culturally over a period of time.

Funabashi (2000) reported that in 1991, in an average week, female Japanese adults spent 4 hours 41 minutes per day on housework and child-rearing while male adults spent 31 minutes, a ratio of 1:9. The comparable ratio in France was 1:1.7 and 1:1.6 in Sweden. Japanese mothers hardly ever receive such support from their husbands and this is closely related to the way men work in Japanese companies. Companies in Japan allow most fathers scant time to co-operate in child-rearing. Thus men, too, are sometimes made victims of the gender-segregated society. This issue again shows how the male gender role defines and confines the female gender role. Since they interact with one another they cannot be considered separately, or as Refsing points out: 'Gender is a relational concept, and male and female gender identities within a specific culture ideally fit into each other like pieces in a puzzle' (Refsing 1998: 200). At the same time, the demand for working mothers to conform to the Japanese style working environment also makes it difficult for them to pursue a career, as the demands made by companies would be too great a sacrifice for most of them. This becomes clear in Creighton's description of how extremely hard work, both physically and mentally, causes most women in high-ranking career posts to remain unmarried (1996: 211–2).

Also, many working mothers in Japan have been coerced into leaving their careers due to the insufficiency of a support system 'in terms of paid pregnancy and maternity leave, guarantees for returning to the same job afterwards, proper childcare facilities, and paid leave when children are ill' (Refsing 1998: 199). Inoue and Ehara (1999) also note the problems faced by working mothers with regard to the inadequacy and inflexibility of registered nurseries (*hoikuen*).[5] For instance, the opening hours are too short, they accept no newborn infants, and they are reluctant to take care of children when they become ill. This leads many mothers to rely on unregistered nurseries, as they are usually more accommodating to the requests of their customers. However, the quality of unregistered nurseries varies, partly because of the lack of government support and control.

Although there has been significant improvement in the institutional support for child-rearing in recent years, cultural resistance has prevented some of these improvements from being enjoyed to the full.[6] As discussed earlier, many Japanese women seem to feel psychological guilt over leaving their children, especially newborn babies, to a third person, including nurseries. Funabashi (2000) reports that about 40 per cent of working mothers today leave their preschool children with their relatives in Japan largely due to their prejudice against nurseries. She continues that nurseries are often regarded as a place for people in 'trouble' because they are welfare facilities. The image of kindergartens (*yōchien*) is very different: people appreciate them as a place to educate children because kindergartens are administered by the Ministry of Education (Funabashi 2000). Not only do women in Japan feel compelled to raise their children by their own hands, but also to educate them 'well' to fulfil the important role of the 'wise mother'.

Increased number of married women participating in part-time work today

Figure 4.4 shows the changes in the proportion of married and single female employees in the non-agricultural sector. The number of females entering the workforce as a whole has risen during the past few decades. Yet it is clear from the figure that the recent increase in female labour force participation is largely due to an increase in the numbers of married working women. In fact, the ratio of married women engaged in the workforce has exceeded that of single women since 1975. Much of this increase in married women's labour has come in the part-time sector (Ministry of Health and Welfare 1998). The percentage of female part-time workers among total female workers doubled from 17.4 per cent in 1975 to 36.5 per cent in 1998, and the corresponding number of female part-timers increased from 1.98 million to 7.56 million (Statistics Bureau, Management and Coordination Agency, Labour Force Survey). This indicates that the recent increase in the female workforce is largely due to a rise in the number of married part-time workers.

Figure 4.5, based on a Ministry of Labour survey of 1995, shows the reasons for choosing part-time work for both sexes. The majority of people replied that the main reason for choosing part-time work was 'to work the hours that are most convenient for oneself'. The term 'convenient for oneself' for women means the time convenient for their family, so that they can carry out housework, child-rearing, and care for the elderly as well (Inoue and Ehara 1999). Female part-timers placed more importance on reducing their working hours rather than on their type of work or labour conditions, compared to their counterpart male-workers. Thus, one might argue that although married women working outside the domestic

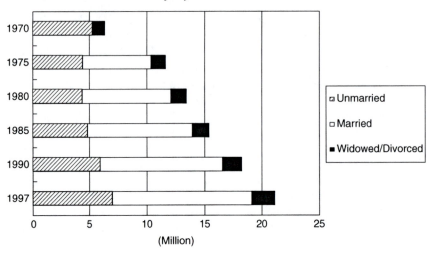

Figure 4.4 Changes in number of female employees based on marital status in the non-agricultural sector.
Source: Inoue and Ehara, 1999 (Based on figures from Management and Coordination Agency, *Rōdōryoku chōsa nenpō* (Annual Report on the Labour Force Survey)).

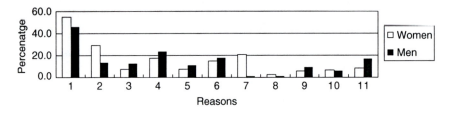

Figure 4.5 Reasons for choosing to work part-time.
1.Work the hours most convenient for oneself 2.Work shorter hours and days 3.Well-paid/Favourable treatment 4.Interested in the work 5.Easy to quit 6.No full-time work opportunities 7.Unable to work full-time due to housework and child-rearing 8.Unable to work full-time due to care of the sick and elderly 9.Unable to work full-time due to own poor physical condition 10.Friends/Acquaintances are working 11.Other.
Note: Students are not included.
Source: Ministry of Labour, *Pōto-taimu rōdōsha sōgō jittai chōsa hōkoku* (General Survey on Part-time Workers), 1995.

domain do not quite fit into the image of *ryōsai kenbo*, who are supposed to be in the private/domestic/reproduction sphere, their income is often used to supplement the family budget, and as long as their part-time work does not interfere with their housework, their 'wage labor *outside* the home became an index of their commitment to the inside, the *uchi* [the domestic domain]' (Kondo 1990: 280). That married women are largely engaged in part-time work again reveals the fact that they are strongly restricted by conventional gender roles.

Case studies

The following section focuses on some case studies that are relevant to the issues I have brought up thus far. The first two cases describe the relationship between my informants and their parents. These two cases clearly illustrate the contrast between a mother-child and a father-child relationship. The third case study describes a role conflict experienced by one of my informants who is a professional woman. As stated earlier in this chapter, what especially distinguishes women today from women born in earlier decades is that they are more likely to seek employment outside the household, which then forces them to choose between the mutually exclusive roles of worker and housewife. This case study clearly reveals this issue through the personal experience of an informant who had to make a tough decision between her career and marriage.

Close bonding with mothers: A case study

Many informants touched on the issue of how their mothers expressed their emotional feelings towards them, in a way that reflected the weak bond between their parents. Sachiko (32) was one interviewee who remarked that the motherhood ideology made contemporary mothers overzealous in their maternal care. She explained to me that since she felt her mother's interference was excessive she decided to live on her own. Living alone meant giving up her 'luxurious life of a parasite single,' as Masahiro Yamada (1999) would put it. In fact, she is currently paying ¥ 43,000 per month for her flat, which accounts for 20 per cent of her income. She finds that price is worth paying just to be away from her mother, who she felt was meddling in her life. For instance, when she was in her second year at university, she took a part-time job in a small shop, which was located about 10 minutes away from her house by bus. One day, her mother came to her workplace bringing lunch for her. This continued for a few days until Sachiko finally asked her mother to stop as her colleagues were teasing her. This incident shows the different ideas in Japan about the appropriate level of maternal care: (a) to Sachiko's mother, presumably this seemed 'what a mother should do' (b) while to Sachiko and her colleagues, it seemed excessive. While the motherhood ideology stresses a close bonding between mothers and children, in practice mothers are often perplexed as to what extent they should take care of their children. Recently the 'excessive care' shown by Japanese mothers has, in fact, been seen by some commentators as causing problems. Ochiai (1997) noted that 'these problems were the result of the decrease in the number of children per couple, which had led parents to concentrate their love and attention so intensely on each child that this love had proved to be a burden' (1997: 126). Looking back on it now, Sachiko feels that her mother was extremely lonely and had too much time on her hands at the time, because her husband was working away from home, having been transferred to a different part of Japan. This is a common practise in Japan and is known as *tanshin funin*.[7] Sachiko's mother married young and bore Sachiko's elder sister when she was 23 years old.

The mother expected her daughters to lead a life similar to her own. Sachiko is in fact planning to get married in the near future and probably have children (see Chapter 5). She plans to marry later than her mother did, however, in order to maintain what she regards as her freedom as a single girl. In her case what she wishes to do while single is to work. Her remarks imply that she believes that she would have to give up work for marriage. I asked if she thought there was any way that she could work and be married without sacrificing anything. She said she is not confident about managing everything at the same time because she believes that she does not have the physical strength to do so. Considering the fact that she is a perfectly healthy woman, her comments clearly reveal that she expects the roles of housewife and child raiser to be extremely demanding, and that this is instrumental in leading her to delay her marriage.

Poor relationship with fathers: A case study

Akira (36), a male interviewee, has been dating a woman from Kenya for about two years and plans to get married in the near future. However, he has only told his mother and not his father about this. This is because he and his mother think that his father will be displeased at his marrying a 'coloured' woman. Akira thinks that his mother is always on his side: she told him that she would convey this issue to the father when the time comes. Even though he is completely leaving this issue to his mother, his story suggests the importance of obtaining final approval from his father. More importantly, this incident reveals much about relationships within the family. There seems to be a strong bond between Akira and his mother, while it appeared to me as if Akira and his father spoke such different languages that they needed an interpreter, i.e. the mother, to fill in the gaps between them. In fact, it has been practically impossible for Akira to communicate with his father on a regular basis. This is because the father, like Sachiko's, has been away from his family due to *tanshinfunin* work transfers since Akira was in primary school. His father works in the real-estate business, trying to develop land that he owns in the countryside, and he usually comes home only once every two months. His mother did not want to go with him for her own and the children's sakes. This suggests that the relationship with her husband was not her main priority. Moreover, Akira said that he and his father are on bad terms and mentioned one incident which aggravated their relationship. Akira's father had wished him to take over the family business but Akira refused, choosing 'freedom' instead by taking a position in an advertising company after graduating from high school. Akira's father has given up the idea by now but their relationship has remained problematic.

Explaining that his father is a 'traditional' Japanese father to whose ideas he has always been opposed. His views on marriage, family, and gender roles seem completely different from those of his father, and his father seems to have served him as an example of how not to behave. Akira said: 'Generally speaking, I'm opposed to the idea that it's okay to have extra-marital affairs, smoke, and drink simply because of being a man.'

Role conflict: A case study

One of my female interviewees, Masako (39), mentioned in Chapter 2, is a professional woman. After graduating from one of the most prestigious universities in Japan, Masako began working for a large firm where she became a successful manager. When Masako was 21 years old, she started to date a man that she met at university. They dated for three years and as their relationship became serious, they began to think about getting married. After they graduated from university, her boyfriend found a job at one of the Japanese television stations and became a reporter. It soon became apparent that he would be transferred to many different places by the company. Then Masako's career became an obstacle to their marriage as it was obvious that Masako had to remain in Tokyo in order to develop her career. She said that she strongly desired to marry him but in the end she chose her career to achieve her ambition. They broke up and Masako became extremely depressed, especially several years later, when she heard that he had married someone else. Right after Masako broke up with her boyfriend, she became intimate with one of her colleagues who was (and is) married. They have had an extra-marital relationship ever since. She said she needed someone to fulfil her emotional and physical emptiness.

In response to my question about having children, Masako replied that she strongly desires to bear and raise children in the future. She does not think that there will be any problem for her to return to her workplace after taking maternity leave because she has already established her position within the company and also she is confident that she is appreciated by the firm. In the past, Masako had a casual talk with her female colleagues about her desire to have children. Their reaction was extremely positive and they said that they would be willing to help her if she becomes a mother. Unusually for a Japanese woman, she said that she would not even mind having children without being married. However, she believed that it would be difficult to raise children by herself. She felt that if her mother lived closer to her, then it might be possible, but since this was not the case, the idea of having a child was totally unrealistic.

Masako's case describes an environment that makes it extremely difficult for a career-oriented woman to play her socially approved gender role of marriage and child-rearing. Despite the fact that both partners strongly wished to get married, her career became an obstacle to their marriage. For Masako, the idea of having children is theoretically not a problem with or without a husband; nor does she have financial problems to worry about. In practice, however, since her work basically takes away all her time, it is practically impossible to raise children alone. She apparently considers support from the private and public sector to be insufficient, or maybe she, herself, does not think that child-rearing help services would be an adequate mother-substitute. Thus she said that the only hope for her to put this into practice would be to have support from her own mother. This again draws attention to the difference between women's work in earlier decades and women's careers today. Compared with pre-war women, Masako's range of career opportunities is of course much wider and her potential for earning and career success greatly improved. However, the fact remains that since Masako is employed outside the home, her career and marriage/child-rearing are virtually incompatible. At the same time, Masako regards her career as a source of gratification and these factors have led her to abandon a potential marriage.

Conclusion

This chapter has argued that ideological structures (such as motherhood ideology) and economic/social structures (such as household-based work versus company-based work) are very important in defining gender roles in contemporary Japanese society. Japanese women's labour pattern, known as the M-shaped curve, clearly illustrates that many women quit their job when they reach the time of marriage or child-rearing. The deepest drop is found during the child-rearing period, meaning that their role as mothers determines their gender roles most decisively in Japan. I have argued that one important reason for this is the motherhood ideology, including the myth of the first three years, in that a significant number of Japanese women are still bound to a belief that severely restricts their behaviour.

Also, the way women participate in the labour force has changed. Previously they could work more easily as an extension of household roles. If they had outside work, it was mainly in a place not too far from home. Nowadays the nature of work has changed, meaning it is more company based. More importantly, the meaning of work has changed and a large number of women today regard their career (rather than mere 'work') as a way to improve themselves or to fulfil their ambitions. More and more women today wish for, and manage to gain, fulfilment from their careers, and thus their gender identity is changing in important ways while men's gender identity remains relatively static and unchanged. The result is a widening disagreement (not necessarily public) about what is legitimate for women.

In this regard, the strong gendered division of labour is an important factor in the recent trend towards postponement or avoidance of marriage in Japan. More women foresee difficulties in pursuing both their careers and housework/child rearing, especially in an environment where the demands made on both these roles are extreme.

In order to further understand gender relations it is useful to examine one specific type of personal relationship – courtship. In the following chapter, I will elucidate some characteristics of, and changes in, Japanese courtship practices, which have been significantly affecting the recent trend towards delayed marriage in Japan.

5 Changes in courtship practices

Introduction

While it is important to study gender roles, it is especially revealing to look at the dynamics whereby relationships are formed. The study of close or personal relationships grew rapidly during the 1980s, involving scholars from a variety of fields, including family studies, sociology, human development, psychology, and communications (Cate and Lloyd 1992). This chapter deals with one type of close relationship known as courtship. Courtship and marriage differ from other relationships in that they are 'probably the only types of voluntary relationships that have an exclusivity about them: part of the whole business of courtship is the cutting off of other sexual relationships and the devotion of oneself to a special partner' (Duck 1988: 73).

Cate and Lloyd (1992: xi) made a comprehensive survey of research on courtship, and define the concept as follows: 'it includes relationships that move to marriage as well as those that end before marriage and might more accurately be called "dating" relationships in that there may be no present intent to marry.' Their definition is rather broad compared to that of other researchers such as Cherlin (1996: 229), who simply defines courtship as 'a publicly visible process with rules and restrictions through which young men and women find a partner to marry'.

It is believed by some scholars that courtship sets the foundation for the later quality and stability of the marriage (e.g. Cate and Lloyd 1992). Many processes that are considered important for marital success are likely to develop during the courtship, and thus it is regarded as significant in terms of its implications for marriage. It is even reported that the longer the partners have dated, the more likely they are to find out whether they are compatible (Benokraitis 1993: 202; Hoult et al. 1978). The study of courtship itself is thus very important. The great number of literary works and films based on romance, love, mate-selection, dating behaviour, and engagement reflect people's interest in this issue.

Analytical perspective beyond Japan

Mating systems across cultures run the spectrum from polygyny (one man to two or more women), through polyandry (one woman to two or more men) and monogamy (one man to one woman), to group marriage (two or more men and two or more women). In recent years same-sex marriage has also come to be approved in several countries and regions. Saxton (1993) reports that 75 per cent of societies worldwide prefer polygyny, albeit without explaining how this figure was arrived at. However, preference, as such, does not necessarily represent the actual state of affairs. Most marriages in those societies are, in fact, monogamous because the sex ratio between marriageable men and women is usually balanced; thus only a small number of men – mostly wealthy ones – have more than one wife. Helen Fisher (1989) goes beyond this and notes that mate selection can be described as serial pairbonding in which individuals are involved in successive monogamous relationships throughout the course of their lives.

Some researchers look at the cultural and historical variations as well as similarities in mate-selection. Gwen Broude (1994: 219), for example, noted that in a sample of 161 societies, as many as 41.1 per cent of marriages are arranged for girls by their parents, while in 29.3 per cent of 157 societies, boys marry a woman chosen by their parents. However, Pamela Regan (2003) argues that there is evidence to show that even in those societies with a strong tradition of arranged marriage, including China, Africa, Russia, and the Middle East, there are tendencies towards marriage based on mutual attraction and individual choice.

What about the qualities desired in a spouse? Many studies in the field of marriage revealed that people tend to marry those who possess traits such as race, age, social class and religion that are similar to their own – the principle of homogamy has been well documented (Smart and Smart 1980: 172). Some researchers stress gender differences in human mate selection criteria. Buss (1987), for instance, examined 37 cultures worldwide and developed evolutionary hypotheses. He concluded that in order to secure sufficient resources for raising their offspring, females value and desire mates possessing resources or potentially capable of acquiring resources (Buss 1987). Men are concerned more with a female's physical attractiveness because this feature is understood to be a good indicator of a female's reproductive capability. Buss notes 'Physical appearance probably provides the strongest set of cues, and these include features such as clear, smooth, and unblemished skin, lustrous hair, white teeth, clear eyes, and full lips' (1987: 341).

But of course, culturally-conditioned views of the attractiveness of marital partners is only one element influencing marriage patterns around the world. Social and economic factors, such as the size, status and wealth of families, also play an important role. Hutter holds that there is a correlation between types of marital arrangements and types of family and states:

> Generally, where a consanguineal family form exists – one that emphasize the rights, obligations, and duties of family members to the larger extended family – there is a tendency for such families to control the marriages of their members. On the other hand, where a conjugal form exists, there is a greater emphasis on individual motivations and, consequently, a greater freedom is allowed family members in choosing their partners. (1981: 230)

One example that illustrates the former case is raised by Schak who writes in his book *Dating and Mate-selection in Modern Taiwan* (1974):

> The ingredients of a modern courtship system are the recognition of court-ship itself as a legitimate social activity, the freedom of young people to choose their own spouses and the recognition and legitimization of roman-tic love as a basis for that choice. In traditional China [the author refers to the years before the Republican revolution in 1911], none of these existed. (p. 81)

Although there were regional as well as social-class differences, Japanese parents also controlled the marriages of their children in pre-war Japan.

The Anglo-American case

Courtship practices in Britain during the mid-nineteenth century, which would be highly influential on American society, dictated that at the early stage of courtship, the principals talked or walked in public places, keeping each other company. They might then move on to evening visiting where a young man would call at the woman's home. At first, there was little privacy because of the woman's parents' presence in the home. After several visits, the couple could have time alone and engage in kissing and fondling, but sexual intimacy had to wait until they became betrothed or married (Cherlin 1996).

This type of courtship, however, began to decline around 1900 in the US, as more people began to live in the expanding cities and became more affluent. Courtship started to give way to dating: it was now moving from the private sphere, i.e. the woman's family home, to more public arenas such as cinemas and restaurants. 'Dating moved courtship into the world of the economy. Money – men's money – was the center of the dating system. Thus, on two counts, men became the hosts and assumed the control that came with that position' (Bailey 1989: 21). This system or style of dating peaked between 1945 and 1960. During this period, college enrollments rose sharply and allowed young couples to date without the restriction of monitoring parents. As a result, as Bailey (1989) discusses in his book, *From Front Porch to Back Seat: Courtship in Twentieth-Century America*, courtship literally went from the front porch of the woman's parents' house to the back seat of the young man's car.

By the 1970s and 1980s, the dating system became less connected with marriage. As the age at first marriage rose to the mid-20s, 'steady' dating in high school seemed to be less associated with finding a spouse (Cherlin 1996; Laner and Ventrone 1998). Thus, 'changes in sexual behaviour and delay of marriage were accompanied by a new stage in the courtship system: cohabitation' (Cate and Lloyd 1992: 30), which shows a profound shift in values. Since a significant increase in unmarried cohabitation began in the early 1960s in the US, Spanier chooses the 1950s as a period for comparison with today. He explains the reasons for the increase in cohabitation as follows:

> premarital sexual activity has become more prevalent, has involved less risk, and has tended to begin earlier. Society accepts such behavior more readily. Contraception more readily available to young people reduces or even eliminates the fear of pregnancy. The availability of abortion and the increased awareness of abortion as a method of controlling fertility undoubtedly also play some role.
>
> (Spanier 1985: 98)

Cohabitation prior to marriage became popular in young adults' lives probably because it offered the advantages of marriage together with the advantages of not being married, i.e., one gets companionship, sexual intimacy, and love without permanent and legal commitment. Cohabitation may also have economic implications because it is usually cheaper for two individuals to live together than to live separately. Although this may be an ambiguous and slightly indeterminate period in their lives, it gives the couple first-hand experience of the advisability and suitability of marriage. Unlike the old-fashioned concept of engagement, which is a definite agreement to marriage, cohabitation provides a deferral of the wedding day (Spanier 1991).

Many scholars emphasize that the characteristics of American courtship contain elements of a participant-run system (Rothman 1984; Cate and Lloyd 1992) in that individual motives play an important role in the selection of a mate.[1] Apparently this does not mean an eligible marriage partner can simply be any unmarried person of the opposite sex. Hutter (1981) explains: 'Rules of endogamy are expressed in ethnocentric beliefs that define "suitable" marriage partners to people of the same social class, religion, ethnic group, and race' (1981: 210) in the US.[2] Indeed people tend to choose a partner who possesses similar background, values, and attitudes, thus limiting the number of eligible partners in a way that can be said to be 'influenced by the principle of preferential mating' (Hutter 1981: 210). At the same time, parents in the US had an indirect influence upon their children's marital selection processes. Goode says that: 'Since youngsters fall in love with those with whom they associate, control over informal relationships also controls substantially the focus of affection' (1959: 45). Furthermore, Hutter reports that the parents in the American upper classes tend to exert influence on their children's mate-selection because of the large amount of wealth involved (1981: 213).

The shift from arranged marriages to love marriages

This section examines courtship practice during the pre- and post-1945 period in Japan. More precisely, I discuss how mate-selection has shifted from arranged marriages to love marriages in Japan and examine some important underlying implications. It is reported that of those who married between 1990 and 1994,

85 per cent married through love and 13 per cent married through arranged marriages. These figures also show that the percentage of arranged marriages declined 12 per cent during the previous 10 years (National Institute of Population and Social Security Research 1998). However, special attention to defining these concepts is required, as it should be recognized that the definitions have changed over time and could even differ among people living in the same era.

Mate-selection in pre-war Japan

Miai kekkon or arranged marriage is a kind of marriage agreement that emphasizes the bond between *ie* (house) and *ie* rather than individualistic ties; whereas *ren'ai kekkon* or love-match marriage is a form of marriage based on an ideology that says love and marriage are related (*Aera Mook*, 1999). In the pre-war years a large number of people, especially those in the upper classes, married through *miai kekkon* or arranged marriages. These were usually arranged by a *nakōdo* or matchmaker, and prospective partners were selected by parents in consultation mainly with relatives. Marriages were based not on mutual attraction but on the interests of the couple's families, and the bride and groom were expected to accept the decision of their elders (Hendry 1981). Kawashima (1954) explained the fundamental social conditions that prescribed these arranged marriages. In his view the strong segregation of the sexes, especially when unmarried, was one of the principal reasons for the extremely high prevalence of arranged marriages in Japan. An old saying 'a boy and a girl must not sit together after they are seven years of age' provides an example of the ideals of sex segregation within traditional Japanese society. Under these social conditions, an intermediary played an indispensable role in matchmaking. Also, as is mentioned by Edwards (1989), young people relied on their families or parents for selecting their mate because they lacked confidence in making their own choice, partly as a result of lack of experience with the opposite sex.

A further fundamental social-condition that prescribed arranged marriages, was the existence of the Japanese family system, the *ie* system. As stated earlier, mate-selection was placed under the control of the head of the family and/or the family members because marriage was not solely an individual matter but was of significant importance to the interests of the family as a whole. Marriage meant the establishment of bonds between families. Thus, marriages were arranged according to perceived appropriateness of background and social status because these would determine both parties' contacts, future opportunities, and social status. Mate-selection meant bringing an outsider, a *yome* or young wife or in some cases *muko* or son-in law, into the house. Continuity was the main consideration of the family. Thus, for example, if the *ie* had no sons, a *muko* or son-in-law would be married in to take over the family responsibilities, and would be known as *muko-yōshi* (Hendry 1987). The introduction of a *yome* to the family was also of extreme importance. The family members needed to have a clear view of whether the *yome* would be able to assimilate into the house and become a dutiful wife. After the *yome* entered her new family, she went through a period of rigid instruction by her mother-in-law in the 'ways of the family' or *kafū* (Dore 1999). Marriage was also a family affair because of the economic issues involved. A *yome* marrying into, or daughter marrying out of, the family meant a gain or loss of work force for the household, and a wedding itself meant a huge expenditure and burden for the family (Kawashima 1954).

During the Tokugawa feudal period (1603–1868), members of the warrior class or samurai were not allowed to marry other classes such as farmers, artisans or merchants, although there were some exceptions in the later years of the period. Furthermore, marriages between residents of different domains were also prohibited in order to avoid power factions developing through marriages (Hoshii 1986). Generally speaking, however, the extent of control held by the head of the *ie* and other family members was stricter among the upper classes compared to the lower classes.

> Even in the Tokugawa period, however, among the poorer urban classes in which the family was already in a process of disintegration, marriage was often a tenuous and only half-formalized contract between individuals, concluded without the benefit of a go-between's negotiation, parental approval or even the wine-drinking ceremony in the presence of relatives which legitimized the match.
>
> (Dore 1999: 108)

This was mainly because Confucianism as a moral code was mostly limited to the high-ranking rulers. Parental control over mate-selection was stricter among the upper classes because marriage in many cases had a greater influence on the cream of society and had social, political, and economic effects whereas the impact of marriage was focused mainly on economic issues among the lower classes (Kawashima 1954). Similar findings have emerged from research in other parts of the world. For example, based on research in Thailand, Cherlin reports that,

> Parents' involvement in finding marriage partners for their children is greater when they have more resources, such as land or investments, to protect; when they control the means children can use to make a living; and when the addition of spouses and children to a family is of crucial importance to the well-being of the larger family unit. (1996: 257)

During the Edo period in Japan, peasants constituted about 80 to 90 per cent of the population (Sekiyama 1985), whereas samurai constituted no more than seven to ten per cent (Hanley 1997). This suggests that the majority of people, mainly peasants, experienced relatively less parental-control compared to those in the upper class over mate-selection. Kawashima (1954) also agrees that among poor tenant farmers, there was less control by the family head. For instance, even if the family head did not agree entirely with the mate-selection of his children, in many cases he consulted with other family members about the issue. And the wishes of the children were often respected, as long as the marriage did not produce any conflict of interest with the family's labour demands. Furthermore, it should be mentioned here that although most commoners married at the around 17 or 18 years of age, marriage was by no means universal. In some poor farm villages, men who were not the first son were often unable to get married due to their financial difficulties (Fukuo 1972).

As for segregation of the sexes, there was a tacit understanding among peasants that social contact between the sexes was acceptable in hidden places, while segregation of the sexes was mostly meant only for public places. In fact, in many villages, there were youth lodges, some for young men, some for young girls and some even for both (Aruga 1935). These lodges provided a place for romantic and sexual exploration for young people (Hendry 1981) and unions were made based on personal choice and mutual attraction. A suitor would visit his lover's lodge (or the girl's home if there were no lodges) at night in an activity commonly known as *yobai*. The term *yobai* meant 'to call' one's lover's name for the proposal of marriage and thus it was regarded as an acceptable step towards marriage. However, with the spread of Confucian patriarchal values, the term acquired a derogatory sense and it came to be written with the characters for 'night' and 'crawl' which had an immoral connotation (Yagi 2001; Hendry 1981). Hendry writes, 'In ancient literature it (*yobai*) referred to a legitimate proposal of marriage, and it seems in various forms to have been sanctioned as a type of courtship leading to marriage in many areas until the Meiji period' (1981: 122).

During the following Meiji period (1868–1912), the political leadership tried to modernize the country while emphasizing Confucian norms and seeking to apply them to the family system throughout society. However, in order to acquire advanced technology from the West, Japan was exposed to Western influence including its family ideals. At the end of the nineteenth century, however, 'a strong reaction occurred against the Western influence that had been incorporated into Japanese society' (Hendry 1985: 203). In response, the government re-adopted Confucianism as the backbone of the moral code, and thus the values of the samurai coloured by Confucian ideology also permeated the lower strata via the stress in the education system on the concepts of *chū* (loyalty) to the Emperor and *kō* (filial piety). As a result of the implementation of this moral code, the effects of Confucianism strengthened during this period. Kawashima notes that the stronger the degree of segregation between sexes, the more virtuous it was believed to be. Consequently, restrictions on mixing between the sexes became stricter even among the peasants, especially those known as *jisakunō* or owner farmers, in order to maintain their status and prestige (Kawashima 1954). In this regard, the Meiji period is often seen as a period in which samurai values were imposed on, and diffused through, the rest of society.

Thus, Edwards states that;

> most marriages were indeed arranged in the literal sense of the word. Partners were selected by the parents in consultation with relatives or friends of their own generation, who were instrumental in conducting negotiations with the other family. In theory a child had the right to veto a particular choice based

on the brief impressions formed at the *miai*, but in practice family pressure often overrode individual protest. (1989: 53–4)

This is an example of how pre-war attitudes or beliefs dominated individual needs. The needs of the family took precedence over individual interests.

Under these circumstances, there was strong social control over *ren'ai kekkon* or love marriages. Goode states that:

> Love is potentially a threat to the stratification system, for it may impel some young people to marry those whom their elders view as inappropriate spouses. It can disrupt the elder's plans to unite two lineages or family inheritances; it can link a high-ranking power with one of low rank, to the embarrassment of the former. Property, power, lineage, honor, totemic relationships, and other family resources in all societies flow from one generation to the next through the kinship lines, linked by marriages. Mate choice thus has many consequences. People who fall in love have braved storms of anger, violence, ostracism and their own inner fears in order to marry the one they loved. To avoid all this, love and mate choice are controlled, so that marriage is not left to the whim of youngsters. (1982: 55)

In other words, if a couple desired to marry for love, it meant that their subjective decisions challenged the objective decisions made by their parents in the case of arranged marriage (Dore 1999). Moreover, marrying an 'undesirable' partner meant a revolt against tradition.

Many writers associate increasing freedom for young people to choose marriage partners with the processes of modernization and industrialization. For example Goode (1963) reports that freedom of mate-selection arose with modernization because modernization had the effect of weakening family authority over individuals. Until modernization, parents controlled their children's mate-selection largely through control over inheritance and also by providing training in work skills.

However, in Japan, a rather different pattern may be observed. Although the onset of modernization coincided with the Meiji Restoration, which was a liberalizing influence on many other aspects of society, the first phase of modernization in Japan actually extended the arranged marriage system. From having been largely limited to the samurai class, it now spread downward to include the peasantry and urban working classes. This is because, as I briefly mentioned earlier, the Meiji reform government of the late-nineteenth century promulgated the Confucian family ethic through public schools. Moreover, from this period, a legal marriage required the permission of the head of the house (Meiji Civil Code, Article 750), and of the parents for a man under 30 and a woman under 25 (Meiji Civil Code, Article 722). Thus the pre-modern system became more firmly entrenched during this period (Blood 1967). This reveals that Goode's assertion that modernization has the effect of weakening family authority is not applicable to the Japanese case. The Meiji government deliberately placed individuals under the control of the family and therefore freedom of mate-selection did not occur with the onset of modernization in Japan.

Mate-selection in post-war Japan

As noted in earlier chapters, the *ie seido* or family system was abolished as a legal entity after the Second World War. This basically came about as a result of the American occupation of Japan which led to the 1947 constitution and associated Civil Code. This replaced the Meiji Civil Code, seen as unsuitable for a Japan which was on its way to becoming a new democratic state. The new constitution allowed freedom of choice of marriage partner, and proclaimed equal rights for women, who were now allowed to own property as well as to inherit. The idea of inheritance by the eldest son alone was completely done away with.

As stated in the previous section, modernization did not initially have a liberalizing effect on mate-selection in Japan. However, there is no question that modernization had a great impact on mate-selection practices in later years. Blood (1967) notes that the modernization and westernization of Japan involved forces that were bound to decrease the segregation of the sexes in the future. He cites a report by Hiroshi Wagatsuma saying that since 1959 the number of female students attending universities previously closed to them had risen to the point where they were now dominating some departments of Literature and Humanities. Blood remarks: 'As student bodies become increasingly coeducational, opportunities for college dating increase correspondingly' (1967: 7). Blood (1967) furthermore says that international travel both before and after the war, as well as exposure to Western literature, movies, and television had a great impact on Japanese culture. In particular, Western individualism and egalitarianism appealed to the younger generation as a rebellion against subordination by their elders. Since the influence of Western ideas was so persuasive, love matches became the preferred choice of the younger generation.

Under these circumstances, the purpose of marriage also started to undergo some changes. One of the most significant aspects was that love between the parties and happiness started to take on more important meanings in the purpose of marriage. This is a significant transition from some of the traditional aims of marriage, namely the continuity of the *ie*, procreation, status, and the fulfilment of a social and economic function in society. Accordingly, a survey by the Institute of Population Problems, Ministry of Health and Welfare in 1983 reported that marriages 'encouraged by those around one' had decreased and instead motivations such as 'felt affection towards the partner' had increased.

Another related issue is that the age gap between the partners in a married couple was decreasing. In the pre-war period, the average age difference between husband and wife was 4 years. This decreased to 3 years in the early post-war period until around 1970, and then gradually became smaller, reaching 2.3 years in 1993 (Yuzawa 1995). Goode (1963) notes that with industrialization, the age discrepancy between spouses became smaller in many societies. This is applicable to the case in Japan and 'With the improved status of women in society,

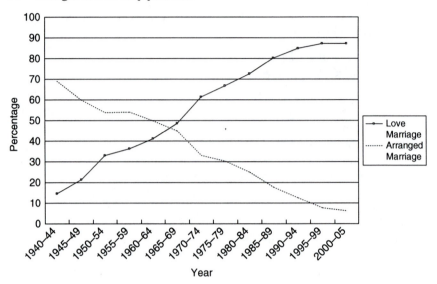

Figure 5.1 Annual trends in arranged and love marriages.
Source: National Institute of Population and Social Security Research, 2007b.

Japanese women have gradually developed a new perspective regarding marriage, seeing it as a companionship between equals in which the ages of the spouses tend to be closer to each other' (Kumagai 1995: 145).

Not surprisingly, the percentage of love match marriages has exceeded arranged marriages since the late 1960s and today the share of love marriages is over 85 per cent (see Figure 5.1). Data from a national survey in 1988 also indicated a decline in the number of arranged marriages. The percentage of arranged marriages for women were as follows: 68 per cent in the 60-year old group and over, 57 per cent in the 50–59-year old group, 48 per cent in the 40–49 group, 36 per cent in the 30–39 group, and 11 per cent in the 20–29 group (Martin 1990).

Apart from the fact that the incidence of arranged marriage has declined dramatically, the definitions of *ren'ai* (love) and *miai* (arranged) marriages have also undergone some changes and could even differ among people living in the same era. Edwards (1989) states that changes in the legal system in the post-war era have weakened people's attitudes towards marriage as a duty to the house, therefore the concepts of *ren'ai* and *miai* have taken on vastly different meanings. He furthermore states that both *ren'ai* and *miai* marriages have come 'to include significant interaction at two levels: as a personal relationship between the principals and through formal negotiations conducted by their families. By the late 1950s this parallelism was making the distinction between ren'ai and miai difficult to apply' (Edwards 1989: 57).

Regarding the concept of the *miai*, Blood says that 'Japanese marriages are no longer [the author refers to the late 1960s] arranged by parents on behalf of unknown children, but arranged by matchmakers on behalf of participating families. "Arrangement" now means primarily the formal introduction of potential marriage partners to each other and secondarily the follow-up message-carrying which cements a promising relationship' (1967: 12). In my view, 'arranged marriages' nowadays seem to be more 'arranged meetings' set up to minimize the trouble of looking for a partner by oneself. The 'arrangers' are no longer just relatives or matchmakers, but can also be colleagues or friends. As for the definition of 'love' marriages, they are often an uncertain concept. Salaff says that the concepts of 'freedom' and 'love' in marriage matters often pertain to 'arranged with consent' marriages and do not always refer to finding a spouse without parental involvement (UN 1990: 199).

Case studies

Ren'ai or Miai? A case study

Hendry notes that, 'Figures (for arranged and love marriages) are sometimes published, but these are notoriously unreliable due to the difficulty of classifying actual marriages as arranged or "love"' (1981: 30). This is clear from the case of one of my female interviewees, Sachiko (32). She entered a dating agency known as '*Zenkoku Nakōdo Renmei*' or National Matchmakers Association in October 1999. An *osewa-gakari* or go-between introduced her to a number of prospective partners. Sachiko was strongly attracted to a particular man to whom she had been introduced. The prospective partner also found himself drawn towards Sachiko and they had been dating ever since. They were seriously thinking of marriage but her partner was considering a job-change. Thus, they planned to get married sometime in the following year (2001) when his job was more settled. What was surprising was the fact that she had not told her parents about their relationship, even though they were the ones who had insisted on her joining the agency. She said that if her parents (especially her mother) had become involved in the matter, things might not have gone as smoothly. Her prospective partner is currently working in one of the major steel companies in Japan and earning a high salary, but he is considering a job-change to a smaller company where he would find his work more satisfactory. Changing jobs means surrendering his status as well as his high salary. She thinks the timing of conveying the news to her parents is an extremely delicate issue and she wishes to inform them when things are more settled. Her comments suggest that she needs to obtain the final approval or agreement of the parents which raises a question about the extent of the power she herself possesses in decision making about her future mate.

To some extent Sachiko's comments illustrate that mate-selection may still be regarded as too important an issue to be handled by the principal and/or determined by love alone, partly because, as Hoult *et al.* argue, the individualism involved in love relationships can tend to undermine important aspects of the social order (1978: 15). Edwards holds that, 'the emphasis in marriage has shifted to the needs of the principals rather than those of their families. Nevertheless, it is not as individuals that their interests hold priority . . . the individual has not replaced the ie as the fundamental unit in cultural values, despite the legal changes' (1989: 144).

When asked her opinion as to whether she regards her future marriage as an arranged- or love-match marriage, Sachiko said after much consideration that 'maybe' it could be regarded as a *miai kekkon* or arranged marriage, simply because they met through a formal *miai* arrangement, namely a dating agency. This case clearly reveals the difficulties in defining the meaning of an arranged marriage today. Blood (1967) raised four main motifs characteristic of pure *miai* marriages: (1) observing traditional formalities; (2) relying on other people's initiative and judgement; (3) lack of premarital interaction; and (4) lack of love. In terms of formality, Sachiko attended a *miai*, and was 'formally' introduced to her prospective partner by an *osewa-gakari* or go-between from the dating agency. Thus, Sachiko regards her future marriage as a *miai* marriage. However, it can be argued that her future marriage cannot be classified simply as a pure *miai* marriage because it does not fully feature the rest of the motifs. For one thing, they were dating in order to judge their compatibility by spending a considerable amount of time together. This is contrary to the motif of 'lack of premarital interaction'. Regarding 'love', they were planning to get married because they were attracted to each other. In fact, she bashfully explained to me that he proposed to her in a very passionate manner. It is extremely difficult to define the word 'love', but if one assumes romantic love as involving physical attraction, emotional involvement, and idealization, their case is far from 'lacking in love', at least from their point of view. In this regard, I agree with Edwards' (1989) and Hendry's (1981) views that *ren'ai* and *miai* are often not easy to separate.

Although Sachiko and her partner were introduced formally through a *miai*, they tested their compatibility, and only after they had found each other attractive did they decide to get married. Before meeting her present boyfriend, Sachiko was formally introduced to many other candidates and declined many. She exercised the right of veto based mainly on her impression formed at a *miai*. Under these circumstances, it would be appropriate to surmize that an arranged marriage today is being regarded as only one method of meeting a prospective partner.

Returning to Edwards (1989), he notes that *ren'ai* and *miai* are best thought of as 'successive strategies'. He suggests that the pressure to have *miai*-type meetings increases as people approach 'the upper ends of their marriageable age'. He continues, 'most people have one or more casual relationships when young, and perhaps one of these develops into marriage of the *ren'ai* type. If not, they begin having formal introductions – *miai* meetings – to ensure they will find a partner before their age makes marriage extremely difficult' (1989: 57).

Miai meetings: A case study

Yuka (31), a female informant, is one of those young women who feel constantly pressured by their parents to get married. Her parents started to arrange *miai* meetings when she was 25 years old and she has had more than 20 *miai* in the past. However she does not think that she will be able to find a suitable marital partner through this kind of arrangement. Yuka believes that she has learned at least one thing from having so many *miai*: those men who attend *miai* meetings usually look for a woman of the *ryōsai kenbo* or 'good wives and wise mothers' type, which she does not fit; neither does she wish to transform herself to fit this stereotype. In the past, she even behaved in a manner that would induce the partner to decline their *miai*. This is because she knew from her experience that if she were the one to decline a *miai*, her parents would criticize her repeatedly for her decision. Yet she continued and will continue this rather unproductive procedure of *miai* meetings, because, as she noted, 'I do it only to please my parents. It makes them relieved, if only temporarily, to think that they are making some kind of effort to move towards *their* ultimate goal.'

She currently lives with her parents but keeps herself busy in order to stay away from them. She said, 'I try to avoid conversations with my mother as much as possible but she catches me whenever she can and repeatedly tells me that I should get married. She even finds time in the morning and if I say I have to leave, she accuses me of avoiding the most important issue of my life!' The worst days are when her mother hears that one of Yuka's girlfriends is getting married. Yuka said, 'I try my best not to let her hear any "got married" news. But she somehow manages to hear the news from one of my girlfriends' mothers. There were six of us who were very close friends from the volleyball club that I joined during my days at high school. Four of them have already got married and two of us are still single. The other unmarried girl sent me a New Year's card saying, *Kotoshi koso shiawase ni narō ne* or "This is the year for us to achieve happiness."' The word *marriage* is not even mentioned because it is too 'obvious': no woman could possibly lead 'a happy life' without it. It can also be interpreted as the only way to get out of their current difficult situation, which discriminates against them because of their status of being single.

Many female informants were unduly concerned about their close girlfriends' marital status; and this in turn can influence their own timing of marriage. One female informant mentioned that she is extremely scared of being 'the last one left on the shelf' but feels it fine to be unmarried as long as her close girlfriends remain single. These girls even joked that they would build a home for the aged if they happen to be unmarried when they become old. In Yuka's case, while she studied a four-year university course, many of her high-school friends went on to vocational schools. Like other girls graduating from this type of school, many of Yuka's friends got married relatively early. This makes Yuka and her parents nervous because she has already passed the *tekireiki* or 'appropriate age at marriage' for her peer group. It shows that *tekireiki* is still operating, at least within each social group, indicating that age at marriage is largely influenced by social class and status. This tendency can also be seen in the wider society. For instance, Hara and Seiyama (1999: 176) show that in 1995, 61.5 per cent of female graduates from four-year universities aged between 25 and 29 were unmarried, while only 22.7 per cent and 32.2 per cent of female high school and women's college graduates respectively were in this position.

Double standards of aging between the sexes: Case studies

It is often asserted that young people today, especially unmarried men, are so preoccupied with their work that they have difficulty finding time to search for a future mate. Thus it is not surprising that the largest proportion of Japanese people find their marriage partners at work and that this share has increased during the past few decades, save for a slight dropping off in the mid-1990s (see Table 5.1). This could cause difficulties to those whose workplace has an imbalanced sex ratio between unmarried men and women, or an unsuitable age profile among its unmarried staff – too young or too old to be prospective partners.

The inability to meet and find 'the right one' was the immediate problem most of my female (and male) interviewees faced. One female informant said that when she broke up with her boyfriend at the age of 30, she realized that she was surrounded only with *ojisan* or 'middle-aged men' who were married or single men who were younger than she was. She thought that she should act positively in order to create a chance to meet a prospective partner and decided to join a tennis club. One day, she went to the club after work, only to find that no single men in their 30s were there. Apparently, those men who are in the prime of life are devoting their energies to their careers.

Some other female informants indicated a more acute problem, i.e. difficulties in getting married because they feel they are 'devalued' as they age. Yuri (32) felt frustrated by these attitudes and said, 'You know men always like *young* women! I, in fact, do not mind dating younger guys as long as *they* don't mind.' There is a double standard of aging between the sexes, which treats men and women differently. Women, in contrast to men, are often regarded as unattractive as they age as Strong *et al.* write:

> As men age, they become distinguished; as women age, they simply get older. Masculinity is associated with independence, assertiveness, self-control, and physical ability; with the exception of physical ability, none of these traits necessarily decreases with age. Because they are considered to

Table 5.1 Summary of where love match couples met

Year of survey	Total %	Love match marriages						Arranged marriages	Others or unknown
		Workplace or through business	Introduced by friends or siblings	School or neigh-bourhood	Met casually or while travelling	Club activities or classes	Part-time job		
1982	100%	25.3	20.5	8.3	8.2	5.8	-	29.4	2.5
1987	100%	31.6	22.4	8.5	6.3	5.4	-	23.3	2.6
1992	100%	35.0	22.3	9.6	6.2	5.5	4.2	15.2	2.0
1997	100%	33.6	27.1	11.9	5.2	4.9	4.6	9.6	3.0

Source: National Institute of Population and Social Security Research, 1998

have lost their attractiveness and because they have fewer potential partners, as women get older, they are less likely to marry. (1998: 98)

At the same time, the female interviewees suggested that they become more and more demanding as they get older. Keiko (37), another female interviewee, noted that she has become quite a connoisseur and said, 'I think about how others would think if I settled down with a "common guy". I waited such a long time to find "the right one" so my partner must be someone "respectable". You become *atamadekkachi* or "stop just going with your feelings" when you are in your 30s. You not only think carefully about the partner, but also about his family. I guess this is partly because I hear so many complaints about marriage and in-law problems through the media or from my married girlfriends. So I try to get as much information as I can about any man who might be my future husband, and that makes it more difficult to make a decision to marry.' Keiko continued, 'I am proud enough not to sell myself at a bargain price. Yet when you look around, those who are really attractive usually turn out to be already married!'

These cases indicate some of the difficulties in getting married for women who are 'at the upper end of marriageable age'. It becomes more and more difficult to get married because one's expectations become higher as one gets older. At the same time, women are indeed aware of the fact that there is a double standard of aging between the sexes, which makes women less desirable as they age. Freedman (1978) noted,

> Under society's continuing double standard, a single older man is a 'confirmed bachelor' or an eligible male; the terms for the single older woman are 'spinster' and 'old maid', hardly comparable. The single man is often considered a social asset, much in demand as an extra at dinner parties. The single woman is a burden, someone to worry about. While the system is totally unfair, that does not make it any less true.
>
> (Freedman 1978: 51)

This statement largely explains why *none* of my female informants are 'confirmed' or voluntary unwedded singles. Although the Japanese language does not distinguish between male and female bachelors, referring to both as *dokushin*, folk expressions such as *urenokori* ('left unsold') and 'Christmas Cake' (see above) are used solely to describe unmarried women perceived to have passed marriageable age. Thus the sexism seen in the English terminology may also be observed in the Japanese case.

Mami (30), another female informant, mentioned that dating with a younger man makes her feel *sukoshi kiga hikeru* or 'feel somewhat uncomfortable and restrained'. She is currently dating a 26-year old, a younger man. She met him at her workplace and they have known each other for about four years. They were brought into a closer relationship a month ago when the two of them were the only ones who were working late one Friday evening and after that they went for a drink. They drank until quite late, and as there were no trains to take him home, he asked her if he could stay at her flat. The next morning she had a personal computer delivered which she had bought a few days earlier. She was quite concerned about setting it up by herself and, as he had had more experience in computers, he came to her aid. She said, 'by the time he had set it up and taught me all the techniques I needed to know to run the computer smoothly, a mere *kōhai* or "junior" had turned into a *sugoi hito* or "incredible man"'.

He asked her at his third visit to her flat if she would be his girlfriend and they have been dating since then. When asked whether she intended to marry him, she replied, 'If I miss this chance, there might be no next time!' Yet Mami also mentioned that she was not confident to what extent he really loves her. He had had a girlfriend he was madly in love with and hoped to marry, but he had been dumped by her recently. Mami often becomes depressed thinking about their intimate relationship. It seemed that his previous girlfriend was the 'dedicated' type who used to do everything for him. She said that he had once mentioned a certain phrase from a Japanese pop song, written and sung by a young Japanese man, to illustrate the relationship with his previous girlfriend: '*Kimi ga inai to nannimo dekinai wake janai to yakan o hini kaketakedo kōcha no arika ga wakaranai*' or 'It's not that I can't do anything without you and in fact I have put the kettle on, but now I realize I don't even know where the tea is stored.'[3] Mami said she learned her boyfriend's expectations and desires through this song and thinks that her boyfriend likes a woman who is dedicated to her partner. She mentioned that although her true feelings or '*honne*' tell her to build an egalitarian relationship with her boyfriend, she often compromises. For instance, Mami usually prepares meals when he visits her flat. She said she enjoys cooking but does not really like washing dishes. Yet she has never asked for his help because she is afraid that this could diminish his attachment to her. This may be one example of how Japanese women participate in their own construction as 'women', in possibly reluctant compliance with men and under the pressures of a patriarchal cultural system – as Simone de Beauvoir puts it, 'One is not born, but rather becomes, a woman' (1997: 295).

Alternative lifestyles: Case studies

Many scholars today suggest that the number of people who will remain unmarried for life will increase in Japan. In my sample, there were, in fact, three informants (one female and two male) who were leading rather unconventional lives. The following three cases explore the informants' relationships with their partners, and discuss the meaning of legal marriage in contemporary Japan. These people were actually leading more diverse lifestyles than I had imagined before conducting my fieldwork. They suggested that the conventional marital situation, including a clear division of labour between the sexes, no longer fitted their lifestyles. The three case studies clearly illustrate the changing attitudes and perceptions towards courtship and marriage in Japanese society today. As indicated earlier, Cate and Lloyd (1992: xi) defined the concept of courtship as follows: '[it] includes relationships that move to marriage as well as those that end before marriage and might more accurately be called 'dating' relationships in that there may be no present intent to marry.' Their broad definition suggests the way changes in norms regarding the institution of marriage influence the definition of courtship itself. Liberal attitudes about cohabitation can affect the concept of courtship.

Alternative lifestyle: Case study one

Fumihiko (38) works in a large Japanese institute as a researcher. He is originally from a rural district of northern Japan but has resided in Tokyo ever since he entered one of the most prestigious national universities in Japan. I met him in one of the busy restaurants near Tokyo station. The first impression I got from him was that he looked very much like a typical Japanese *sararīman* or 'white-collar salaried worker', wearing a sober grey suit and silver-framed glasses. However, notwithstanding his ordinary, almost conformist appearance, I discovered that he was leading a rather unconventional lifestyle. In response to my question of whether he dates anyone, he said he has an intimate female partner who resides in a different part of Japan. They live apart because they both work as researchers in a government institution, but in different branches. They have maintained their relationship in this manner for the past nine years. They speak over the phone every day for about one hour and meet each other twice a month during weekends. She lives hundreds of miles away from him and since it was he who first fell in love with her, he has to visit her in order to have dates. Although the travel costs soon became a large expenditure for Fumihiko, the situation improved once they became partners based on a mutual *verbal* agreement. They decided to have a mutual fund that pays all the expenses incurred on their dates. Exactly the same amount of money from each is put into a purse they have named 'wallet for two'. Their shared wallet signifies and symbolizes their egalitarian relationship.

Fumihiko then started to describe his partner, Kyoko, and I learned that she was in her forties, a few years older than he. Fumihiko described Kyoko as an extremely serious-minded type of a person, *ishibashi o tataite wataru yōna hito* or 'she is someone who acts with the utmost caution.' Fumihiko also mentioned that Kyoko was a feminist and had studied the subject enthusiastically when she was a university student. The study seemed to have had a tremendous influence on her lifestyle. Kyoko strongly believes that her relationship with Fumihiko is a private issue that needs no interference from the state. Thus she has no intention to register the partnership at a government office. Fundamentally she is against conventional *ie* ideas based on a belief that historically it has been suppressing women. She believes that the *ie ishiki* or '*ie* consciousness' still exerts its influence upon Japanese society today. For instance, Kyoko strongly wishes to maintain her surname, which is part of her identity. However, as noted earlier, the marriage law today requires a couple to choose one common surname, either the husband's or the wife's, prior to marriage and today almost all couples (97 per cent) choose the husband's surname (Nishikawa and Nishikawa 2001). It is often asserted, especially among Japanese feminists like Kyoko, that this figure reveals the fact that the idea of women marrying into the husband's family still exists in contemporary Japanese society. In other words, the patriarchal family system survives in the law and family registration system known as *koseki*. Consequently, many Japanese feminists have been fighting for *fūfu bessei*, a system in which both husband and wife can keep their original surnames after marriage.

At first, Fumihiko gave me the impression that he was satisfied with his current relationship with Kyoko. He said he defines marriage as a sexually exclusive relationship and under this broad definition, he considers their relationship as one type of marriage. Yet he also showed his desire to marry her *legally* to give the proper public appearance to their relationship. While his wishes are somewhat contradictory, the fact remains that he takes Kyoko's beliefs very seriously and gives unconditional priority to them. In this regard, I naturally wanted to find out why Fumihiko was so understanding of Kyoko's beliefs. As our conversation progressed I learned that this basically came from his childhood, hearing about his mother's hardships and sufferings as a *yome* or 'daughter-in-law'. His mother was born and raised in a small village in a remote rural part of northern Japan. At the time of her marriage, she had to wait some time until she was considered an eligible bride. In other words his mother helped the prospective groom's family with their farming for a while so that the family members could assess her eligibility as a *yome*. Fumihiko's mother became a 'de jure' member of the family (meaning she was registered as a family member at a government office) only when she became pregnant with her first son, Fumihiko's elder brother. She went through all these hardships even though at first she had been reluctant to marry Fumihiko's father. She knew him prior to their marriage but he did not make a very good impression on her. Thus when she was informed about the plan for their *miai* meeting through her father, she tried to decline the proposal. Her father, however, persuaded her to marry him because he came from a fairly well-off family. The family owned large farmlands and so she would not have to suffer poverty. This indicates the purpose of marriage in remote parts of rural Japan at a time when financial security overrode personal satisfaction, and reveals the comparatively modest emotional expectations of marriage in those days. Fumihiko told me of another incident of hardship his mother faced when she was about to deliver her second child, Fumihiko himself, in the month of June. She was told by a member of her husband's family that she should have an abortion because it was the busiest season for farming. Today it is hard to imagine this as a true story, but as noted by Hara and Seiyama (1999), women in those days had to endure extremely hard farming labour. Fumihiko is unable to forget that he was nearly killed before birth by his own relatives, though it is unclear how serious their attempts to persuade his mother to abort him really were. Hearing all these stories from his own mother made Fumihiko very supportive of Kyoko's ideas that women have been oppressed by the constraints of the *ie* system and its ideological survival.

Knowing nothing about Fumihiko's intimate partner, his colleagues, mainly his senior bosses, told him on several occasions that they would introduce him to a prospective marriage partner. Fumihiko does not see the point in telling them about his personal life. Also he gave me the impression that as both Fumihiko and his partner work in the same company this makes them even more reluctant to disclose their relationship because it would only disturb some of their colleagues who believe in legal marriage. Thus when his bosses tried to set up a *miai* meeting, Fumihiko told them that it was not necessary, as he would try to find a partner by himself.

It was intriguing to learn that many male interviewees besides Fumihiko pointed to their colleagues as the ones who pressured them to marry, while many female informants cited their parents. For example, one male interviewee said that he had been told by his boss that if he got married he would work harder simply because he would have more responsibilities as a husband and father. Underlying this, is the social belief that marriage is an important milestone on the road to becoming a fully-fledged man. More importantly, this is also an indication of the bias against unmarried men. The informant was considered to be not working as hard as he could because he had 'fewer responsibilities as a single man'.

For Fumihiko, his parents' reaction was of the most serious concern. In fact, he kept the relationship secret for the first few years and only told his parents when he became more confident about the stability of the relationship. At first, his parents were confused about Fumihiko's 'unconventional' and 'ambiguous' partnership but they soon became relieved that Fumihiko was at least on intimate terms with someone. Fumihiko then became worried about how his mother's neighbours would react to his relationship. His lifestyle could be read as meaning that he was disobeying the rules which have prevailed in the village for many years. He feared that his situation might make his parents feel uncomfortable in keeping up *sekentei* or 'appearances', and even thought about his parents facing a situation similar to *murahachibu* or ostracism in their remote village. Yet his mother was still determined to tell the neighbours and one day she attempted to explain her son's situation. After hearing her story, the neighbours said to the mother, '*uso darō*' which means they could hardly believe that such a partner really existed. The mother, upset by all these neighbourly doubts, then went to meet Kyoko and brought back a photo showing Kyoko and Fumihiko together as 'proof' of their relationship. The photo produced satisfactory results – the neighbours finally accepted Kyoko's existence. This incident contains many intriguing factors. First, it was not Kyoko who went to see or greet the mother. In other words, Kyoko's status as a single woman exempted her from shouldering all the responsibilities of a *yome* or 'a daughter-in-law' according to the idea of *ie* consciousness, which is exactly what Kyoko is against. Second, the mother's enthusiasm in obtaining a photo suggests her eagerness to gain acceptance from the general public and at the same time shows the struggle she was facing. The mother probably thought that Fumihiko's reputation as a single man was worse than anything else and she was determined to tell the neighbours that in fact he was in a close heterosexual relationship.

It became evident that Fumihiko's concern regarding his status was excessive. He said that he had not realized how far the villagers' *ie* consciousness had eased. Fumihiko illustrated the changing attitudes towards marriage in his remote home village through the example of a young couple, who had had a wedding ceremony recently in their village but apparently invited none of their relatives. He noted that this is one of many examples that show a totally different attitude towards marriage by young villagers compared to the time when he was a small boy. He said that in those days the purpose of a marriage ceremony was *ohirome* which means publicly announcing the marriage to the people attending the wedding banquet. He remembers clearly that newly wedded couples often visited their neighbours, bringing a gift of *tenugui* (a hand towel) in order to obtain acceptance and recognition in becoming village members. He also mentioned that young couples used to hold their weddings at the groom's house instead of wedding banquet halls, inviting all their relatives. He thinks that these customs have changed significantly with the changing attitudes towards marriage.

His parents' expectations have also changed and said that they will live by themselves while they are healthy and then will go to a home for the aged. The eldest son, Fumihiko's elder brother, works and lives in the Tokyo metropolitan area with his family and has no intention of returning and living in the village. Although Fumihiko visits his parental home twice a month or goes to help them with the farming, he also cannot stay permanently to take care of them. Fumihiko said that emotionally he still clings to the idea of the *ie* system but cannot do anything about it in reality. He repeatedly expressed his guilt towards his parents because none of the children are able to take care of them in their old age because the new generation's lifestyles are not compatible with life in rural areas. A similar view was expressed by the researcher Hareven who states, 'The pressure on the nuclear family today, combined with economic and technological stresses, would make it difficult if not impossible for families to sustain continued assistance and support for their kin, especially for aging relatives' (1983: 89).

People have an idealized image of the family as an institution that fulfils both emotional and physical needs, but families in real life suffer great stresses, which as Hareven states, 'reflect the difficulties that the family faces in its adaptation to recent social changes, particularly in the loss of diversity in household membership it had in the past, the reduction of the variety of its functions, and, to some extent, the weakening of its adaptability' (Hareven 1983: 83). Fumihiko is indeed caught between his idealized image of being a son (and/or the cultural expectations of being a son) and the reality. Yet Fumihiko's story shows how a son living in an urban area is still connected emotionally with his parents in rural Japan. It also illustrates the extent and limit of changes in attitudes to marriage in Japan today. It shows that there has been significant change, in Kyoko and Fumihiko's acceptance of feminist influences and in the changes in attitudes in a small remote village, but it also indicates the limits of the change, illustrated by the fact that Fumihiko feels he cannot tell his colleagues about his relationship. In addition, it is an example of the privileging and preferring of 'love' (i.e. an emotional relationship) over 'family' (i.e. a marriage of the conventional sort – based on the idea of forming a household).

Alternative lifestyle: Case study two

I was able to conduct an interview with a female informant called Rie (35) who has not registered her marriage legally. She and her partner even had a luxurious wedding banquet six years ago when Rie was 29 years old. They have nonetheless remained legally unmarried up to now, simply because they have not had the time to go to a government office as they both work full-time. In other words, they have remained legally unmarried without any philosophical or ideological reason, at least in the first few years of their marriage. Currently they live in a flat that they purchased after they had their banquet. Rie and her partner view themselves just like any other couple whose marriage is registered. Neither of them sees any disadvantages in their marital arrangement. They both work for the same company and the firm has treated them as if they were a 'legally' married couple since the wedding banquet. As an example, under their company rules, if a married couple both work at the same company, they can obtain a greater housing allowance by registering the one who gets the larger salary as *setainushi* or 'household head'. Rie's partner receives a larger salary than she does and therefore he is registered at the company as the head of the household.

Rie said that their unregistered marriage is not a big issue unless they mention it to people who might consider it a 'problem'. People around them automatically assume that they had their marriage registered after the banquet: it was a *fait accompli*. Rie therefore said that she did not have to lie to anyone because no one had ever asked them if they were 'legally' married. Her friends and her relatives, however, all know about their unmarried status. She assumed that her partner's relatives would consider it a problem and therefore has never told them about their status. Underlying this issue is the continuing dominance of the legal marriage system and, more importantly, a prevailing norm that makes people believe that a woman should marry into her husband's family. After the wedding banquet she became aware of the fact that some of her married female colleagues kept their maiden names (at least for use within the company) because they looked upon the legally required name change as a survival of the old *ie* system. Once she realized this, she became reluctant to legalize her union. She said that they would register their marriage only when it became necessary, i.e. when she became pregnant. Thus what started out as a casual failure to visit the local ward office to register the marriage, has gradually taken on a somewhat deeper significance.

Both Fumihiko and Rie consider their partnerships as a marriage or a type of marriage, despite the fact that they are not legally married. People around them, however, treat them differently in that Fumihiko is assumed to be unmarried while Rie is assumed to be 'legally' married, only because she had a wedding banquet. This highlights the fact that public announcements are vital in Japanese marriage customs. At the same time, these cases clearly reveal the difficulties in defining the meaning of 'marriage'. Stephens defines marriage as follows: 'Marriage is a socially legitimate sexual union, begun with a public announcement and undertaken with some idea of permanence; it is assumed with a more or less explicit marriage contract, which spells out reciprocal rights and obligations between spouses, and between the spouses and their future children' (1982: 5). Strictly speaking, under this legalistic definition, the two cases examined cannot be defined as 'marriage', simply because: 'From a legal standpoint, a marriage is valid only if performed in conformity with the laws and customs of the country by a person legally authorized to officiate the marriage ceremony and properly registered to do so' (UN 1988: 51). Yet, the cases of Rie and Fumihiko are significant because both interviewees are examples of the changing perceptions of marriage in Japanese society today. Both informants, however, keep their relationships secret from certain people. The cases show the difficulties faced by some people who try to live according to their own ideas about a desirable marriage and lifestyle. It is important to recognize that in a number of societies marital unions are not strictly limited to those registered and/or legally recognized. For instance, in a country like Sweden, where cohabitation is practiced by a wide range of the population, it is perceived as a social institution. Cohabiting couples regard their relationship as one type of marriage rather than mere courtship and view themselves as essentially married (Macklin 1987). Alternative lifestyles are still not tolerated by the majority of people in Japan: individuals are supposed to conform to the prevailing norms in their culture. In this regard, Keller points out that, 'Since most individuals are unable to step outside of their cultures, they are unable to note the arbitrary and variable nature of their conventions. Accordingly, they ascribe to their folkways and creeds an antiquity, an inevitability, and a universality these do not possess' (1983: 139).

Alternative lifestyle: Case study three

Among all my informants, Hiroshi (37) was the least enthusiastic about the idea of getting married. After he entered one of the most prestigious publishing companies in Japan, he started to live alone in a flat located in the Tokyo Metropolitan area. It would have been possible to commute from his parents' house, but he knew that he would become extremely busy with his work and decided to rent a flat close to his office. When he first moved in, he thought that he would eventually have to move out of this flat. He had a vague idea that he would one day get married just like any other 'ordinary guy' and the one-room flat would soon become too small to start a family. Since then, 14 years have passed and he still lives in the same flat, still unmarried.

Hiroshi has had a number of girlfriends and he once fell deeply in love with a woman when he was 25 years old. He dated her for three years and in fact thought of marrying her. Yet he was not confident enough that he could 'make her happy' for the rest of her life. Hiroshi seemed to feel that a man has the responsibility to make his wife happy rather than creating happiness based on mutual effort. In response to my asking what he meant by 'his' responsibilities, he replied that a woman's life can be enormously affected by the man she marries and therefore he feels a heavy responsibility, especially in maintaining a secure financial position as well as social status. Underlying this comment are the beliefs that a man shoulders a heavy responsibility as a breadwinner and that his own status directly determines that of his wife.

As the interview progressed, he became frank with me and indicated that he was hesitant to make a commitment to love a single woman for the rest of his life. It seemed that the more seriously he considered the meaning of marriage, the less inclined he was to make a commitment. It was also intriguing to hear the resentment he expressed against Japanese wives in general. He believes that Japanese women are very powerful and that once they become wives they take control of the money within the household. In his view, housewives also tend to neatly avoid problems when difficulties occur within the family, expecting their husbands to shoulder all the burdens. He said that they are just like Japan's Ministry of Finance, which has enormous power and money but takes no responsibility.

He basically feels that there are no inconveniences in living alone on a daily basis. He keeps himself extremely busy with his fulfilling job as an editor and at the same time enjoys a lively personal life with many of his friends. Hiroshi also mentioned that many single men of his age are unwilling to prepare their own meals and therefore getting a proper diet is a crucial issue. Yet there are many *konbini* or 'convenience stores' in Japan, open round the clock and selling a variety of decent cooked meals, which fulfil the needs of customers like himself perfectly.

Hiroshi has lived by himself for 14 years without encountering any serious problems: city life suits him and offers all the services a bachelor could require. Moreover, he does not have a very favourable view of Japanese wives in general. The decline of the husband's authority within the family makes him less inclined to enter into matrimony, as he expects fewer privileges as a 'man' and even perceives marriage as a deprivation of his own rights. In the definition of Van de Walle and Henry, marriage 'involves rights and obligations fixed by law and custom' (Van de Walle and Henry (eds) 1982 cited in UN 1988: 51). For Hiroshi, the obligations and hindrances of marriage weigh much heavier than its rights. As long as he continues to dwell upon the disadvantages and costs of abandoning his bachelor lifestyle, he probably will not be attracted to family life, nor will marriage be his personal goal. Macklin summarizes this calculating view of lifestyle choices as follows:

> It makes sense to assume that, at any given time, one's lifestyle is the result of past opportunities and of decisions made with regard to those opportunities. Social exchange theory would suggest that whether or not one moves to, and stays in, a given lifestyle depends on the degree of perceived satisfaction with one's present lifestyle, the barriers to or perceived costs of leaving that lifestyle, the number of perceived alternatives or options to the present lifestyle, and the perceived costs and benefits of those possible alternatives (1987: 342).

Some of the case studies show the dilemmas and conflicts surrounding gender identity in Japan today, as well as how these dilemmas and conflicts influence courtship and marital behaviour. For instance, Yuka's case illustrates an example of inter-generational conflict over gender identity. Her parents have been constantly putting pressure on Yuka to marry. However, Yuka who feels very uncomfortable about conventional gender identity, finds it difficult to find a suitable prospective partner. Another informant is happy to be unmarried as long as she is not 'the last one left on the shelf' among her close girlfriends: when they marry, her social and emotional support will disappear. On the other hand, Mami feels she has to get married and clearly feels pressure from conventional ideas of gender identity. Kyoko, Fumihiko and Rie are influenced by feminist thinking and also by their dislike of the patriarchal *ie* system. Kyoko's case, in particular, is a good example illustrating the impact of feminist discourse on the way a woman leads her life. She is determined to remain unmarried because the conventional notion of the *ie* system inhibits her independence, individuality and autonomy. What these case studies illustrate is that there are gender identity conflicts on several levels: between society and young women, among young women themselves, and in fact, also in the *minds* of many of these young women. In other words, the problems exist both on the social and psychological levels.

Many of my informants in this chapter also suggested that individual emotional satisfaction has become much more important than before among younger people in Japan (as shown by the cases of Sachiko, Keiko, Fumihiko and Kyoko, and Hiroshi). This means that an increasing number of people are unwilling to submit to marriages that are primarily for the purposes of the family or for financial security, as in the past. However, this increasing attachment to individual emotional satisfaction has not been translated into a new *public* discourse that is dominant, or even a major alternative to the traditional one, as is the case in some other countries. The traditional discourses about marriage may have less and less of a hold on private individuals, but they remain strong at the level of public discourse. This is illustrated by the cases of Yuka, Yuri, Mami, Fumihiko and Kyoko, and Rie.

The result of this may be that the resistance to traditional discourses and behaviour patterns is privatized – that is, confined to private decisions which are often hidden from the wider public world as much as possible, and may even be kept completely secret. A useful parallel can be drawn with Sharon Kinsella's argument in her article 'Cuties in Japan': that the cute behaviour so pervasive in Japan is a way of resisting or rebelling against traditional norms and behavior patterns in a covert, rather than overt, way. Kinsella notes, 'The idea underlying cute was that young people who had passed through childhood and entered adult life had been forced to cover up their real selves and hide their emotions under a layer of artifice' (1995: 240). She continues,

> Cute fashion was perceived correctly as one more example of social disaffection and malaise amongst youth. Rather than attempting to grow up and take on social obligations that adulthood brings with it, youth were quite obviously attempting to avoid all these oppressive demands made on them by aspiring not to grow up at all and immersing themselves in cute culture.
>
> (Kinsella 1995: 247)

One result of this privatization of resistance may be that alternative types of relationship remain illegitimate in the dominant public discourse in Japan, despite their growing frequency in the private sphere. In addition, this continued public illegitimacy of alternative types of relationships may lead some younger people in Japan to abandon old forms of relationships to which they no longer feel sufficiently attracted, while hesitating to develop new forms.

Influence of changes in courtship practices on the timing of first marriage in Japan

The following section examines how changes in mate-selection practices have been affecting the timing of first marriage in Japan. Edwards (1989) notes that in pre-war arranged marriages the principals often had only one meeting before the decision to marry because marriage was a familial matter. In contrast, young people today wish to get married on the basis of romantic love. As noted in the following section, they spend a relatively long time in their courtship process because the process itself is extremely important in that they are testing their compatibility before making a commitment.

As Japan's National Institute of Population and Social Security Research (1998) indicates (Table 5.2), the number of dating years before marriage is shortest among arranged marriage couples, whose average is as low as one year. On the other hand, the longest dating period is observed among love-match couples

Table 5.2 Methods or places of couples meeting – average age of first encounter, first marriage and years of dating period in Japan

Methods or places of meeting	Husbands		Wives		Years of dating period
	Average age at first encounter	Average age at first marriage	Average age at first encounter	Average age at first marriage	
Love match marriages					
Educational institution	18.3	25.7	17.7	25.1	7.4
Part-time job	22.6	26.3	20.6	24.3	3.7
Met casually or while travelling	24.4	27.8	22.1	25.4	3.3
Introduced by friends or siblings	25.3	28.1	23.1	25.8	2.7
Club activities or classes	24.6	28.3	22.7	26.4	3.7
Workplace or through business	25.2	28.4	22.4	25.6	3.2
Arranged marriages (including dating agencies)	31.3	32.3	27.1	28.1	1.0

Source: National Institute of Population and Social Security Research, 1998.

Table 5.3 Average age at first encounter, first marriage and years of dating period in Japan

Year of investigation	Husbands		Wives		Average years of dating period
	Average age at first encounter	Average age at first marriage	Average age at first encounter	Average age at first marriage	
1987	25.7	28.2	22.7	25.3	2.5
1992	25.4	28.3	22.8	25.7	2.9
1997	25.1	28.4	22.7	26.1	3.4
2002	24.9	28.5	23.2	26.8	3.6
2005	25.3	29.1	23.7	27.4	3.8

Source: National Institute of Population and Social Security Research, 2007b.[4]

who met each other at school. The report reasons that this is because when they first met they were relatively young, naturally extending the years of dating. This longer period spent in dating before love-match marriages is an important factor in delaying the timing of first marriage.

What is particularly interesting here is that contrary to the accepted view of arranged marriage as 'an important determinant of early marriage in Asia' (UN 1990: 198), those couples whose marriages were arranged also contributed to the lengthening delay before marriage despite their short dating periods; because they tended to be of more advanced years when they first met. In other words, the UN report is referring to arranged marriages as they used to be in Japan, i.e. when they were dominant in the society and an expression of parental control. Nowadays, arranged marriages do not contribute to early marriage because they are a much smaller proportion and used largely as a 'last resort', and therefore the role of arranged marriage has changed in Japan. Edwards agrees on this point and holds, 'Most young people prefer to find a partner by themselves, but as they grow older and it becomes clear that their chances of meeting suitable prospects on their own are poor, they usually slide into the miai pattern' (1989: 63). Thus this is another intriguing factor delaying marriage in contemporary Japanese society.

Furthermore, it is reported that the length of the dating period before marriage is becoming longer each year. The average age when a couple meets each other for the first time is stable (see Table 5.3). However, the average dating period lengthened from 2.5 years in 1987 to 3.8 years in 2005. Thus, the report surmises that this increase in the length of the dating period is another crucial cause of the recent delay of marriage.

Conclusion

In this chapter I first discussed how courtship processes and practices differ across societies. To some extent, courtship practices in the Anglo-American case and Japan illustrate two contrasting patterns. I explored how the long tradition of different family systems has produced different marital arrangements. Courtship processes and practices also differ within a society and at different points of time in history. In Japan there has been a shift in tendency from arranged marriages to love marriages. This has affected the timing of the first marriage and the longer time spent in dating is a significant reason for the trend towards later marriages in Japan. This, at the same time, suggests the importance young people place on finding their ideal partner by testing their compatibility before marriage. I emphasized the point that it is extremely difficult to make a clear distinction between arranged and love marriages in Japan today. If one examines these two marriage arrangements in detail, it becomes clear that the concepts of arranged and love marriages are not only shifting but also overlapping with one another. Thus, I conclude that although the majority of Japanese people have been *reporting* that they have got married through 'love marriages', their marriage arrangements are still influenced by the long tradition of marriage customs in Japan. The blurring of the distinction between romantic and arranged marriages makes it all the more important to use refined qualitative research methods rather than merely relying on statistics.

As pointed out in this chapter, Japan is a country that continues to maintain relatively conventional attitudes towards marriage. The following chapter will further help us understand the Japanese marital situation by placing it in an international comparative perspective.

6 Beyond Japan
Crossnational comparisons

Introduction

This chapter will provide an overview of the marriage situation in some selected countries in East Asia, namely Japan, Hong Kong, and the Republic of Korea, and the West such as France, Italy, Sweden, and the US.[1] Along the way the chapter examines cultural traditions and the norms governing the institution of marriage in Japan by placing them in an international perspective. James White reports that 'all social institutions within a given society continually adapt to the changes in the world economic, social, and political system' (1992: 209). He also notes that even though different cultures adapt to changes in the world environment at different speeds, adaptations to the concept or institution of marriage seem surprisingly uniform throughout all societies and cultures. Both the East Asian regions and Western countries I examine share many similarities such as the fact that they are all developed and urbanized countries. Nonetheless, compared to Western countries, East Asian regions appear to share significant cultural similarities that contribute to shaping people's ideas about marriage, such as Confucian values about the strong division of labour between the sexes. In this chapter, it is argued that cultural tradition is a significantly important factor influencing changes in marriage patterns in the societies being studied. Japan is a good example to illustrate this. Hendry (1985) even claims that the patterns of marital change in Japan are, more or less, shaped by Japanese culture rather than by world economic development.

Comparative perspectives in East Asia: Japan, Hong Kong and the Republic of Korea

The following cross-cultural study provides an overview of the marriage situation over the last century in selected societies in East Asia, namely Japan, Hong Kong and Korea. In order to provide a basis for comparison, conventional family systems before the Second World War in these three regions will be briefly examined. East Asian social traditions share Confucian influences that stress the importance of the family and filial piety. The conventional family assumed its importance because people depended on the family for their economic, social and emotional needs. In principle, arranged marriage was the norm, and prospective marriage partners were selected mainly by the father under patrilineal family systems (Martin 1990; Maykovich 1978; Chang 1978; Siu 1988).

In terms of the ideal household, there were substantial differences between the three regions before the Second World War. The Chinese household was characterized by a joint-stem family. If the family was rich, all the sons brought their wives to the parental house. This extended family system allowed young people to get married before they were economically independent. Thus, the average age at first marriage was very low (Goode 1963). In Korea and Japan, the ideal was a stem family, in which the first son would live permanently with his parents, but other sons had to leave the family of origin. Furthermore, the Korean stem family stressed consanguineous lineality (blood inheritance), whereas the Japanese family was characterized by including fictive kinship (non-blood) ties through adoption from outside the kin group. This shows that the goal was to preserve the *ie* (or family) rather than to preserve the bloodline in Japan. In terms of ideal inheritance practices, all Chinese and Korean sons received shares, with the eldest son obtaining more in Korea. In Japan, however, the eldest son took all the inheritance, with a few regional exceptions (Martin 1990; Lee 1984; Befu 1971).

Marriage patterns – timing and prevalence

Timing of first marriage – since World War II

Traditionally, marriage norms encouraged early marriages in Asian countries. This trend has remained in a number of Asian countries among girls, but only a few societies still cling to this trend among boys. Relative to this Asian standard, people in East Asia marry late, South-East Asian people marry very early, and in between are those living in West Asia (UN 1990).

In East Asia, singulate mean age of marriage (SMAM) for men was already relatively high in the 1950s and had become even higher by the mid-1990s (see Table 6.1).[2] Also, high female SMAMs are reported, notably in Hong Kong (1996).

Prevalence of marriage – Since World War II[3]

Prevalence of marriage (by age 50) has remained high in most Asian countries, as Table 6.2 demonstrates.

The three East Asian countries or sub-regions examined here have largely maintained high-marriage prevalence for both sexes, notably in the Republic of Korea (see Table 6.2).[4] As for Japan, marriage prevalence remained at 91 per cent for men and 94.9 per cent for women in 1995.[5] The decrease of 7.8 per cent for men and 3.6 per cent for women since 1955 is still relatively small compared to some countries in the West, as will be discussed later.

As I stated earlier, based on a worldwide scale, Asian women marry early and there is nearly universal marriage for both sexes in Asia. However, in Japan, Hong Kong and the Republic of Korea, although overall marriage prevalence

Table 6.1 Singulate mean age at marriage, by sex, 1955–1995

Subregion and country	Men		Women	
	1955 (HK 1961)	1995 (HK 1996)	1955 (HK 1961)	1995 (HK 1996)
Japan[6]	27.0*	28.5***	24.7*	26.3***
Hong Kong	28.7*	30.7**	21.9*	28.6**
Republic of Korea	24.6*	29.3**	20.5*	26.1**

Source: *United Nations, 1990. **United Nations, 2000.
***Statistics and Information Department, Ministry of Health, Labour and Welfare, *Jinkō Dōtai Tōkei* (Statistics of Population Dynamics), 2006.
Note: I have used 1995 data for Japan to facilitate comparison with the other countries and regions surveyed. More recent data from Japan's Ministry of Health, Labour and Welfare shows SMAM of 28.8 for men and 27.0 for women in 2000.

Table 6.2 Marriage prevalence – percentages ever married at age 50, by sex, 1955–1995

Subregion and country	Men		Women	
	1955 (HK 1961)	1995 (HK 1996)	1955 (HK 1961)	1995 (HK 1996)
Japan	98.8*	91.0***	98.5*	94.9***
Hong Kong	95.4*	92.5**	92.2*	94.1**
Republic of Korea	99.7*	98.7**	99.8*	99.0**

Source: *United Nations, 1990. **United Nations, 2000.
***Statistics Bureau, Ministry of Internal Affairs and Communications, *Kokusei Chōsa* (Population Census), 2005.
Note: As with Figure 6.1, I have used 1995 data for Japan to facilitate comparison with the other countries and regions surveyed. More recent data for Japan shows an ever-married percentage of 87.4% for men and 94.2% for women in 2000, indicating a further drop of 3.6 percentage points in marriage prevalence among Japanese men, and of 0.7 percentage points for women since 1995.

remains relatively high, the timing of marriage is late. The question therefore arises, what are the factors influencing the recent trend of delayed marriage despite relatively high marriage prevalence in all three regions?

Influence of industrialization on the timing of marriage

Industrialization brought economic and social changes that have influenced family relations. Modern industrial societies based on advanced technology require educated employees with skills. In this regard, Caldwell (1976) says that education was one of the most important factors in changing the family. Educational attainment has improved in all three regions under study, and this phenomenon has been especially conspicuous among women. Increased educational attainment and expanded work opportunities increased chances for women to work outside the family before they got married. Therefore, longer years spent in school, together with premarital work, set the stage for an increase in the average age at first marriage (UN 1990).

After industrialization in Japan

Modernization in Japan followed the Meiji Restoration in 1868. The most important factor here in regard to the relationship between industrialization and age at first marriage is that, 'contrary to what happened during the industrialization of Europe, where age at marriage fell, in Japan modernization, with the help of the State, strengthened the traditional family system and enhanced conditions for delayed marriages' (UN 1990: 42). This is because the Meiji government, as discussed earlier, hoped to modernize the economic system while strengthening Confucian norms in the family system. The new Civil Code legislated in 1898 strengthened the power of the household head and affirmed patrilineal authority and filial piety. This parental control over children had a significant impact on the timing of the first marriage. At the same time, the idea of succession exclusively by the eldest son spread to all classes, which caused difficulties for other children in getting married (UN 1990). This is another factor influencing both age at first marriage and marriage prevalence.

After World War II

As mentioned earlier, one significant change made in the Japanese family system after the Second World War was the abolition of the '*ie*' or 'family system' as a legal entity. The enactment of the 1947 constitution and associated Civil Code dis-established the family system of the Meiji Civil Code. The constitution assured freedom of choice of spouse and equal rights of women to own property and to inherit. Inheritance solely by the eldest son was no longer required, and all children now had rights to equal shares. Also parents were no longer automatically entitled to receive care from family members. With the abolition of the legal foundation for household headship, husbands were no longer given primacy over wives.

In terms of the household, the abolition of the *ie* system together with enhanced urbanization contributed to structural change in the Japanese family, so that large numbers of people began to live in nuclear families. In the nuclear families, the married couple became the basic social and economic unit and became independent from their extended families. The nuclearization process was relatively gradual between the 1920s and the mid-1950s, with an average of five members per household. However, with the progressive decline in the birthrate in the 1960s, the average household unit decreased to 3.41 members in 1970. At present, the traditional stem-family and the new nuclear-family coexist in Japan, but the increase in the proportion of nuclear families has been marked.

Nuclear families amounted to 59.2 per cent of all Japanese households while the average household had 2.69 members in 2000 (Ministry of Health, Labour, and Welfare 2001).

After industrialization in Hong Kong

In the last 50 years, Hong Kong has developed as a major manufacturing, then service centre. Chinese immigrants and capital flowed into Hong Kong during several periods, including pre-World War, the immediate post-war period, and thereafter. Today, Hong Kong is a market- and consumer-driven society with multinational influences. These have apparently had a drastic impact on the role of marriage and family. Traditional concubinage was prohibited under the Marriage Reform Ordinance in 1971, and in the following year no fault divorce was instituted. In 1990, the Law Reform Commission proposed to reduce the waiting period to one year in order for consenting couples to get divorced. As noted by Levy (1949), the conventional family system and industrialization were not compatible. Therefore with the rise of industrialization, family units became smaller, on average 3.1 persons per household, with 66.2 per cent of the population living in nuclear families in 2001 (Hong Kong Population Census Office 2001).

The largest increase in mean age at first marriage in the three regions under study was reported for Hong Kong women (from 21.9 to 28.6) from the early 1960s to the mid-1990s (see Table 6.1). This increment is significant when compared with that of Hong Kong men, from 28.7 to 30.7. One of the most important reasons behind this delayed marriage for Hong Kong women is progress in the levels of educational attainment.

Traditionally, Chinese women seldom had opportunities for formal education. There was even the common saying that 'the virtuous woman is the unlearned woman'. However, during the four and a half decades since the end of the Second World War, with tremendous social and economic development, female participation in educational institutions in Hong Kong has expanded rapidly. In 1978, compulsory education was instituted for all children up to the age of 15, providing opportunities for the schooling of girls. Since then, the gender differences in levels of educational attainment have narrowed significantly. For instance, in the Chinese University of Hong Kong, from its founding in 1963 to 1983, the ratio of male to female students varied between 6:4 and 2:1. The gap has been narrowing since 1983, and the ratio was about 1:1 in 1989–1990 (Chinese Education Translation Project 1990: 56).

Salaff (1976) comments that, ideally, marriages are slightly hypergamous for Hong Kong women [i.e. Hong Kong women tend to 'marry up' in socio-economic status], although this is not always achieved in practice. According to marriage registration data for 1970–71, women employed in menial and semi-skilled occupations generally married men with higher status. Twenty-four per cent of these women chose partners with the same occupation while the remainder selected men of superior status. The largest group of women, those employed as skilled operatives, were somewhat less successful in marrying upwards, only 25 per cent married above their status, 62 per cent married other skilled operatives, and 14 per cent in fact married below their status. The cultural norm of educational hypergamy implies that the pool of marriageable men declines as women's education increases (Mare and Winship 1991). If Hong Kong women desire to improve or even maintain their status through marriage, they may end up failing to get married at all. The situation is similar in Japan in that Japanese women with higher educational attainment postpone their marriage (Tsuya and Mason 1995) and this is closely linked to strong educational homogamy or hypergamy for women (Raymo 1998). As noted earlier, Shirahase (2008) also argues that women with high levels of education and men with low levels of education tend to have difficulty in securing marriage partners.

Also, it is well known that many unmarried daughters make economic contributions to their families of origin in Hong Kong (Salaff 1976). This suggests that the later they marry, the longer their parents can benefit from their incomes. This may be rooted in the patrilineal family system which is based on the idea that girls can only contribute to their natal families while they are unmarried, because they would eventually 'marry out' (Greenhalgh 1985). Yet the situation is rather different in Japan. A 1991 survey cited in the *Economist* magazine indicated that Japanese women in their 20s shun marriage because it means giving up both jobs and comfort. A 1991 survey in Tokyo found that 76 per cent of unmarried women in their 20s lived with their parents; few did any housework or contributed to the household budget (*Economist*, 1994: 32). Yamada (2000), therefore, argues that the fact that Japanese unmarried women can live comfortably with their parents increases the attractiveness of single life. These discussions show a contrasting situation between Japanese women and Hong Kong women.

After industrialization in Korea

Until recently, especially in rural areas, there has been no major change in family type in South Korea. The rapid industrialization in the 1960s, however, resulted in mass immigration to urban areas; the 58 per cent of the population living in rural areas in 1960 decreased to less than 45 per cent in 1970. In addition, family planning to limit the family to two children has caused significant change in the family pattern. Today, the Korean family is certainly more consonant with the conjugal family type and even the number of conjugal families comprising old couples in rural areas is increasing (Lee 1984).

As discussed earlier, the first son received a greater share of the inheritance in traditional Korean society to form a stem family, and a large number of the first sons today receive better education than their younger brothers. When the first sons finish their education, they usually live in urban areas for the sake of their careers and invite their parents living in rural areas to the city so that they can support them in their old age. Nonetheless, old couples often return home because they find it difficult to adjust to city life (Lee 1984: 197). In Korea, the conventional family system is not compatible with industrialized society. This is because people today change their residence as a result of the needs of industry, and this makes it difficult for sons to serve their parents (Meyers 1989). However, as noted by Lee,

> On the surface the modern family has become an isolated unit of small size. But in the subjective experience of the people, the family is never isolated, it has just been extended geographically. The conjugal family of an old couple in a rural area is, in many cases, connected economically and psychologically with that of their offspring in an urban area. The structural principle of family and functional cooperation of the families maintains continuity even in a fast-changing society. (1984: 199)

This reveals a complexity in examining how industrialization causes change in the family situation. It would require in-depth empirical studies to clarify the processes that are affecting the family.

This rural to urban migration is very important in terms of the timing of first marriage because, in general, rural residents marry earlier than urban residents. Korea is no exception in this regard: in 1974 its female SMAM for rural residents was 22.2 whereas the urban SMAM was 23.7 (UN 1990). The urban–rural difference also applies to the Japanese case, where both men and women in rural regions marry earlier than their urban counterparts (National Institute of Population and Social Security Research 1998; Kumagai 1995). For instance, the average age at first marriage in Tokyo was 29.9 for men and 27.7 for women, whereas in rural areas such as Kagawa prefecture, the comparable figure was 27.6 for men and 25.9 for women in 1998 (Statistics and Information Department, Ministry of Health and Welfare 1998).

Influence of industrialization on mate-selection

Goode (1982 [1964]) states that as societies modernize, young people gain greater freedom of choice in making decisions about their prospective marriage partners. Formal schooling and a work place outside the home increasingly become important factors in acquiring adult status. In other words, with societal modernization, young people gain more opportunities to obtain tangible and intangible benefits outside the family unit. This increases the independence of children and at the same time decreases parental control, with consequent loss of influence in the selection of mates. The incidence of arranged marriages has dramatically declined in Japan, Hong Kong, and South Korea (see Table 6.3). Delayed marriage in East Asia is expected to be influenced by socio-economic determinants, such as education and occupation. However, marital behaviour is not solely affected by these factors. Cultural factors such as parental control contribute to shaping marriage norms as they interact with socio-economic factors to influence marriage decisions. The change in the number of arranged marriages is very important because, 'The custom of arranged marriage is an important determinant of early marriage in Asia . . . This custom, often associated with the

Table 6.3 The share of arranged marriages in the three regions

(a) Percentages of arranged marriages among Japanese women by age group

Age Group	60+	50–59	40–49	30–39	20–29
%	68	57	48	36	11

Source: 1988 Japanese National Family Survey cited from Martin, 1990.

(b) Percentages of arranged marriages among Hong Kong women by birth cohort and age group

Birth cohort	1921–25	1931–35	1941–45	1946–50
Age group*	64–68	54–58	44–48	39–43
%	58.3	38.8	20	16.7

Source: Siu, 1988.
* Calculated from birth cohort figures.

(c) Percentages of arranged marriages among Korean women by marriage cohort[7]

Marriage Cohort	1950–59	1960–69	1970–79	1980–86
%	90	81	55	45

Source: 1987 Korean Institute of Population and Health, cited from Martin, 1990.

prevalence of the extended family, leads, in general, to very young marriages' (UN 1990: 198). Furthermore, the UN report notes that dowry obligations are strongly linked to arranged marriages as obtaining a dowry without parental help is quite difficult. Therefore, changes in dowry customs that reduce parental obligation may simultaneously reduce their influence in enforcing arranged or early marriages (UN 1990: 200).

It is clear from the preceding discussion that some important socio-economic determinants, such as education, occupation, and rural or urban residence, affect the timing of marriage. Cultural factors, such as declining parental control over marriage decisions, are another extremely important component influencing the timing of first marriage. At the same time, all three regions have displayed relatively high marriage prevalence despite the delay of marriage, indicating that marriage remains an important social norm among people living in these three sub-regions.

Comparative perspective in the West

The first decades of the twentieth century

In terms of timing and prevalence of first marriage, France, Italy, Sweden, and the US displayed an opposite pattern to that of East Asia in the first decades of the twentieth century. They were characterized by late marriage (SMAMs for men

exceeded 27 years and for women 23 years) and a low-prevalence pattern origi-
nating in pre-industrial times. The US was an exception, and displayed a pattern
between that of the developing and the developed countries (UN 1990: 214).

During the first decades of the twentieth century, the late-marriage and low-
prevalence pattern observed in these countries' pre-industrial societies was shifting towards earlier marriage and higher-prevalence. By the mid-1930s and 1940s,
SMAM levels had already declined substantially in all four regions except Italy
(UN 1990). The trend towards earlier marriage seems to have come from the last
part of the transition in the late-nineteenth and early-twentieth centuries from
an 'agricultural-rural' to an 'industrialized-urbanized' society (UN 1990: 37).
Dramatic increases in the number of nuclear families in the West are believed to
be another outcome of industrialization. This family type is usually associated
with the delay of marriage because it requires more time for young couples to
acquire the economic resources required to live independently from their parents.
The nuclear family became compatible with early marriages in early-twentieth
century Europe, because 'declining family authority, greater job independence,
associated with greater job opportunities and decline of the large landholdings
permitted couples to achieve their social and economic independence earlier and
hence to marry earlier' (UN 1990: 37).[8] Some of the studies revealed that less
constraining obligations towards the extended family also allowed young couples
to choose earlier marriages. Other reasons, such as dissemination of birth control,
made earlier marriage compatible with the limitation of family size. Also, urbanization and large industrial-centres produced larger marriage markets, favourable
to earlier and more frequent marriages. This is an intriguing phenomenon because
urbanization has often been associated with the delay of marriage. This issue is
discussed further at the end of this chapter.

Among the four countries examined, only in Italy did the SMAM level not
decline substantially during the mid-1930s and 1940s. The trend towards younger
marriage occurred a little later in Italy because industrialization and demographic
transition (e.g. migration caused by better employment opportunities in urban
areas) took place later compared to the northern and western parts of Europe.
Strong adherence to conventional courtship practice and marriage behaviour also
served to delay marriage in Italy (UN 1990).

After World War II

Timing of marriage – SMAM

By the early 1950s, male SMAMs had fallen to 26.3 in France, 27.1 in Sweden,
and 23.8 in the US (see Table 6.4). SMAMs fell further in the early to mid
1970s, to levels ranging from 23 in the US to around 26 in Sweden. In Italy, as
in other Southern European countries, the male SMAM remained high despite
the decline; the figure did not fall below 27 years in the early 1970s. By the
early 1980s, all regions except Italy reported higher levels of SMAM, notably in
Sweden. As for female SMAMs, they had fallen to 23.2 in France, 22 in Sweden,

Table 6.4 Singulate mean age at marriage by sex: Europe and US, 1950/51–1980/81

Men

Country	Year of census			
	1950 or 1951	*1960 or 1961*	*1970 or 1971*	*1980 or 1981*
Italy	28.7	28.5	27.2	27.1
France	26.3*	26.4**	25.3†	26.4‡
Sweden	27.1	26.4	26.2	30.0
USA	23.8	23.3	23.5	25.2

Women

Country	Year of census			
	1950 or 1951	*1960 or 1961*	*1970 or 1971*	*1980 or 1981*
Italy	24.6	24.2	22.6	23.2
France	23.2*	23.3**	23.0†	24.5‡
Sweden	22.0	22.5	23.7	27.6
USA	20.8	20.3	21.5	23.3

Source: United Nations, 1990.
*1954
**1962
†1975
‡1982

and 20.8 in the US in the early 1950s. Female SMAMs remained relatively stable in the early 1960s and 1970s. By the early 1980s the trend was for later marriage, displaying a delayed marriage pattern. Rapid increases in SMAMs for both sexes were reported between 1970 and 1980, notably in Sweden, which recorded a rise from 23.7 to 27.6 for women and from 26.2 to 30.0 for men. In fact, these were the highest SMAMs recorded in a 1980 census among European countries. Italy, like the rest of Southern Europe, did not follow the general pattern found in other European countries and still displayed the pre-war late-marriage pattern in the 1950s (UN 1990).

Prevalence of marriage

It is clear from Table 6.5 that male and female prevalence levels formed an upward, and then a downward trend, between 1950 and 1980 except in Italy. The post-war revival of the marriage institution had already taken place by the period 1950–60, displaying higher prevalence levels than before. After 1970, however, prevalence levels fell below the 1950–60 level. In the 1970–80 period, marriage prevalence was much lower than before, notably in Sweden, where it fell to 68.1 per cent for men and 68.7 per cent for women.

Table 6.5 Marriage prevalence[9]

Men

Country	Year of census	Intercensal prevalence[10]		
	1950 or 1951	1950 – 1960	1960 – 1970	1970 – 1980
Italy	91.3	91.9(a)	90.8(b)	93.6(c)
France	89.7(d)	..	92.0(e)	87.4(f)
Sweden	84.3	89.0	88.7	68.1(g)
USA	91.5	94.8	94.1	90.0

Women

Country	Year of census	Intercensal prevalence		
	1950 or 1951	1950 – 1960	1960 – 1970	1970 – 1980
Italy	85.2	88.6(a)	91.9(b)	93.8(c)
France	89.7(d)	..	94.1(e)	91.2(f)
Sweden	80.9	94.1	92.9	68.7(g)
USA	92.2	96.2	93.3	90.4

Source: United Nations, 1990
(a)1951–61 (b)1961–71 (c)1971–81 (d)1954 (e)1963–68 (f)1977–82 (g)1975–80

The following explains the reasons behind (1) the initial decline in SMAM and high prevalence in the first phase of post-war trends; and (2) the delayed marriage and low prevalence in the second phase of post-war trends.

(1) The trend towards earlier marriage and its higher prevalence was partly a hangover effect from the pre-war period. As a UN study points out,

> changes in the ratio of women to men, resulting from the decline in the heavy emigration flows, the effect of the former decline in the birth rate, the end of the depression of the 1930s, the end of the First World War, changes in the sex ratio of marriageable population and earlier marriages stimulated by the draft prior to the Second World War are all involved.
>
> (UN 1990: 260)

This trend was further enhanced by the immediate post-war 'marriage boom' (UN 1990). Lethaeghe (1995) says that social historians like Ariés and Sauvey stress that rising real wages among men led to earlier marriage and earlier parenthood. They note that this trend has emerged since the 1880s in most Western countries. It also arises in part from an increase in the numbers of working women, another contributing factor favourable to marriage formation (UN 1990).

(2) Since around the early 1970s, a reversal of the previous trend can be observed. Marriages were increasingly delayed and there was a fall in marriage

prevalence. There are a number of reasons that have been cited to explain the trend, such as unfavourable economic and demographic conditions, decreased social pressure to marry or to marry early, changes in attitudes towards reproduction, and so on. Urbanization is often raised as an explanation for the delay of marriage. The declining proportion of the rural population in industrial societies and the emergence of large urban metropolitan regions may have increased the mean age at marriage at the aggregate level (UN 1988; 1990).

There are two further interesting factors inducing delayed and low prevalence of marriage that clearly reveal how changes in values and social norms affect marriage behaviour: women's greater participation in the labour force and the new lifestyle choice of cohabitation. The increase in the number of working women is now cited as a factor contributing to delayed marriage. More women today go on to higher education and a career. Consequently, they have become reluctant to marry early or to have children when they launch into their new careers (Davis 1985; UN 1988; Edwards and Demo 1991). This phenomenon is contrary to the situation observed in the first phase of the post-war trend, when career and income were factors contributing to early marriages. Higher levels of income/employment for women can thus be associated either with earlier or later marriage. This suggests that these factors may not inevitably *cause* either phenomenon; rather, it depends on people's assumptions about what the income/ employment is for. In other words, values and social norms pertaining to the meaning of income/employment affect what happens to marriage behaviour.

The 1970s saw the emergence of a new consensual union known as cohabitation. This phenomenon is observed notably in the Nordic countries and other European countries and is particularly popular among the young who have never been married. The increased number of people in nonmarital cohabitation has been accompanied by the decline in marriage prevalence in a number of European countries as well as in the United States (Macklin 1983). The following section assesses the effect of cohabitation on timing and prevalence of marriage in France, Sweden, and the United States.

Data on cohabitation is more difficult to gather than data on marriage. Despite these difficulties, Cherlin (1992) makes an intriguing comparison between the United States, France, and Sweden. Unfortunately, his analysis does not include Italy, but this is not surprising if one considers that cohabitation in Italy is low, with only 1.3 per cent of all couples living in non-legal marital unions as of the early 1980s (UN 1990: 252). Cherlin says that the United States is different from France and Sweden in two important respects. First, the prevalence of cohabitation is much higher in France and Sweden than in the United States. By 1980, 15 per cent of all Swedish households were cohabiting, compared with 2 per cent in the United States. In France, 6 per cent of households consisted of cohabiting couples in 1982. Second, the time spent in cohabitation is longer in France and Sweden than in the United States, where almost half of all cohabiting couples marry within three years of starting to live together. In Sweden the comparable rate is only 20 per cent. By the end of the 1980s, approximately 50 per cent of all births in Sweden were to cohabiting women. Furthermore, he says that cohabitation seems to be more of a substitute for marriage in Sweden than it is in the US. In France, 30 per cent of cohabitive relationships last at least 5 years, as compared with 10 per cent in the US (Cherlin 1992). These findings clearly indicate that the emergence of cohabitation has a considerable impact on marriage timing and prevalence in the three countries, notably in Sweden with its higher prevalence of, and longer time spent in, cohabitation. The phenomenon observed in these countries evolved concomitantly with changing attitudes towards marriage, especially among youth. Macklin (1983) explains this fairly sudden change in social values and behaviour in the US as follows:

> A major factor has been technology and the increased availability of effective contraception, which gave a fresh boost to the gradual evolution in sexual behaviors that began in the early part of the century. Since the 1920s, increasing urbanization, mobility, and education of women, and the resulting opportunities for anonymity and privacy, have led to gradually increasing nonvirginity rates for women and a growing acceptance of sexual involvement before marriage. By the late 1960s, sexual intercourse among college students in a "going steady" relationship was taken for granted, and in 1972, it was estimated that 70 per cent of single students of both sexes were nonvirginal by their senior year. (54–5)

Conclusion

Findings from cross-cultural studies have clearly highlighted the fact that changes in marital behaviour are neither uniform nor unidirectional. The influence of industrialization on marital behaviour, including marriage timing and prevalence, varied in all the countries studied in this chapter. One important variable in the development process was the family system. Industrialization enhanced the postponement of marriage in East Asia. In Japan, industrialization was associated with the conditions for the delay of marriage because of the Meiji government's policy of imposing the patriarchal samurai model of the family onto the entire society. In early twentieth century Europe, by contrast, industrialization was associated with *earlier* marriage because it had the effect of weakening family authority over individuals, and provided greater opportunities for economic independence, enabling young couples to live independently.

In terms of prevalence of marriage, industrialization is usually associated with low rates of marriage (UN 1990). The phenomenon of low prevalence is observed today in the Western countries discussed (except Italy), with a rise in the number of people cohabiting. This reflects changes in attitudes towards marriage, which have resulted in increasing numbers of people trying to build relationships based on egalitarian values between the sexes and seeking alternative lifestyles that accommodate their diversified demands. On the other hand, the prevalence of marriage has remained fairly high in East Asia; this indicates a continuing adherence to legal marriage as both a personal commitment and an economic union. Furthermore it is interesting to see that the latest figures quoted for prevalence of marriage in Italy, a country where cohabitation is relatively rare, are quite close to those for Japan. In this regard, Ochiai is correct in asserting that Southern Europe and Japan 'still maintain a relatively conservative approach to the social norms regarding marriage' (1997: 176).

These findings imply that a single phenomenon such as industrialization (or modernization, urbanization, increasing numbers of working women, etc.) must be considered in its sociocultural context. A single factor cannot be assumed to have identical consequences everywhere and always; rather, consequences depend on how it combines with other factors such as indigenous cultural traditions and norms.

Conclusion

It should be clear by now from the preceding discussion of the recent marriage pattern in Japan that no single factor such as the general process of industrialization can be assumed to have identical consequences in different cultures and different historical periods on the timing of marriage. The various timings of first marriages and prevalence of marriage in some selected industrialized countries highlight the necessity of illuminating the theoretical perspectives by placing them in the context of indigenous cultural settings. It is thus suggested that structural changes interact with people's values, ideologies, belief systems and customs – phenomena known collectively as cultures – therefore making it hard to predict their influence on factors such as marriage patterns and family formations.

One important structural change that has affected the timing of first marriage in Japan is the shift in courtship practices. I have analyzed how these practices led from arranged marriages to romantic love marriages, especially after the Second World War. Even though this shifting pattern suggests a decline in parental control, both arranged and love marriages continue to be influenced by the long tradition of marriage customs in Japan. Furthermore, Goode (1963) points out that freedom of mate-selection arises with modernization. I would argue that Goode's generalization is too simple, and that the Japanese case shows that the modernization in Japan coincided with the restoration of the imperial system; and since the government systematically imposed samurai norms on the whole population, the conventional marriage and family system became firmly entrenched, meaning that freedom of mate-selection did not simply occur with the onset of modernization. This analysis again supports the earlier argument that a single phenomenon such as modernization (or industrialization) must be considered in *context*.

Both historical and cross-societal comparative perspectives provide useful insights into the norms surrounding marriage in Japan. For instance, I argued that most of my informants have internalized their ideas about marriage and believe that it is 'normal' to get married. The Japanese concepts of normal behaviour within their society dispose people towards the idea of marriage inasmuch as they feel it is better to live a married life rather than a single one. Because of these culturally constructed ideas or social norms, compared to some other industrialized countries in the West, marriage is perceived as culturally mandatory rather than a matter of individual choice. Accordingly, more than 85 per cent of unmarried young Japanese men and women responded that they intend to get married in the future (Ministry of Health and Welfare 1998). Japanese men, in particular, still cling to the conventional gender roles supported by the image of the dominant masculine role model. I explored how the male gender role, male identity, and masculinity as perceived by Japanese men themselves are based on an assumption that there are always norms or models that people are expected to conform to in order to act and behave 'acceptably and appropriately' (Buchbinder 1994). In Japan, one widely accepted ideal image – though it has been weakening in recent years – is that of the *sarariman* who works as a corporate warrior, sacrificing his entire life for his company (Henshall 1999). As a wage earner he must be aggressive to move up the social ladder, at the same time, however, he is expected to be considerate and understanding of others' feelings (Steiner 1963). Nowadays, many contradictory roles are expected of Japanese men that make them confused about which roles they are supposed to play. This shows the ambiguity, the ambivalence, and the uncertainty that many Japanese men feel about their masculine identity.

Even though the majority of Japanese still cling to the conventional ideas about gender roles and marriage, the main theme of this book is change. New discourses of gender identity, including feminist ones, are influencing young Japanese women. It seems that gender identity, especially connected to the conventional notions of the *ie* system, is a major issue for many Japanese women. In other words, the *ie* system, one of the main objects of the feminists' wrath, still acts against women's autonomy as individuals, and this affects their behaviour concerning marriage.

Feminist discourses on sexuality are also affecting Japanese women. A considerable change is under way in women's sexual behaviour, especially regarding premarital sex. This is indeed affecting their identity as women. However, unlike some countries in the West where more liberal attitudes concerning sexuality are prevalent, even younger Japanese seem to show rather conservative attitudes when it comes to marriage. This is mainly caused, in my view, by the conventional understanding of legitimacy: reproduction outside marriage is still considered not legitimate.

The institution of marriage is nonetheless shifting in important ways, especially among one segment of Japanese population, i.e. young highly-educated Japanese women living in urban areas. With increasing honesty, these women are questioning the accepted attitudes towards family and marriage as well as the worth and rewards of marriage itself. One of the greatest problems facing highly-educated women is the fact that they are more aware of the sacrifices they have to make when entering into marriage – and have more to lose than the average woman. They look at these sacrifices not only from a financial and personal achievement point of view but also from an egalitarian point of view. The potential rewards to be gained from pursuing a career makes women not only delay the timing of their first marriage but also lead them to view conventional marriage as being in competition with the pursuit of their careers. As noted by Brinton (1992), there is little variation for most people in the timing of life transitions (educational institutions to work organizations to family) in Japan, and such irreversible transitions are usually not overlapping. In this regard, there is a strong awareness of following life events 'on schedule' and 'in order' (Brinton 1992). This means that the nature and content of future gender roles has indeed the potential power to define marriage in Japan. Young women are fully aware of the fact that age barriers to career re-entry are high in Japan. Once women quit their job for marriage or child rearing, it is extremely difficult to re-enter the labour market unless they are prepared to endure working as a part-time worker with less responsibility and lower wages. This shows a continued occupational segregation by gender, which limits the pay and occupational mobility of women. This phenomenon reveals how sexual inequality is rooted in the institutions of work and the family. This discussion also shows how cultural values concerning the institution of marriage, education, and career often interact with one another to determine the patterns of marriage.

There also exists a generation gap of which many of my informants mentioned. I started my discussion about the changing attitudes towards marriage with one of my girlfriends, Sayuri, who had originally given me the inspiration to write my doctoral thesis which is the basis for this book. Sayuri's story shows just how huge the generation gap between parent and child can get, and what serious conflict it can create. For instance, I noted that there was a disagreement between them about the level of 'appropriate educational attainment for a woman'. Sayuri went to one of the most prestigious universities in Japan. Her father, however, attempted to persuade her to go to a women's college because he believed that this would make her more valuable in the marriage market rather than going to a higher educational institution. Just like many other parents in Japan, Sayuri's parents probably thought that: 'Long-range goals, mastery, and self-determination cannot hold a high place in the lives of persons who know that plans may be disrupted at any point' (Scanzoni and Scanzoni 1981: 176). Her parents thus attempted to raise her as a 'traditional' future bride who could easily adapt to the needs of a future husband and/or his role as a breadwinner. However, Sayuri knew that 'traditional' sex-role socialization practices could limit her potential as an individual. Thus she prepared for her career. She spent many years on her education and after she got her PhD degree, she became an associate professor. This case illustrates that education is an important variable associated with female employment, which has the potential power to define women's future roles and their position within the family as discussed in the following section.

Implications

Female economic activity has increased over the past three decades in Japan and education is a prerequisite for effective economic participation. Japan has made significant progress in this respect and today women's college advancement rate is about the same as for their male counterparts. In 2005, for instance, the rate of advancement to higher education for women was 49.8 per cent against

53.1 per cent for men. However, this situation of near-equality was largely due to the number of women attending junior colleges, two-year institutions widely viewed as being a kind of finishing school for women. In the same year in 2005, 13.0 per cent of female high-school graduates went on to junior college against 1.8 per cent for males (School Basic Survey, Ministry of Education, Culture, Sports, Science and Technology 2005). The proportion of female students attending four-year college courses (36.8 per cent) remains relatively low compared to that of their male counterparts (51.3 per cent) in 2005. As indicated in the earlier chapter those highly-educated women (especially four-year college course graduates) are ahead of the curve in regard to changing views towards marriage and gender roles. I explored some significant changes in their consciousness and aspirations. Women's higher educational achievements increase both their market value and the earnings available to them. Female economic independence, in turn, enhances greater gender equality. These, then, are crucial issues that demand future study.

Finally, intensive interviews with my informants have revealed a variety of lifestyles practised by individuals who are classified simply as 'single' by quantitative research. One of the main sources of information on which we rely, the legal categories of marital status, are thus limited in scope, giving only limited insight into the reality of the actual lives of the people questioned. Qualitative research, that listens attentively to the voices of unmarried individuals, is the only way to understand what is really going on in their lives. In addition, Macklin (1987) emphasizes that it is extremely important to be aware of the fact that each individual's lifestyle is unique to that person and is also changing continuously. She continues that alternative or non-'traditional' lifestyles are 'best seen as evolving modifications of the structure of the family, caught at a moment in time in the family's continual process of adaptation to changing societal conditions' (1987: 343). One of the least understood groups or categories is that of young unmarried people, due mainly to the fact that they are assumed to be in a transitional period (Macklin 1987). As I mentioned in an earlier chapter, Japan is seeing an increase in the numbers of people who will stay single for life. This is a relatively slow movement compared to some other industrialized nations in the West, like Sweden, but definitely a sign of a new trend in Japanese society. Research on this segment of the population is becoming increasingly important in many ways, not only because of its significant demographic effects, such as its influence on the falling birth rate, but also in broader contexts surrounding the future of social welfare and policy in Japan. In particular, an increase in the number of lifelong single persons would definitely place the state under greater pressure to provide all sorts of services such as medical care, welfare, and other functions formerly supplied by families.

Appendices

Appendix 1: Profile of interviewees

Age	30–31	32–33	34–35	36–37	38–39	Total
Men	2	4	1	5	1	13
Women	6	5	3	1	1	16

Academic Background	High School	Vocational School	Junior Collage	University	Graduate School	Total
Men	4	0	0	8	1	13
Women	0	1	2	13	0	16

Occupation	Student	Temp-Staff	Part-time Worker	Full-time Staff	Total
Men	1	1	0	11	13
Women	0	3	2	11	16

Income (Unit: ¥ mil)	−2.5	2.5–4.0	4.0–6.0	6.0–8.0	8.0–	Total
Men	1	3	5	1	3	13
Women	5	2	5	3	1	16

Living Arrangement	Alone	Member(s) of Family	Cohabiting	Total
Men	10	3	0	13
Women	10	5	1	16

Boyfriend(s)/ Girlfriend(s)	Involved	Uninvolved	Total
Men	4	9	13
Women	6	10	16

Appendix 2: Interview questions

A) Profile: name, age, sex, place of residence, family structure, occupation (and place of occupation), academic background, income, siblings (and their marital status).

B) Marriage timing in general

What do you think about the recent marriage timing?

Why do people delay (or not delay) their first marriage?

C) Personal questions

1. Views on marriage

Would you like to marry in the future?

If yes:

Why do you want to get married (more specifically merits in getting married and demerits in remaining single)?

At what age do you wish to get married or from what age did you start to think about marrying?

What do you expect from your prospective partner?

What kinds of environment or conditions have caused you to delay marriage?

Have you taken any action in order to get married in the past one year?

If no:

Why do you want to stay single (more specifically merits in remaining single and demerits in getting married)?

2. Issues which may influence marriage

Do you wish to have children and why/why not?

What do you think about having an extra-marital sexual relationship, extra-marital children and cohabiting with your girlfriend or boyfriend?

What do you think about the possibility of divorcing your future spouse?

Do your family or any other acquaintances put pressure on you to marry?

Do you have a girlfriend or boyfriend?

If yes:

How long have you been dating him or her?

Are you planning to get married to him or her?

How long do you think it would take to get married?

What would need to happen before proposal and marriage?

If no:

Can you tell me about your previous boyfriend or girlfriend?

What kind of person are you looking for and what qualities are important?

Have you taken any actions in order to find a boyfriend or girlfriend?

3. Lifestyle related questions

How much free time do you have? How do you spend your free time?

4. Question to the participants of the Tokyo 21st Century College

Why did you come to the Tokyo 21st Century College?

D) Subsidiary questions on gender roles

Do you think there are basic differences between men and women?

What are those differences?

What do you think about gender roles in general?

What kind of roles do you think you will wish to play if you get married (real and ideal) and why?

Appendix 3: Tokyo 21st Century College

Year	School name	Programme title	School fees * (Unit: JPY)	Qualifications for admission	Teaching method
1989	Bridegroom School	'To become a cool guy'	40,000	Married or unmarried men above high-school students	Lectures only
1990	Bridegroom School	'To become a cool guy'	40,000	Married or unmarried men above high-school students	Lectures only
1991	No lectures were given this year				
1992	Bridegroom School	'Finding a new way of life for men'	40,000† 20,000‡	Married or unmarried men and women above high-school students	Lectures only**
1993	Bridegroom School	'Finding a new way of life for men'	70,000	Married or unmarried men and women age above 18	Lectures only
1994	Bridegroom School	'Finding richer relationships (between men and women)'	60,000	Married or unmarried men and women age above 18	Lectures and self-guided seminars
1995	Bridegroom School	'Lectures on men's liberation and independence'	60,000	Married or unmarried men and women age above 18	Lectures and self-guided seminars
1996	Bridegroom School	'Lectures on men's liberation and independence'	65,000	Married or unmarried men and women age above 18	Lectures and self-guided seminars
1997	Bridegroom School	'Lectures on men's liberation and independence'	34,000	Married or unmarried men and women age above 18	Lectures and self-guided seminars
1998	Tokyo 21st Century College	'Lectures on getting to know someone and building a relationship'	Free of charge***	Married or unmarried men and women no age restrictions	Lectures and self-guided seminars
1999	Tokyo 21st Century College	'Interesting mechanisms of gender – through an experience of being a journalist'	Free of charge***	Married or unmarried men and women age above 18	Lectures and self-guided seminars

* School fees are the total amount provided that students participate in all programmes.
** Women were allowed to attend certain programmes.
*** Funded by the Ministry of Education since 1998 and thus students participated in the school free of charge.
† Men
‡ Women

Notes

Introduction

1. I have paid careful attention to preserving the anonymity of my informants by changing their names and disguising their workplaces, titles, and so on.
2. There is no adequate translation for the word *ie* in English and it is usually translated as family, house, or household depending on the context. Hendry translated the term *ie* as 'house' because both words signify a building and have a connotation of continuity, but she also states that at an ideological level, this unit is better described using the indigenous term *ie* (Hendry 1987). It is perhaps closest in meaning to the dynastic use of the word 'house', as in 'the House of Windsor' or 'the House of Usher'. The *ie* is an institution which emphasizes the continuation of the family lineage and business over generations (Ochiai 1997). This feudalistic family structure was considered a corner stone of Japanese society until the end of the Second World War (Wagatsuma and de Vos 1962; Kumagai 1995). Its key principles include patrilocal marriage, along with inheritance and continued residence in the parental household of the eldest son.
3. For example, in 2000, 612,148 boys were born against 578,399 girls, giving a ratio of 105.8 boys per 100 girls (Statistics and Information Department, Ministry of Health, Labour and Welfare, *Jinkō Dōtai Tōkei* (Statistics of Population Dynamics).
4. The 1998 White Paper on Social Welfare (1998: 10) reported that, as of 1995, 70 per cent of male divorcees remarried compared with 60 per cent of female divorcees. Moreover, among divorcees with children, roughly 40 per cent of men said they wanted to remarry if they got the chance, against just 20 per cent of women.
5. In this book, the concept of multiplicity is discussed in Chapter 3 through the idea of 'masculinities' within Japanese culture and the analysis of how hegemonic and non-mainstream discourses challenge and reinforce one another.
6. JYF is an organization dedicated to supporting young people in Japan, the descendent of the old Youth Association (*Seinendan*). It provides room space for the 21st Century College to run classes, while Yoko Itamoto, head of the marriage consultation office run by JYF, is also organizer of the school.

Chapter 1   Perceptions and expectations of marriage

1. Recruit is a company publishing various kinds of information magazines.
2. The term 'parasite single' was coined by a sociologist, MasahiroYamada of Tokyo Gakugei University, and refers to 'young men and women who continue living with their parents even after they become adults, enjoying a carefree and well-to-do life as singles' (Yamada 2000: 49).
3. The divorce rate per 1,000 of the population in Japan was 2.15 in 2004, up from 1.57 in 1994 and 1.50 in 1984 (Statistics Bureau/Statistical Research and Training Institute, Ministry of Internal Affairs and Communications 2007).

4. *Tekireiki* (marriageable age or appropriate age for marriage) is the norm that predisposes unmarried Japanese people to marry before a certain age. It was reported in the late 1970s that the range for women was 22–24, and for men, 26–30 (Prime Minister's Statistical Office 1979: 577) and it was (and to some extent still is) believed that if one passes these ages, it becomes difficult to find a partner.

5. Nagase also agrees on this point and says that because her female interviewees perceived it difficult to balance both work and family life those 'with a higher education, income and position and better work conditions were particularly reluctant to get married' (2006: 51).

6. See Figure 2 in the Introduction

7. The approximate exchange rate during my study was $1 = ¥130.

8. '*Tō ga tatte iru*' originally meant that foods like vegetables become tough and you can no longer eat them.

Chapter 2   The impact of feminist discourses on marriage and fertility

1. Chapter 3, Article 14, paragraph 1, item 4; 'A designated physician may perform an abortion if the continuation of pregnancy or childbirth is likely to seriously damage the mother's health for physical or economic reasons' (Norgren 2001: 149).

2. Japan, however, had one of the highest divorce and illegitimacy rates in the world in the nineteenth century (Fuess 2004). See also, Smith and Wiswell 1982, who illustrate the weak link between sex and marriage in the 1930s.

3. The birthrate rate in 1989 was lower than the rate of 1.58 in 1966, the year of the Fiery Horse (*Hinoeuma*) in the Chinese zodiacal calendar. It is said that women born in the year of Fiery Horse, which recurs once every 60 years, will bring ruin to their husbands, and consequently there tends to be a sharp drop in the birthrate, especially for girls. The '1.57 shock' was the sudden realization that what was once a dramatic exception to the usual birthrate was now the norm.

4. In the decade between 1990 and 2000, about 60 per cent of the TFR (Total Fertility Rate) decline was attributable to the change of marital fertility behaviour (National Institute of Population and Social Security Research 2008).

5. The upper house of the Japanese Diet.

6. Some readers might argue that Masako has already 'snatched' another woman's husband. Her comment reflects a very Japanese stress on the importance of the legal status of marriage, rather than a sexual relationship, in determining the 'ownership' of a member of the opposite sex.

7. The word *furin* literally means, quite simply 'immorality'. It became widespread in Japan from the 1980s onwards, thanks to various popular works of fiction dealing with extra-marital affairs. These stories included a television programme in 1983 called *Kinyōbi no Tsumatachi e* (Friday Wives), and a 1996 bestseller by Junichi Watanabe, *Shitsurakuen* (Paradise Lost). Although these stories are fictional, their tremendous success indicates the fascination of *furin* for the Japanese.

8. See Appendix 1: Profile of Interviewees for details.

9. Under the Civil Code, for instance, the inheritance of an illegitimate child is half that of a legitimate child.

Chapter 3   Male gender roles and masculinity

1. For instance, Margaret Mead's first ethnography, *Coming of Age in Samoa* (1928) was criticized by Derek Freeman (1983; 1999), who claimed that she had been hoaxed by her informants. He argued that Mead relied on totally false information, which led her to the erroneous theory of cultural determination of sex roles.

2. *Bōsōzoku* literally means the 'violent running tribe', who engage in misdeeds such as exceeding the speed limit, ignoring traffic signals, and driving illegally modified vehicles in a group. They are mostly in their late teens or early 20s. Some drive modified cars, but motorcycles are the main choice of vehicle.

3. Nitobe explains that Bushido means 'literally Military-Knight-Ways the ways which fighting nobles should observe in their daily life as well as in their vocation; in a word, the "Precepts of Knighthood," the *noblesse oblige* of the warrior class' (1998: 33).

4. According to *Kōjien* (Japanese dictionary) 1991, the word 'samurai' is a conjugated form of '*saburau*' which literally means to serve.

5. In fact, Clark (1988) argues that the notion of firm-as-family and employee loyalty to company only became popular during the first two decades of the twentieth century. Although people assume these concepts have remote historical antecedents, they are actually quite modern.

6. This illustrates a stereotypical 'inexpressive male,' who does not express emotions to any women including his wife (Strong and DeVault 1992). Silence is often highly valued in Japanese traditional culture.

7. Although 'madonna' is a word from English, the Japanese meaning is somewhat different from the English meaning. In Yamada's films, she is usually depicted as an unmarried woman whose beauty, character, and manner impress not only men but also women of all ages. Because of all these attributions she is seen by unmarried men as an 'unattainable' woman or *takane no hana*.

8. In 1985 the never-married rate was particularly high for men aged 27–37, i.e. those immediately below the *dankai* generation (aged 36–38 that year). There appear to have been two main reasons for this. Firstly, when there are rapid changes in the birthrate, such as a baby boom, a gender imbalance will develop in the population of those who find it hard to get married, unless there is a change in the pattern of women tending to marry older men. Secondly, since women tend to marry earlier than men, a further imbalance will be shown if a survey is conducted after most of the women have started getting married but before most of the men have. In the case of this particular survey, an increase in the overall mean marriage age further accentuated this factor.

9. *Jōyō Shinbun* is a provincial newspaper with headquarters in Ibaraki prefecture.

10. Shigeo Saito, who enthusiastically supported the school, suddenly passed away in April 1999. A memorial service was held at JYF and as many as 700 people gathered to offer their condolences.

11. '*W*' is a magazine published by the marriage consultation office of JYF.

Chapter 4   Gender roles: the roles of wife and mother

1. I use the term productive labour to distinguish it from unpaid housework and child-rearing. Although it means paid work in a broad sense, it does not necessarily imply that women have always received their share. For instance, many married women born in the 1920s participated in the family business but their income was paid to the head of the household (Ochiai 1997: 16–7).

2. The occupation of the remaining 0.3 per cent could not be classified in primary, secondary or tertiary industries.

3. *Jokō aishi* (The Pitiful History of Women Factory Workers) was written by Wakizo Hosoi and published in 1925. Hosoi wrote about the severe labour conditions, poverty, and abuse faced by factory workers. Hosoi himself was employed as a factory worker from 1908–1923 (Kidd 1978).

4. Saxonhouse (1976) reports that by 1890, the amount of cotton yarn imported exceeded the amount that was produced within the country. Japan dominated the world's cotton-textile markets from WWI through the 1930s.

5. There were 22,401 registered nurseries in 1997 and 9,644 unregistered nurseries in 1998 (Ministry of Health and Welfare 1998).
6. For example, at companies with five or more employees, the proportion of women workers who took maternity leave when they had a child increased from 56.4 per cent in 1999 to 72.3 per cent in 2005. In the same period, the proportion of companies with over 30 employees that offered childcare leave rose from 77.0 per cent to 86.1 per cent (Ministry of Health, Labour, and Welfare (2006).
7. *Tanshin funin* means to take up a post away from one's family. It is estimated that the number of *tanshin funin* rose from 204,700 in 1990 to 317,000 in 2004 (Minister's Secretariat, Ministry of Labour 1990; Ministry of Health, Labour and Welfare 2004).

Chapter 5   Changes in courtship practices

1. Individual motives can include elements such as romantic love, sexual desire, loneliness, desire for children, or the feeling of attainment of adulthood (Hutter 1981).
2. The term endogamy refers to the requirement that an individual marry someone within a particular group. This group could be a kinship group, a clan, a religious organization, or any other social category (Hutter 1981: 201).
3. *Mō koi nante shinai* (I won't fall in love again) was released in 1992, by singer-song writer Noriyuki Makihara.
4. Observant readers may notice that these figures differ somewhat from those given on p. 3 above (29.8 for men and 28.0 for women in 2005). This reflects the fact that the data were compiled by different bodies. The earlier data came from the MHLW, using slightly different statistical techniques to the NIPSSR studies cited here.

Chapter 6   Beyond Japan: crossnational comparison

1. The material used for the crossnational comparisons in this chapter are largely obtained from a UN report in 1990 that provides comparable data to compare societies.
2. SMAM is the estimated average age at first marriage. (For more information, see UN 1990: 23 for details.)

	Men (SMAMs)	Women (SMAMs)
Early-marriage	–	21 or under
Intermediate-marriage	–	20–23
Late-marriage	27 or over	23–28

United Nations, 1990

3. The index of marriage prevalence is defined by the UN as 'the percentage ever married in age group 45–49 or by age 50.' This age limit was chosen because by age 50, the majority of first marriages have already taken place.

High marriage prevalence	95% or more ever married at ages 45–49 or 50
Intermediate prevalence	90-95% ever married at ages 45–49 or 50
Low prevalence	90% or under ever married at ages 45–49 or 50

(UN 1990)

4. There is of course, no empirical rule to determine what constitutes 'high' or 'low' prevalence of marriage. The United Nations favours a definition whereby a rate of 95 per cent or over by age 50 is 'high,' 90–95 per cent is 'intermediate,' and 90 per cent or under is 'low.' Under this definition, the data in 6.2 would show the Republic of Korea with a high rate, Japan and Hong Kong with an intermediate rate for men and an intermediate rate, bordering on high, for women in the mid-1990s. But this definition

assumes that marriage is a norm. Absent that assumption, and it seems reasonable to define all three countries' rates, ranging from 91.0–99.0 per cent as 'high.' Under this definition, only Sweden and France (men) among the countries discussed here have fallen out of that category.

5. These figures are calculated by the author based on figures published by the Statistics Bureau, Ministry of Internal Affairs and Communications. For an explanation of the gap between male and female never-married rates, see pp. 4–5 above.

6. Note also that there is a discrepancy between UN data and Japanese government data on SMAM. According to the UN report 'World Marriage Patterns 2000,' the SMAM for Japan was already as high as 30.3 for men and 26.9 for women in 1990. This discrepancy means that the comparative data presented here must be treated with some caution. Incidentally, the UN data for Japan only goes up to 1990, which is why I have chosen to use Japanese government data instead.

7. Percentages of arranged marriages among Korean women by age group were not available (International Cooperation Division, Korea National Statistical Office 2002).

8. It should be mentioned here that the U.N. report also noted that this model is 'too general to fit all situations' and thus it is used as 'a hypothetical framework to derive some of the mechanics of these changes' (1990: 37).

9. It may be objected that the data presented here is out of date. Unfortunately, the UN changed its methodology for generating statistics on this issue after 1990, presenting point-in-time data rather than intercensal data. Moreover, data for different countries was collected in different years. The latest data on marriage prevalence for these four countries is as follows: Italy, 90.2 for men and 92.5 for women in 1991; France, 90.2 for men and 92.3 for women in 1990; Sweden, 76.0 for men and 83.5 for women in 1997; USA, 91.9 for men and 93.9 for women in 1995. Source: United Nations, *World Marriage Patterns 2000*.

10. Intercensal Percentage – The estimated marriage prevalence at each age during a period between two censuses. For more information, see U.N., 1990: 247.

Bibliography

Adler, L. L. (ed.) (1993) *International Handbook on Gender Roles*, Westport, CN: Greenwood Press.

Aera Mook (1999) *Ren'aigaku ga wakaru* (Understanding the Study of Love), No.51, Tokyo: Asahi Shinbun.

Allen, S. M. and Kalish, R. A. (1984) 'Professional Women and Marriage', *Journal of Marriage and the Family*, 46(2): 375–82.

Allison, A. (1994) *Nightwork: Sexuality, Pleasure, and Corporate Masculinity in a Tokyo Hostess Club*. Chicago: University of Chicago Press.

Applbaum, K. D. (1995) 'Marriage with the Proper Stranger: Arranged Marriage in Metropolitan Japan', *Ethnology*, 34(1): 35–51.

Aruga, K. (1935) 'Wakamononakama to kon'in (‖)' (Association of young men and marriage in the village life (‖)), *Shakai Keizaishi Gaku* (The Journal of The Social and Economic History Society), VI(12): 1311–40.

—— (1954) 'The Family in Japan', *Journal of Marriage and the Family*, 16(4): 362–8.

Asahi Shinbun, 1 January 1998, '*Kekkon no inshō*' (The image of marriage).

——, 13 March 2000, *Study Finds More Teens Having Sex*. Available online http://www.asahi.com/english/asashi (accessed 13 March 2000).

Bailey, B. L. (1989) *From Front Porch to Back Seat: Courtship in Twentieth-Century America*. Baltimore: Johns Hopkins University Press.

Bardwick, J. M. (1980) *Women in Transition: How Feminism, Sexual Liberation, and the Search for Self-Fulfillment have Altered Our Lives*. Sussex: Harvester Press.

Basu, A. (ed.) (1995) *The Challenge of Local Feminisms: Women's Movements in Global Perspective*. Oxford: Westview Press.

Beasley, W. G. (1990) *The Rise of Modern Japan*. New York: St. Martin's Press.

Beck, U. and Beck-Gernsheim, E. (1995) *The Normal Chaos of Love*. Cambridge: Polity Press.

Becker, G. S. (1981) *A Treatise on the Family*. Cambridge, MA: Harvard University Press.

Befu, H. (1971) *Japan: An Anthropological Introduction*. San Francisco: Chandler Publication Co.

—— (2001) *Hegemony of Homogeneity: An Anthropological Analysis of Nihonjinron*. Melbourne: Trans Pacific Press.

Benokraitis, N. V. (1993) *Marriages and Families: Changes, Choices, and Constraints*. New Jersey: Prentice-Hall, Inc.

Bernard, J. (1976) *The Future of Marriage*. Harmondsworth: Penguin. (Originally published in 1972).

Bernstein, G. L. (ed.) (1991) *Recreating Japanese Women, 1600–1945*. Berkeley: University of California Press.

Blood, R. O. (1967) *Love Match and Arranged Marriage: A Tokyo-Detroit Comparison*. New York: Free Press.

Bowlby, J. (1951) *Maternal Care and Mental Health: A Report Prepared on Behalf of the World Health Organization as a Contribution to the United Nations Programme for the Welfare of Homeless Children*. Geneva: World Health Organization.

Brinton, M. C. (1988) 'The Social-Institutional Bases of Gender Stratification: Japan as an Illustrative Case', *American Journal of Sociology*, 94(2): 300–34.

—— (1992) 'Christmas Cakes and Wedding Cakes', in T. S. Lebra (ed.) *Japanese Social Organization*. Honolulu: University of Hawaii Press. pp. 79–107.

Brinton, M. C., Lee, Y.-J. and Parish, W. L. (1995) 'Married Women's Employment in Rapidly Industrializing Societies: Examples from East Asia', *American Journal of Sociology*, 100(5): 1099–130.

Broude, G. (1994) *Marriage, Family, and Relationships: A Cross Cultural Encyclopedia*. Santa Barbara, CA: ABC-CLIO.

Bruer, J. T. (1999) *The Myth of the First Three Years: A New Understanding of Early Brain Development and Lifelong Learning*. New York: The Free Press.

Buchbinder, D. (1994) *Masculinities and Identities*. Carlton, Vic.: Melbourne University Press.

Buckley, S. (1994) 'A Short History of the Feminist Movement in Japan', in J. Gelb and M. L. Palley (eds) *Women of Japan and Korea: Continuity and Change*. Philadelphia: Temple University Press. pp. 150–86.

—— (1997) *Broken Silence: Voices of Japanese Feminism*. Berkeley: University of California Press.

Burgess, E.W. and Locke, H. J. (1945) *The Family: From Institution to Companionship*. New York: American Book Co.

Buss, D. M. (1987) 'Mate selection criteria: An evolutionary perspective', in C. Crawford, M. Smith, and D. Krebs (eds) *Sociobiology and Psychology: Ideas, issues and applications*. Hillsdale, NJ: Lawrence. pp. 335–51.

Cabinet Office, Government of Japan. (2005) *Heisei 17 nen Kōrei Shakai Hakusho* (Annual Report on the Aging Society: 2005) Tokyo: Gyōsei.

Cafagna, L. (1972) 'The Industrial Revolution in Italy 1830–1914', in C. M. Cipolla (ed.) *The Fontana Economic History of Europe: The Emergence of Industrial Societies*. Part One, Volume IV. Glasgow: Collins/Fontana. pp. 279–328.

Caldwell, J. C. (1976) 'Toward a Restatement of the Demographic Transition Theory', *Population and Development Review*, 2: 321–66.

Caldwell, R. and Caldwell, P. (1983) 'The Causes of Marriage Change in South India', *Population Studies* (London), 37(3): 343–61.

Casler, L. (1974). *Is Marriage Necessary?* New York: Human Science Press.

Cate, R. M. and Lloyd, S. A. (1992) *Courtship*. California: Sage publications, Inc.

Chang, D. H. (1978) 'The Korean Family', in M. S. Das and P. D. Bardis (eds) *The Family in Asia*. New Delhi: Vikas Publishing House. pp. 277–343.

Cherlin, A. J. (1981) *Marriage, Divorce, Remarriage*. Cambridge, MA: Harvard University Press.

—— (1992) *Marriage, Divorce, Remarriage*, rev. ed. Cambridge, MA: Harvard University Press.

—— (1996) *Public and Private Families: An Introduction*. New York: Mc.Graw-Hill, Inc.

Chinese Education Transportation Project (1990) *Women and Education in China, Hong Kong and Taiwan*. N.Y.: Comparative Education Centre, Graduate School of Education Publications, Graduate School of Education, State University of New York at Buffalo.

Clark, R. (1988) 'The Company as Family: Historical Background', in D. I. Okimoto and T. P. Rohlen (eds) *Inside the Japanese System: Readings on Contemporary Society and Political Economy*. Stanford: Stanford University Press. pp.103–5.

Collinson, D. and Hearn, J. (1996) '"Men at Work": Multiple Masculinities/ Multiple Workplaces', in M. Mac an Ghaill (ed.) *Understanding Masculinities: Social Relations and Cultural Arenas*. Buckingham, UK: Open University Press. pp.61–76.

Connell, R. W. (1995) *Masculinities*. Berkeley, CA: University of California Press.

Cornwall, A. and Lindisfarne, N. (eds) (1994) *Dislocating Masculinity: Comparative Ethnographics*. London: Routledge.

Cox, F. D. (1990) *Human Intimacy: Marriage, the Family, and Its Meaning*. St. Paul: West Pub. Co. (Originally published 1978.)

Creighton, M. R. (1993) 'Review of Kamikaze Biker: Parody and Anomy in Affluent Japan', *American Ethnologist*, 20(4): 887–9.

—— (1996) 'Marriage, Motherhood, and Career Management in a Japanese "Counter Culture"', in A. E. Imamura (ed.) *Re-Imaging Japanese Women*. Berkeley: University of California Press. pp. 192–220.

—— (1998) '"Kramer vs. Kramer" vs. Suspense Theatre: the perception gap in constructions of self, gender, and family', in K. Nagatani and D. W. Edgington (eds) *Japan and the West: the Perception Gap*. Aldershot: Ashgate. pp. 81–107.

Curtin, J. S. (1999) *Japan's Divorce Decade: an Analysis of Legal and Social Trends in Divorce During the 1990s*. Hokkaido: Research Institute Asahikawa University.

Dahlstrom, E. (1967) *The Changing Roles of Men and Women*. London: Duckworth.

Dasgupta, R. (2000) 'Performing Masculinities? The 'Salaryman' at Work and Play', *Japanese Studies*, 20(2): 189–200.

Davis, K. (ed.) (1985) *Contemporary Marriage: Comparative Perspectives on a Changing Institution*. New York: Russell Sage Foundation.

De Beauvoir, S. (1997) *The Second Sex*, London: Vintage. (Originally published as *Le Deuxième Sex* in 1949).

Dixon, R. B. (1971) 'Explaining Cross-Cultural Variations in Age at Marriage and Proportions Never Marrying', *Population Studies*, 25(2): 215–33.

Dore, R. P. (1999) *City Life in Japan: A Study of a Tokyo Ward*. Richmond, Surrey: Curzon Press. (Originally published 1958.)

Duck, S. (1988) *Relating to Others*. Milton Keynes: Open University Press.

Economic Planning Agency (1995) *Heisei 7 nendo kokumin seikatsu hakusho* (White Paper on the National Lifestyle Fiscal Year 1995), Tokyo: Zaimushō insatsu kyoku.

—— (1997) *Heisei 9 nendo kokumin seikatsu hakusho* (White Paper on the National Lifestyle Fiscal Year 1997), Tokyo: Zaimushō insatsu kyoku.

Economic Planning Agency, Quality-of-Life Policy Bureau (eds) (1994) *Katei to shakai ni kansuru ishiki to jittai chōsa hōkokusho* (Report on Attitudes and the Actual Conditions of the Family and Society), Tokyo: Ōkurashō Insatsu Kyoku.

Economist, 12 November 1994, '*Japan's Missing Children*', p.32.

Edin, K. and Kefalas, M. (2005) *Promises I can keep: why poor women put motherhood before marriage*. Berkeley; London: University of California Press.

Edwards, J. N. and Demo, D. H. (eds) (1991) *Marriage and Family in Transition*. Boston: Allyn and Bacon.

Edwards, W. (1989) *Modern Japan through Its Weddings: Gender, Person, and Society in Ritual Portrayal*. Stanford, CA: Stanford University Press.

Ehara, Y. (1993) 'Japanese Feminism in the 1970s and 1980s', *U.S.-Japan Women's Journal, English Supplement*, 4 (Jan): pp.49–69.

—— (2000) 'Hahaoyatachi no daburubaindo' (Mothers in a Double-Bind), in Y. Meguro and S. Yazawa (eds) *Shōshika jidai no jendā to hahaoya ishiki* (Gender and Motherhood Attitudes in an Era of Falling Birthrate), Tokyo: Shinyōsha. pp. 29–46.

Ember, C. R. (1979) 'A Cross-Cultural Perspective on Sex Differences', in R.H. Munroe, R.L. Munroe, and B.B. Whiting (eds) *Handbook of Cross-Cultural Human Development*, New York: Garland STPM Press. pp. 531–80.

Eun, K.-S. (1995) *The Transition to Adulthood in Korea: Sequences of Life Events and Their Consequences on the Timing of Marriage*. PhD. Dissertation, University of Pennsylvania.

Eyer, D. E. (1992) *Mother-Infant Bonding: A Scientific Fiction*, New Haven, CT: Yale University Press.

Federico, G. (ed.) (1994) *The Economic Development of Italy Since 1870*. Aldershot: Edward Elgar.

Feldman, H. (1985) *Current Controversies in Marriage and Family*. Beverly Hills, CA: Sage.

Fisher, H. (1989) 'Evolution of Human Serial Pairbonding', *American Journal of Physical Anthropology*, 78(3):331–54.

Fōramu josei no seikatsu to tenbō (eds) (1994) *Zuhyō de miru onna no genzai* (Women Today Observed Through Charts), Kyoto: Mineruva Shobō.

Freedman, J. L. (1978) 'Love and Marriage = Happiness (still)', *Public Opinion*, 1(5): 49–53.

Freeman, D. (1983) *Margaret Mead and Samoa: The Making and Unmaking of an Anthropological Myth*. Cambridge, MA: Harvard University Press.

—— (1999) *The Fateful Hoaxing of Margaret Mead: A Historical Analysis of Her Samoa Research*. Boulder, CO: Westview Press.

Friedan, B. (1982) *The Feminine Mystique*. Harmondsworth: Penguin, (First edition 1963).

Fry, J. (1979) *Limits of the Welfare State: Critical Views on Post-War Sweden*, Farnborough: Saxon House.

Fuess, H. (2004) *Divorce in Japan: family, gender, and the state, 1600–2000*. Stanford, CA: Stanford University Press.

Fujiwara, M. (1984) *Japanese Women in Turmoil*. Tokyo: Hakuhōdo Institute of Life and Living.

Fukuo, T. (1972) Nihon kazokuseidoshi gaisetsu (Historical Outline of The Japanese Family System), Tokyo: Yoshikawa Kōbunkan.

Funabashi, K. (2000) '"Kōfuku na katei" shikō no kansei – Henyō suru chichioyazō to hahaoyakihan' (Pitfalls in the "Happpy Family" Ideal – Changing Images of Fatherhood and Motherhood Norms), in Y. Meguro and S. Yazawa (eds) *Shōshika jidai no jendā to hahaoya ishiki* (Gender and Motherhood Attitudes in an Era of Falling Birthrate), Tokyo: Shinyōsha. pp. 47–67.

Gauthier, A. (1996) *The State and the Family: A Comparative Analysis of Family Policies in Industrialized Countries*. Oxford: Clarendon Press.

Gerschenkron, A. (1962) *Economic Backwardness in Historical Perspective: A Book of Essays*. Cambridge, MA: Belknap Press.

Giddens, A. (1992) *The Transformation of Intimacy: Sexuality, Love and Eroticism in Modern Societies*. Cambridge: Polity Press.

Gittins, D. (1985) *The Family in Question: Changing Households and Family Ideology.* Basingstoke: Macmillan.

Glenn, N. D. (1996) 'Values, Attitudes, and the State of American Marriage', in D. Popenoe, J. B. Elshtain and D. Blankenhorn (eds) *Promises to Keep: Decline and Renewal of Marriage in America*, Lanham, Maryland: Roman & Littlefield Publishers, Inc. pp.15–33.

Goldman, N. (1993) 'The perils of single life in contemporary Japan', *Journal of Marriage and the Family*, 55(1): 191–205.

Goldstein-Gidoni, O. (1997) *Packaged Japaneseness: Wedding, Business and Brides.* Richmond, Surrey: Curzon Press.

Goode, W. J. (1959) 'The Theoretical Importance of Love', *American Sociological Review*, 24(1): 38–47.

—— (1963) *World Revolution and Family Patterns.* New York: Free Press of Glencoe.

—— (1982) *The Family.* Englewood Cliffs, NJ: Prentice-Hall. (Originally published 1964).

Goodenough, W. H. (1970) *Description and Comparison in Cultural Anthropology.* Cambridge: Cambridge University Press.

Greenhalgh, S. (1984) 'Networks and Their Nodes: Urban Society on Taiwan', *China Quarterly*, 99(September): 529–51.

—— (1985) 'Sexual Stratification: The Other Side of "Growth of Equity" in East Asia', *Population and Development Review*, 11(2): 265–314.

Hajnal, J. (1953) 'Age at Marriage and Proportions Marrying', *Population Studies*, VII(2): 111–36.

Hancock, M. D. (1972) *Sweden: The Politics of Postindustrial Change.* Hinsdale, IL: Dryden Press.

Hanley, S. B. (1997) *Everyday Things in Premodern Japan: The Hidden Legacy of Material Culture.* London: University of California Press.

Hara, J. and Seiyama, K. (1999) *Shakai kaisō: Yutakasano nakano fubyōdō* (Social Stratification: Inequality in an Affluent Society), Tokyo daigaku shuppan kai.

Hareven, T. K. (1983) 'American Families in Transition: Historical Perspectives on Change', in A. S. Skolnick and J. H. Skolnick (eds) *Family in Transition: Rethinking Marriage, Sexuality, Child rearing, and Family Organization.* Boston: Little Brown and Company. (4th edition). pp. 73–91.

Hendry, J. (1981) *Marriage in Changing Japan.* London: Billing and Sons Limited.

—— (1985) 'Japan: Culture Versus Industrialization as Determinant of Marital Patterns', in K. Davis (ed.) *Contemporary Marriage: Comparative Perspectives on a Changing Institution.* New York: Russell Sage Foundation. pp. 197–222.

—— (1987) *Understanding Japanese Society.* London: Croom Helm.

Henshall, K. G. (1999) *Dimensions of Japanese Society: Gender, Margins and Mainstream.* New York: St. Martin's Press.

Higuchi, K., Saito, S. and Itamoto, Y. (1990) *Hanamuko Gakkō – Ii otoko ni naru tame no 10 shō* (The Bridegroom School – 10 Lessons for Becoming a Nice Guy), Tokyo: Sanseidō.

Hochschild, A. (1990) *The Second Shift: Working Parents and the Revolution at Home.* London: Piatkus.

Hong Kong Population Census Office (2001) *Population Census*, Census and Statistics Department of Hong Kong.

Hoshii, I. (1986) *The World of Sex. Volume 2: Sex and Marriage.* Kent: Paul Norbury Publications, Inc.

Hoult, T. F., Henze, L. F. and Hudson, J. W. (1978) *Courtship and Marriage in America: A Text with Adapted Readings*. Boston: Little, Brown.

Hunter, J. (1995) 'Men and Women', in T. Megarry (ed.), *The Making of Modern Japan: A Reader*. London: Greenwich University Press. pp. 467–83.

Hurst III, G. C. (1990) 'Death, honour and loyalty: The bushido ideal', *Philosophy East & West*, 40(4): 511–27.

Hutter, M. (1981) *The Changing Family: Comparative Perspectives*. New York: John Wiley & Sons.

Ikegami, M. (1984) *Sisters of the Sun: Japanese Women Today*. London: Change International.

Inoue, S. (1998) 'Family Formation in Japan, South Korea, and the United States: An Overview', in K. O. Mason, N. O. Tsuya, and M. K. Choe (eds) *The Changing Family in Comparative Perspective: Asia and the United States*, Honolulu: University of Hawaii Press. pp. 19–41.

Inoue, T. and Ehara, Y. (eds) (1999) *Josei no dēta bukku* (Women's Data Book). Tokyo: Yūhikaku (Originally published 1991).

Inoue, T., Ueno, C. and Ehara, Y. (1994–5) *Nihon no feminizumu*. (Feminism in Japan), 8 vols, Tokyo: Iwanami Shoten.

Institute of Population Problems, Ministry of Health and Welfare (eds) (1983) *Kekkon ni kansuru jinkōgakuteki chōsa* (Demographic Exploration of Marriage), Tokyo: Kōseishō jinkō mondai kenkyūjo.

—— (1993) *Dai 10 kai (heisei 4 nen) shusshō dōkō kihon chōsa* (The Tenth Japanese National Fertility Survey, 1992), Tokyo: Kōseishō jinkō mondai kenkyūjo.

Ito, K. (1993) '*Otokorashisa' no yukue*, (The Future of Masculinity). Tokyo: Shinyōsha.

Itoi, K. (1998) 'A Tax on Mommy', *Newsweek*, Vol. cxxxii, No. 17, October 26, p.18.

Iwao, S. (1993) *The Japanese Woman: Traditional Image and Changing Reality*. New York: The Free Press.

Iwao, S. and Kato, C. (eds) (1997) *Joseigaku kīwādo* (Keywords in Women's Studies). Tokyo: Yūhikaku.

Jolivet, M. (1997) *Japan: The Childless Society?* New York: Routledge. (Originally published as *Un pays en mal d'enfants* in 1993.).

Jones, C. L., Tepperman, L. and Wilson, S. J. (1995) *The Futures of the Family*. New Jersey: Prentice Hall.

Jones, G. (2002) '"Ladies' Comics": Japan's Not-So-Underground Market in Pornography for Women', *U.S.-Japan Women's Journal, English Supplement*, No.22: 3–31.

Jong, E. (1973) *Fear of Flying*. New York: Holt, Rinehart & Winston.

Jōyō Shinbun, 29 September 1989, '*Motto josei o shiritakute*', (Wishing to know more about women).

Ju, Y. (1993) 'Mate Selection as Cultural Choice: Reflections on Findings in China, Japan and Korea', in A. M. Nicotera & Associates (eds), *Interpersonal Communication in Friend and Mate Relationships*. Albany: State University of New York Press. pp. 201–18

Kanai, Y. (1996) 'Issues for Japanese Feminism', in AMPO (ed.) *Voices from the Japanese Women's Movement*. New York: M.E. Sharp. pp. 3–22.

Kano, M. (1991) '"Bosei"no tanjō to tennōsei' (The birth of motherhood and the Emperor system),, in Inoue, Ueno, and Ehara (eds) *Bosei-nihon no feminizumu* (Motherhood-Feminism in Japan), Tokyo: Iwanami Shoten. pp. 56–61.

Kawashima, T. (1954) *Kekkon* (Marriage). Tokyo: Iwanami Shinsho.

Kayser, K. (1993) *When Love Dies: the Process of Marital Disaffection*. New York: Guilford Press.

Keller, S. (1983) 'Does the Family Have a Future?', in A. S. Skolnick and J. H. Skolnick (eds) *Family in Transition: Rethinking Marriage, Sexuality, Child rearing, and Family Organization*. Boston: Little Brown and Company. (4th edition). pp. 137–50.

Kelsky, K. (2001) *Women on the Verge: Japanese Women, Western Dreams*. Durham, NC: Duke University Press.

Kendall, L. (1996) *Getting Married in Korea: Of Gender, Mortality, and Modernity*. Berkeley, CA: University of California Press.

Kephart, W. M. and Jedlicka, D. (1991) *The Family, Society, and the Individual*. New York: HarperCollins Publishers Inc. (7th edition).

Kidd, Y. A. (1978) *Women Workers in the Japanese Cotton Mills, 1880–1920*. Ithaca, N.Y.: China-Japan Program, Cornell University.

Kim, C. I. E. and Chee, C. (eds) (1969) *Aspects of Social Change in Korea*. Kalamazoo, Michigan: The Korea Research and Publications, Inc.

Kinsella, S. (1995) 'Cuties in Japan', in L. Skov and B. Moeran (eds), *Women, Media and Consumption in Japan*. Richmond, Surrey: Curzon Press. pp. 220–54.

Kondo, D. K. (1990) *Crafting Selves: Power, Gender, and Discourses of Identity in a Japanese Workplace*. Chicago: The University of Chicago Press.

Korn, C. J. and Nicoter, A. M. (1933) 'Friend and Mate Relationship Literature, Empirical Propositions, and Methodology', in Anne Maydan Nicoter & Associates (eds), *Interpersonal Communication in Friend and Mate Relationships*. Albany, NY: State University of New York Press. pp. 13–42.

Kumagai, F. (1992) 'Research on the Family in Japan', in *The Changing Family in Asia: Bangladesh, India, Japan, Philippines, and Thailand*. Bangkok: UNESCO Principal Regional Office for Asia and the Pacific. pp. 159–237.

—— (1995) 'Families in Japan: Beliefs and Realities', *Journal of Comparative Family Studies*, 26(1): 135–63.

Laner, M. R. and Ventrone, N. A. (1998) 'Egalitarian Daters/Traditionalist Dates', *Journal of Family Issues*, 19(4): 468–77.

Lee, K. K. (1984) 'Family and Religion in Transitional and Contemporary Korea', in G. A. DeVos and T. Sofue (eds) *Religion and the Family in East Asia*. Berkeley, CA: University of California Press. pp. 185–99.

Lethaeghe, R. (1995) 'The Second Demographic Transition in Western Countries: An Interpretation', in K. O. Mason and A.-M. Jensen (eds), *Gender and Family Change in Industrialized Countries*. Oxford: Clarendon Press. pp. 17–62.

Levine, A. and Cureton, J. S. (1998) *When Hope and Fear Collide: A Portrait of Today's College Student*. San Francisco: Jossey-Bass.

LeVine, R. A. (1990) 'Gender Differences: Interpreting Anthropological Data', in M. T. Notman and C. C. Nadelson (eds) *Women and Men: New Perspectives on Gender Differences*. Washington, DC: American Psychiatric Press. pp. 1–8.

Levy, M. J., Jr. (1949) *The Family Revolution in Modern China*. Cambridge, MA: Harvard University Press.

Lewis, J. (2001) *The End of Marriage?: Individualism and Intimate Relations*. Cheltenham: Edward Elgar.

Lindsey, L. L. (1990) *Gender Roles: A Sociological Perspective*. Englewood Cliffs, NJ: Prentice Hall.

Lockwood, W. W. (1968) *The Economic Development of Japan*. Princeton: Princeton University Press.

Lunsing, W. (2001) *Beyond Common Sense: Sexuality and Gender in Contemporary Japan*. London: Kegan Paul Limited.

—— (2003) 'Parasite' and 'Non-parasite' Singles: Japanese Journalists and Scholars Taking Positions', Social Science Japan Journal, 6: 261–5.

Mackie, V. (1996) 'Feminist Critiques of Modern Japanese Politics', pp. 260–87, in M. Threlfall (ed.). *Mapping the Women's Movement: Feminist Politics and Social Transformation in the North*, London: Verso.

—— (1997) *Creating Socialist Women in Japan – Gender, Labour and Activism, 1900–1937*. Cambridge: Cambridge University Press.

—— (2003) *Feminism in Modern Japan: Citizenship, Embodiment and Sexuality*. Cambridge: Cambridge University Press.

Macklin, E. D. (1983) 'Nonmarital Heterosexual Cohabitation: An Overview', in *Contemporary Families and Alternative Lifestyles: Handbook on Research and Theory*. Beverly Hills, CA: Sage. pp. 49–74.

—— (1987) 'Nontraditional Family Forms', in M. B. Sussman and S. K. Steinmetz (eds). *Handbook of Marriage and the Family*. New York: Plenum Press. pp. 317–53.

Macklin, E. D. and Rubin, R. H. (1983) *Contemporary Families and Alternative Lifestyles: Handbook on Research and Theory*, Beverly Hills, CA: Sage.

Mainichi Shinbun, 28 December 1989, *Kōhyō datta 'Hanamuko Gakkō'* ('Bridegroom School' gains favourable reputation).

Mare, R. D. and Winship, C. (1991) 'Socioeconomic Change and the Decline of Marriage for Blacks and Whites', in C. Jencks and P.E. Peterson (eds) *The Urban Underclass*. Washington, DC: Urban Institute. pp. 175–202.

Martin, L. (1990) 'Changing Intergenerational Family Relations in East Asia', *The Annals*, 510: 102–14.

Mason, K. O. and Jensen, A.-M. (eds) (1995) *Gender and Family Change in Industrialized Countries*. Oxford: Clarendon Press.

Masuda, K. (ed.) (1974) *Kenkyūsha's New Japanese-English Dictionary*. Tokyo: Kenkyūsha. (4th edition).

Matthews, G. (2003) 'Can "a Real Man" live for His Family?': *Ikigai* and Masculinity in Today's Japan', in J. E. Roberson and N. Suzuki (eds) *Men and Masculinities in Contemporary Japan: Dislocating the Salaryman Doxa*, London: RoutledgeCurzon. pp. 109–25.

Matsubara, J. (1988) *Kurowassan shōkōgun* (The Croissant Syndrome), Tokyo: Bungeishunjū.

Maykovich, M. K. (1978) 'The Japanese Family', in M. S. Das and P. D. Bardis (eds), *The Family in Asia*, New Delhi: Vikas Publishing House. pp. 277–343.

McLanahan, S. and Booth, K. (1989) 'Mother-only Families: Problems, Prospects and Politics', *Journal of Marriage and the Family* 51(Aug.): 557–80.

McLelland, M. J. (1999) *Male Homosexuality in Modern Japan: Cultural Myths and Social Realities*, PhD Dissertation, University of Hong Kong.

Mead, M. (1935) *Sex and Temperament in Three Primitive Societies*. New York: William Morrow.

—— (1953) [1928] *Coming of Age in Samoa: A Psychological Study of Primitive Youth for Western Civilization*. New York: Modern Library.

Meyers, R. R. (1989) *An Analysis of the Confucian Marriage and Family System in Modern Korea and a Christian Alternative*, PhD Dissertation, Fuller Theological Seminary.

Ministry of Education, Culture, Sports, Science and Technology (2005) *Gakkō kihon chōsa*. (School Basic Survey*)*. Available Online http://www.mext.go.jp/b_menu/toukei/001/04073001/pdf/sanzu07.pdf (accessed 26 August 2008).

Ministry of Health and Welfare. (1996) *Heisei 8 Nenban – Kōsei Hakusho* (White Paper on Social Welfare, 1996), Tokyo: Gyōsei.

—— (1998) *Heisei 10 nenban – Kōsei hakusho* (White Paper on Social Welfare, 1998), Tokyo: Gyōsei.

Ministry of Health, Labour, and Welfare (2001) *Kōsei rōdō hakusho* (*Annual Reports on Health and Welfar, 2001*), Available online http://wwwhakusyo.mhlw.go.jp/wpdocs/hpax200101/b0010.html (accessed 10 February 2008).

—— (2004) *Shūrō jōken sōgō chōsa* (General Survey on Working Conditions). Available online http://www.mhlw.go.jp/toukei/itiran/roudou/jikan/syurou/04/4-4.html (accessed 5 May 2008).

—— (2005a) *Heisei 17 nendo kokumin seikatsu hakusho* (White Paper on the National Lifestyle Fiscal Year 2005), Tokyo: Jijigahō sha.

—— (2005b) *Heisei 17 nen jinkō dōtai tōkei geppō nenkei (gaiyō) no gaikyō* (Report on Vital Statistics Monthly), Tokyo: Kōsei Tōkei Kyōkai.

—— (2006) *Josei koyō kanri kihon chōsa kekka hōkokusho*, 2005 (Report on the Basic Survey on Management of Female Employment, 2005). Tokyo: Equal Employment Policy Division, Equal Employment, Children and Families Bureau, Ministry of Health, Labour, and Welfare.

Ministry of Health, Labour and Welfare and Statistics and Information Department (2008) *Heisei 19 nen chingin kōzō kihon tōkei chōsa* (Basic Survey on Wage Structure 2007). Available online at http://www.mhlw.go.jp/toukei/itiran/roudou/chingin/kouzou/z07/kekka1-2.html (accessed 15 April 2008).

Ministry of Labour. (1995) *Pāto–taimu rōdōsha sōgō jittai chōsa hōkoku* (General Survey on Part–time Workers), Tokyo: Ōkurashō Insatsu Kyoku.

Mitchell, R. E. (1972) *Family Life in Urban Hong Kong.* Taipei: Orient Cultural Service.

Miyake, Y. (1991) 'Doubling Expectations: Motherhood and Women's Factory Work Under State Management in Japan in the 1930s and 1940s', in G. L. Bernstein (ed.) *Recreating Japanese Women, 1600–1945.* Berkeley: University of California Press. pp. 267–94.

Money, J. and Ehrhardt, A. A. (1972) *Man and Woman, Boy and Girl.* Baltimore: Johns Hopkins Press.

More. 1 January 1979. No. 19, Tokyo: Shūeisha.

Murdock, G. P. (1949) *Social Structure*, New York: Macmillan.

Nagase, N. (2006) 'Japanese Youth's Attitudes Towards Marriage and Child Rearing', in M. Rebick and A. Takenaka (eds). *The Changing Japanese Family.* New York: Routledge. pp. 39–53.

National Institute of Population and Social Security Research. (eds) (1998) *Heisei 9 nen nihonjin no kekkon to shussan – Dai 11 kai shusshō dōkō kihon chōsa* (Japanese Marriage and Fertility – The Eleventh Japanese National Fertility Survey in 1997), Tokyo: Kōsei Tōkei Kyōkai.

—— (2001) *Zenkonin oyobi shokon no heikin konin nenrei: 1899–1999* (Average Age of All Marriages and First marriages: 1899–1999), (Web Site Table 6–12). Available online http://www1.ipss.go.jp/scripts/qf/FrwdWeb.EXE/a?QFWebSearch (accessed 25 October 2001).

—— (2002) *Heisei 14 nen wagakuni fūfu no kekkon katei to shusshōryoku – Dai 12 kai shusshō dōkō kihon chōsa* (Marriage Process and Fertility of Japanese Married Couples – The Twelfth Japanese National Fertility Survey in 2002), Tokyo: National Institute of Population and Social Security Research.

—— (2003) *Ippan jinkō tōkei* (*Latest Demographic Statistics*), Tokyo: National Institute of Population and Social Security Research.

—— (2007a) *Heisei 17 nen wagakuni dokushinsō no kekkonkan to kazokukan – Dai 13 kai shusshō dōkō kihon chōsa* (Attitudes toward Marriage and the Family among Japanese Singles – The Thirteenth Japanese National Fertility Survey in 2005), Tokyo: National Institute of Population and Social Security Research.

—— (2007b) *Heisei 17 nen wagakuni fūfu no kekkon katei to shusshōryoku – Dai 13 kai shusshō dōkō kihon chōsa* (Marriage Process and Fertility of Japanese Married Couples – The Thirteenth Japanese National Fertility Survey in 2005), Tokyo: National Institute of Population and Social Security Research.

—— (2008) *Dai 12–kai kōsei seisaku seminā hōkokusho – Chō shōshika to kazoku · Shaki no henyō – Yōroppa no keiken to nihon no seisaku kadai* (Report on the 12th Health and Welfare Policy Seminar: 'Ultra–low Fertility and Changes in the Family and Society: the European Experience and Japan's Policy Agenda'), Tokyo: National Institute of Population and Social Security Research.

New York Times (11 February 1990) 'Who Needs Love! In Japan, Many Couples Don't', Vol. 145, Issue 50334.

NHK Broadcasting Culture Research Institute (ed.) (1998) *Gendai nihonjin no ishiki kōzō* (Attitudinal Structure of Contemporary Japanese), Tokyo: Nippon hōsō shuppan kyōkai.

Nicotera, A. M. (1993) 'Where Have We Been, Where Are We, and Where Do We Go?', in A. M. Nicotera and Associates (eds) *Interpersonal Communication in Friend and Mate Relationships*. Albany, NY: State University of New York Press. pp. 219–36.

Nihon Keizai Shinbun, 10 May 1989, *Kekkonnan jidai no hanamuko kōza*, (Lectures for Bridegrooms in an Era of Marriage Difficulties).

—— 18 October 1995, *Hanamuko gakkō* (The Bridegroom School).

—— (eds) (1998) *Onnatachi no shizukana kakumei: "Ko" no jidai ga hajimaru* (Women's Quiet Revolution: The Dawn of the "Individualist" Era), Tokyo: Nihon Keizai Shinbun.

Nishikawa, T. and Nishikawa, H. (2001) *Kekkon no atarashii katachi* (New Styles of Marriage). Tokyo: Takarajima sha.

Nitobe, I. (1998) [1900]. *Bushido*. Tokyo: Kodansha International Ltd. (English text first published in 1900).

Niwa, A. (1993) 'The Formation of the Myth of Motherhood in Japan', *U.S.-Japan Women's Journal, English supplement*, (4): 70–82.

Nock, S. L. (1998) *Marriage in Men's Lives*. New York: Oxford University Press.

Nolte, S. H. and Hastings, S. A. (1991) 'The Meiji State's Policy Toward Women, 1890–1910', in G. L. Bernstein (ed.) *Recreating Japanese Women, 1600–1945*. Berkeley: University of California Press. pp. 151–74

Norgren, T. (2001) *Abortion before Birth Control: The Politics of Reproduction in Postwar Japan*. Princeton: Princeton University Press.

Ochiai, E. (1997) *The Japanese Family System in Transition*. Tokyo: LTCB International Library Foundation, (Originally published 1994).

Ogawa, N. and Hodge, R. W. (1991) *Fertility Change in Contemporary Japan*. Chicago: University of Chicago Press.

Ogino, M. (1994) 'Abortion and Women's Reproductive Rights: The State of Japanese Women, 1945–1991', in J. Gelb and M. L. Palley (eds), *Women of Japan and Korea: Continuity and Change*. Philadelphia: Temple University Press. pp. 69–94.

Oguma, E. (2002) A Genealogy of 'Japanese' Self-Images, Melbourne: Trans Pacific Press.

Ohashi, T. (2000) 'Mikonka · bankonka · singuruka no haikei', (The Background of the Postponement and Avoidance of Marriage), in Yoshizumi (ed.) *Kekkon to pātonā kankei: Toinaosareru fūfu* (Marriage and Partner Relationships: Reconsidering Married Couples), Kyoto: Mineruva Shobō. pp.27–55.

Ohinata, M. (1995) 'Boseigainen o meguru genjō to sono mondaiten' (The Present Circumstances of the Concept of Motherhood and Its Problems), in Inoue, Ueno, and Ehara (eds) *Nihon no feminizumu.* (Feminism in Japan), 8 vols, Tokyo: Iwanami Shoten. pp.29–55

Okamoto, H. (2000) 'Nihongata koyō kankō no henka to hahaoya ishiki – Shūhenka suru josei rōdō', (Changes in Japanese Employment Practices and Mothers' Attitudes – Female Workforce Working at the Margins), in Y. Meguro and S. Yazawa (eds) *Shōshika jidai no jendā to hahaoya ishiki* (Gender and Motherhood Attitudes in an Era of Falling Birthrate), Tokyo: Shinyōsha. pp. 131–48.

Okano, K. H. (1999) 'Review of Kamikaze Biker: Parody and Anomy in Affluent Japan', *Asian Studies Review*, 23(4): 514–6.

Oppenheimer, V. K. (1988) 'A Theory of Marriage Timing', *The American Journal of Sociology*, 94(1): 563–91.

Oppenheimer, V. K. and Lew, V. (1995) 'American Marriage Formation in the 1980s: How Important was Women's Economic Independence?', in K. O. Mason and A.-M. Jensen (eds) *Gender and Family Change in Industrialized Countries*. Oxford: Clarendon Press. pp.105–38.

Ortner, S. B. (1972) 'Is Female to Male as Nature is to Culture?', pp. 21–42, Reprinted in S. B. Ortner, *Making Gender: The Politics and Erotics of Culture, Boston: Beacon Press* (1996).

—— (1981) 'Gender and Sexuality in Hierarchical Societies: The Case of Polynesia and Some Comparative Implications', in S. B. Ortner and H. Whitehead (eds) *Sexual Meanings: The Cultural Construction of Gender and Sexuality*. London: Cambridge University Press. pp. 359–409.

—— (1984) 'Theory and Anthropology Since the Sixties', *Comparative Studies in Society and History*, 26(1): 126–66.

—— (1996) *Making Gender: The Politics and Erotics of Culture*. Boston: Beacon Press.

Parsons, T. (1956) 'Family Structure and the Socialization of the Child', in T. Parsons and R. F. Bales, *Family: Socialization and Interaction Process*. London: Routledge & Kegan Paul Limited. pp. 35–131.

Patrick, H. (ed.) (1976) *Japanese Industrialization and Its Social Consequences*, Berkeley, CA: University of California Press.

Peterson, S L. (1998) *The Changing Meaning of Feminism: Life Cycle and Career Implications from a Sociological Perspective*. San Francisco: International Scholars Publications.

Podmore, D. B. L. (1974) 'Family Norms in a Rapidly Industrializing Society: Hong Kong', *Journal of Marriage and the Family*, 36: 400–7.

Popenoe, D., Elshtain, J. B. and Blankenhorn, D. (eds) (1996) *Promises to Keep: Decline and Renewal of Marriage in America*. Lanham, Maryland: Roman & Littlefield Publishers, Inc.

Prime Minister of Japan and His Cabinet. *The Constitution of Japan*. Available online http://www.kantei.go.jp/foreign/constitution_and_government_of_Japan/constituion_e. html(accessed 14 August 2008).

Prime Minister's Statistical Office. (1979) *Yoron chōsa nenkan* (Opinion Survey Yearbook), Tokyo: Sōrifu.

Prinz, C. (1995) *Cohabiting, Married, or Single?: Portraying, Analyzing & Modeling New Living Arrangements in the Changing Societies in Europe*. Aldershot, Hants.: Avebury.

Quality-of-Life Policy Bureau, Economic Planning Agency (eds) (1992) *Senkōdo chōsa* (National Survey on Lifestyle Preferences Fiscal Year 1992), Tokyo: ōkurashō Insatsu Kyoku.

—— (1994) *Katei to shakai ni kansuru ishiki to jittai chōsa hōkokusho* (Report on Attitudes and the Actual Conditions of the Family and Society), Tokyo: ōkurashō Insatsu Kyoku.

—— (1996) *Heisei 7 nendo kokumin seikatsu senkōdo chōsa* (National Survey on Lifestyle Preferences in 1995), Tokyo: ōkurashō Insatsu Kyoku.

Raymo, J. M. (1998) 'Later Marriages or Fewer? Changes in the Marital Behaviour of Japanese Women', *Journal of Marriage and the Family*, 60(4): 1023–34.

Rebick, M. and Takenaka, A. (eds) (2006) *The Changing Japanese Family*. New York: Routledge.

Recruit, 13 September 2007, 'Dekichatta kon tte dō omou?' (What do you think about 'shotgun weddings'?) *L25*, 33, p.13.

Refsing, K. (1998) 'Gender Identity and Gender Role Patterns in Cross-cultural Marriages: The Japanese-Danish Case', in R. Breger and R. Hill (eds), *Cross-Cultural Marriage: Identity and Choice*. Oxford: Berg. pp. 193–208.

Regan, P. (2003) *The Mating Game: A Primer on Love, Sex, and Marriage*. Thousand Oaks, CA: Sage Publications.

Reischauer, E. O. (1989) *Japan, Tradition & Transformation*. Boston: Houghton Mifflin. (Originally published 1978).

Riviere, P. (1971) 'Marriage: A Reassessment', in R. Needham (ed.), *Rethinking Kinship and Marriage*. London: Tavistock Publications. pp. 57–74.

Roberson, J. E. and Suzuki, N. (eds) (2003) *Men and Masculinities in Contemporary Japan: Dislocating the Salaryman Doxa*. London: RoutledgeCurzon.

Roberts, G. S. (1994) *Staying on the Line: Blue-Collar Women in Contemporary Japan*, Honolulu: University of Hawaii Press.

Rodd, L. R. (1991) 'Yosano Akiko and the Taisho Debate over the "New Woman"', in G. L. Bernstein (ed.) *Recreating Japanese Women, 1600–1945*. Berkeley: University of California Press. pp. 175–98.

Rothman, E. K. (1984) *Hands and Hearts: A History of Courtship in America*. New York: Basic Books.

Rutter, M. L. (1972) *Maternal Deprivation Reassessed*. Harmondsworth: Penguin.

Sacks, K. (1979) *Sisters and Wives: The Past and Future of Sexual Equality*. London: Greenwood Press.

—— (1989) 'Toward a Unified Theory of Class, Race, and Gender', *American Ethnologist*, 16(3): 534–50.

Saito, M. (2003) *Modan gāru ron* (A Theory of Modern Girls). Tokyo: Bungei Shunjū.

Saito, S. (1982) *Tsumatachi no shishūki* ('Autumnal Wives'), Tokyo: Kyōdō Tsūshin Sha.

Sakamoto, K. (1999) 'Reading Japanese women's magazines: the construction of new identities in the 1970s and 1980s', *Media, Culture & Society*, 21(2): 173–93.

Salaff, J. W. (1976) 'The Status of Unmarried Hong Kong Women and the Social Factors Contributing to Their Delayed Marriage', *Population Studies*, 30: 391–412.

Sano, C. (1973) *Changing Values of the Japanese Family*. Westport, Conn.: Greenwood Press.

Sato, I. (1991) *Kamikaze Biker: Parody and Anomy in Affluent Japan*. Chicago: The University of Chicago Press.

Saxonhouse, G. R. (1976) 'Country Girls and Communication among Competitors in the Japanese Cotton–Spinning Industry', in Hugh Patrick (ed.) *Japanese Industrialization and Its Social Consequences*, Berkeley, CA: University of California Press. pp.97–125

Saxton, L. (1993) *The individual, marriage, and the family*. (8th ed), Belmont, CA: Wadsworth Pub. Co.

Scanzoni, L. D. and Scanzoni, J. (1981) *Men, Women, and Change: A Sociology of Marriage and Family*. New York: McGraw-Hill.

Schak, D.C. (1974) *Dating and Mate–Selection in Modern Taiwan*. Taipei: The Orient Cultural Service.

Schoppa, L. J. (2006) *Race for the Exits: The Unraveling of Japan's System of Social Protection*. Ithaca: Cornell University Press.

Schwartz, M. A. (1997) *Marriages and Families: Diversity and Change*. N.J.: Prentice Hall.

Sechiyama, K. (1996) *Higashi ajia no kafuchōsei* (East Asian Patriarchal Systems), Tokyo: Keisō Shobō.

Sekiyama, N. (1985) *Kinsei nihon no jinkō kōzō* (Population Composition in Premodern Japan), Tokyo: Yoshikawa Kōbunkan.

Shinmura, I. (ed.) (1991) *Kōjien*. Tokyo: Iwanami Shoten (4th edition).

Shirahase, S. (2008) '*Shōshika shakai ni okeru kaisō ketsugō toshiteno kekkon — Korekarano shakai kaisōron o saguru*' (Marriage as a Basic Unit of Social Stratification in the Society with Low Fertility: Searching the New-version of Social Stratification Theory in the Aging Society), pp. 63–81, in H. Takada (ed). *Kaisō·Kaikyū kōzō to chii tassei (Class structure and status attainment)*.

Shostak, A. B. (1987) 'Singlehood.' in Marvin B. Sussman and Suzanne K. Steinmetz (eds). *Handbook of Marriage and the Family*. New York: Plenum Press. pp. 355–67.

Sievers, S. (1983) *Flowers in Salt: The Beginnings of Feminist Consciousness in Modern Japan*. Stanford, CA: Stanford University Press.

Silverman, D. (2000) *Doing Qualitative Research: A Practical Handbook*. London: Sage Publications.

Simpson, R. F. (1966) *Comparative Statistics on Economic and Educational Development in Asian Countries*. Hong Kong: Hong Kong Council for Educational Research.

Siu, Y.-m. (1988) *Family Structure, Marriage and Fertility in Hong Kong: Demographic Effects of the Changing Chinese Family*. Thesis (PhD.), University of Michigan.

Skolnick, A. S. and Skolnick, J. H. (1989) *Family in Transition: Rethinking Marriage, Sexuality, Child Rearing, and Family Organization*. Boston: Scott, Foresman and Company. (6th edition).

Smart, S. L. and Smart, M. S. (1980) *Families: developing relationships*. New York: Macmillan. (2nd edition).

Smith, D. E. (1986) 'Institutional Ethnography: A Feminist method', *Resources for Feminist Research/Documentation sur la recherche feministe*, 15(1): 6–13.

Smith, P. C. (1980) *Urbanization, Education, and Marriage Patterns: Four Cases from Asia*. Honolulu: East-West Center, no.70.

Smith, R. J. (1987) 'Gender Inequality in Contemporary Japan', *Journal of Japanese Studies*, 13(1): 1–25.

Smith, R. J. and Wiswell, E. (1982) *The Women of Suye Mura*. Chicago: University of Chicago Press.

Spanier, G. B. (1985) 'Cohabitation in the 1980s: Recent Changes in the United States', in K. Davis (ed.) *Contemporary Marriage: Comparative Perspectives on a Changing Institution*. New York: Russell Sage Foundation. pp. 91–111.

—— (1991) 'Cohabitation: Recent Changes in the United States', in Edwards and Demo (eds) *Marriage and Family in Transition*. Boston: Allyn and Bacon. pp. 94–102.

Spence, J. T., Deaux, K. and Helmreich, R. L. (1985) 'Sex Roles in Contemporary American Society', in G. Lindzey and E. Aronson, (eds), *Handbook of Social Psychology*, New York: Random House. pp. 149–78.

Sprecher, S. and Hatfield, E. (1996) 'Premarital Sexual Standards among U.S. College Students: Comparison with Russian and Japanese Students', *Archives of Sexual Behavior*, 25(3): 261–89.

Standish, I. (1998) 'Akira, Postmodernism and Resistance', in D.P. Martinez (eds), *The Worlds of Japanese Popular Culture: Gender, Shifting Boundaries and Global Cultures*. New York: Cambridge University Press. pp. 56–74.

Statistics and Information Department, Ministry of Health and Welfare (1998) *Jinkō dōtai tōkei nenpō* (Annual Report on Statistics of Population Dynamics), Tokyo: Kōsei Tōkei Kyōkai.

Statistics and Information Department, Ministry of Health, Labour and Welfare. (2006) *Jinkō dōtai tōkei* (Statistics of Population Dynamics). Available online http://www.mhlw.go.jp/toukei/saikin/hw/jinkou/tokusyu/konin06/konin06-1.html (accessed 10 February 2008).

—— (2008) *Heisei 19 nen chingin kōzō kihon tōkei chōsa* (Basic Survey on Wage Structure 2007). Available online http://www.mhlw.go.jp/toukei/itiran/roudou/chingin/kouzou/z07/kekka1-2.html (accessed 15 April 2008).

—— *Seibetsu shusshō sū oyobi shusshō seihi—1970~2000* (Number and ratio of male/female births, 1970 and 2000). Available online http://www.mhlw.go.jp/shingi/2002/01/s0130-6b5.html (accessed 4 September 2008).

Statistics Bureau, Management and Coordination Agency (1997) *Shūgyō kōzō kihon chōsa kekka no gaiyō* (Summary Results and Analyses of Employment Status Survey). Available online http://www.stat.go.jp/data/shugyou/2007/index.htm (accessed 10 February 2008).

—— (1998) *Rōdōryoku chōsa* (Labour Force Survey), Tokyo: Nihon Tōkei Kyōkai.

Statistics Bureau, Ministry of Internal Affairs and Communications (2005) *Kokusei Chōsa* (Population Census). Available online http://www.stat.go.jp/data/kokusei/2005/kihon1/00/zuhyou/a00611.xls (accessed 10 February 2008).

—— (2005) *Rōdōryoku chōsa* (Labour Force Survey (Time Series)). Available online http://www.stat.go.jp/data/roudou/longtime/03roudou.htm (accessed 10 February 2008).

—— (2007) *Nihon tōkei nenkan* (Japan Statistical Yearbook), Tokyo: Nihon Tōkei Kyōkai. (57th edition).

—— *Rōdōryoku chōsa* (Labour Force Survey (Time Series)). Available online http:/www.stat.go.jp/data/roudou/index.htm (accessed 10 February 2008).

Steiner, L. R. (1963) *Romantic Marriage: The Twentieth Century Illusion*. Philadelphia: Chilton Books.

Stephens, W. N. (1982) *The Family in Cross-Cultural Perspective*. Washington, D.C.: University Press of America (Originally published in 1963).

Strong, B. and DeVault, C. (eds) (1992) *The Marriage and Family Experience*. St. Paul, MN: West Publication Co. (5th edition).

Strong, B., DeVault, C. and Sayad, B. W. (1998) *The Marriage and Family Experience: Intimate Relationships in a Changing Society*. CA: Wadsworth Publishing Company. (7th edition).

Sugimoto, Y. (2003) *An Introduction to Japanese Society*. Cambridge: Cambridge University Press. (2nd edition).

Sussman, M. B. and Steinmetz, S. K. (eds) (1987) *Handbook of Marriage and the Family*. New York: Plenum Press.

Suzuki, T. (2006) *Lowest-Low Fertility and Governmental Actions in Japan*. Available online http://www.ier.hit–u.ac.jp/pie/English/discussionpaper/dp2006/dp294/text.pdf (accessed 19 December 2007).

Suzuki, Y. (1995) *Kekkonkan·rikonkan no henyō* (Changes in Attitudes towards Marriage and Divorce), Gendai no esupuri 341 Seikatsu ishiki no henyō

Tanaka, K. (1995) 'The New Feminist Movement in Japan, 1970–1990', pp. 343–52, in K. F. Fanselow and A. Kameda (eds), *Japanese Women: New Feminist Perspectives on the Past, Present, and Future*, New York: The Feminist Press.

Tanaka, Y. (1995) *Contemporary Portraits of Japanese Women*. Westport, Connecticut: Praeger.

Tannen, D. (1994) *You Just Don't Understand: Women and Men in Conversation*. New York: Ballantine Books.

Thornton, A. (1996) 'Comparative and Historical Perspectives on Marriage, Divorce, and Family Life', in D. Popenoe, J. B. Elshtain and D. Blankenhorn (eds) *Promises to Keep: Decline and Renewal of Marriage in America*. Lanham, Maryland: Roman & Littlefield Publishers, Inc. pp. 69–87.

Tokuza, A. (1999) *The Rise of the Feminist Movement in Japan*. Tokyo: Keio University Press.

Toshitani, N., Yuzawa, Y., Sodei, T. and Shinotsuka, E. (eds) (1996) *Kōgakureki jidai no josei* (An Era of Women with High Educational Background). Tokyo: Yūhikaku.

Tovar, P. (2000) 'Marriage: Overview', in C. Kramarae and D. Spender (eds) *Routledge International Encyclopedia of Women*, Vol. 3, New York: Routledge. pp. 1301–3.

Tsurumi, E. P. (1990) *Factory Girls: Women in the Thread Mills of Meiji Japan*. Princeton, N.J.: Princeton University Press.

Tsuya, N. O. and Mason, K. O. (1995) 'Changing Gender Roles and Below–Replacement Fertility in Japan', in K. O. Mason and A.-M. Jensen (eds) *Gender and Family Change in Industrialized Countries*. Oxford: Clarendon Press. pp. 139–67.

Ueno, C. (1996) 'The Making of a History of Feminism in Japan', *Asian Journal of Women's Studies*, 2: 170–91.

—— (1997) 'Ueno Chizuko: Professor, University of Tokyo; Sociologist', in S. Buckley, *Broken Silence: Voices of Japanese Feminism*, Berkeley: University of California Press. pp. 272–301.

Unger, R. and Crawford, M. (1992) *Women & Gender: A Feminist Psychology*. New York: McGraw-Hill.

United Nations. Economic and Social Commission for Asia and the Pacific. (1974) *The Demographic Situation in Hong Kong*. Bangkok: United Nations.

—— (1985) *The State of World's Women, 1985. World Conference to Review and Appraise the Achievements of the United Nations Decade for women: Equality, Development and Peace. Nairobi, Kenya (July 15–26)*, Oxford: New Internationalist Publication.

—— (1988) *First Marriage: Patterns and Determinants*. New York: United Nations.

—— Department of International Economic and Social Affairs (1990) *Patterns of First Marriage: Timing and Prevalence*, New York: United Nations.

—— Department of International Economic and Social Affairs (2000) *World Marriage Patterns*. Available online http://www.un.org/esa/population/publications/worldmarriage/worldmarriagepatterns2000.pdf (accessed 25 April 2008).

—— Department of Economic and Social Affairs, Statistical Office (2004) *Demographic Yearbook*. New York: United Nations.

Uno, K. S. (1991) 'Women and Changes in the Household Division of Labor', in G. L. Bernstein (ed.) *Recreating Japanese Women, 1600–1945*. Berkeley: University of California Press. pp. 17–41.

—— (1999) *Passage to Modernity: Motherhood, Childhood, and Social Reform in Early Twentieth Century Japan*. Honolulu: University of Hawai'i Press.

US Bureau of the Census (2007) *Stastical Abstract of the United States: 2008*. Washington, D.C.: US Department of Commerce, Bureau of the Census. (127th edition).

Van de Kaa, D. J. (1987) 'Europe's Second Demographic Transition', *Population Bulletin*, 42: 1–59.

Vogel, E. F. (1963) *Japan's New Middle Class: The Salary Man and His Family in a Tokyo Suburb*. Berkeley, CA: University of California Press.

W, 10 August 1999, 'Tsuitō – 'Hanamuko gakkō' o umi sodateta jānarisuto' (Memorial Writing – A Journalist Who Founded and Promoted the Bridegroom School), p.2.

Wagatsuma, H. and De Vos, G. A. (1962) 'Attitudes Towards Arranged Marriage in Rural Japan. Human Organization', *Journal of the Sociology for Applied Anthropology*, Vol. 21, pp.187–200.

—— (1984) *Heritage of Endurance: Family Patterns and Delinquency Formation in Urban Japan*, Berkeley, CA: University of California Press.

Waite, L. J. and Gallagher, M. (2000) *The Case for Marriage – Why Married People are Happier, Healthier, and Better Off Financially*, New York: Doubleday.

Watanabe, J. (1997) *Shitsurakuen (Paradise Lost)*, Tokyo: Kodansha.

Watanabe, T. (1986) *Datsu Dansei no Jidai: Andorojinasu o Mezasu Bunmeigaku* (The Age of Escape of Masculinity: Studies Towards an Androgynous Civilization), Tokyo: Keiso Shobō.

Watkins, S. C. (1981) 'Regional Patterns of Nuptiality in Europe, 1870–1960', *Population Studies (London)*, 35(2): 199–215.

Weekly ST Report, 5 November 1993, *'Bridegroom School' Helps to Bring the Sexes Together*, p.6.

Wharton, A. S. (1995) 'Gender', in D. Levinson (ed.) *Encyclopedia of Marriage and the Family*, New York: Simon & Schuster Macmillan. pp.328–36.

White, J. M. (1992) 'Marriage: A Developing Process', in K. Ishwaran, *Family and Marriage: Cross-Cultural Perspectives*, Toronto, ON.: Thompson Education Publishing, Inc. pp.197–211.

White, L. E. (1999) 'Feminism Within and Beyond Japan: Women's Movements in Tokyo in 1995', Thesis (PhD.), University of Colorado.

Whyte, M. K. (1992) *From Arranged Marriages to Love Matches in Urban China*, HK: Hong Kong Institute of Asia–Pacific Studies, The Chinese University of Hong Kong.

Wolf, R. (1996) *Marriage and Families in a Diverse Society*, New York: HarperCollins College Publications.

Wong, F.-m. (1974) *Industrialization and Family Structure in Hong Kong*, Hong Kong: Social Research Centre, Chinese University of Hong Kong.

Xerox, P. (1992) *Trends in Female and Male Age at Marriage and Celibacy in Asia*, Honolulu: East-West Center.

Yagi, T. (2001) *Nihon no tsūkagirei* (A rite of passage in Japan), Tokyo: Shibunkaku.

Yamada, M. (1996) *Kekkon no shakaigaku* (Sociology of Marriage), Tokyo: Maruzen Library.

—— (1999) *Parasaito shinguru no jidai* (*The Age of Parasite Singles*), Tokyo: Chikuma Shobō.

—— (2000) 'The Growing Crop of Spoiled Singles', *Japan Echo* 27(3): 49–53.

Yamada, Y. (1979–1980) *Yamada Yoji sakuhinshū*, v.5&8 (Pieces of Work by Yamada Yoji, v.5&8), Tokyo: Rippū Shobō.

Yomiuri Shinbun, 3 July 1990, in Ogino 1994, p. 90.

Yorburg, B. (1974) *Sexual Identity: Sex Roles and Social Change*. New York: Wiley-Interscience.

Yuzawa, Y. (1995) *Zusetsu – Kazoku mondai no genzai* (An Illustrated Study of Family Issues in Modern Japan), Tokyo: Nihon Hōsō Shuppan Kyōkai (Originally published 1973).

Index

The entries from Notes sections are denoted with an 'n' and followed by the chapter number and note number.

age at first marriage, average 3–4
Allison, A. 57–8
alternative lifestyles; case study 104–13; courtship practices 104–13
appendices; interview questions 135–6; interviewees profile 134; profile of interviewees 134; Tokyo 21st Century College 137
arranged marriage 17–18, 90; incidence 123; shift to love marriages 92–9

bankonka (postponement of marriage) 2–4
Beck, U. and Beck-Gernsheim, E. 7–8
Becker, Gary 22
Bernard, Jessie 9
births, extra-marital 16
Blood, R. O. 18, 97, 100
bonding with mothers, case study 85–6
Bridegroom School; development 67–8; gender gap 71; gender views 63–4; male gender roles 63–71; marriage difficulties for men 65; men's studies 64–5; organizers/aims 65–7; programme 68–9; rise/fall analysis 69–71
Burgess, E.W. and Locke, H. J. 8
bushido 56–7

case study; alternative lifestyles 104–13; bonding with mothers 85–6; courtship practices 99–113; double standards 102–4; fathers, poor relationship with 86; female gender roles 85–8; feminism 48–51; feudalistic family structure (*ie* system) 48–9; lifestyles, alternative 104–13; marriage 99–113; marriage, views 49–51; *miai* meetings 100–1; *ren'ai or miai?* 99–100; reproduction, views 49–51; role conflict 87–8; sexuality, views 49–51
Cherlin, A. J. 89
comparisons, crossnational *see* crossnational comparisons
courtship practices 89–115; alternative lifestyles 104–13; analytical perspective beyond Japan 89–92; Anglo-American case 91–2; case study 99–113; double standards 102–4; Edo period 94–5; lifestyles, alternative 104–13; love marriages, shift from arranged marriages 92–9; mate-selection, post-war Japan 97–9; mate-selection, pre-war Japan 93–7; Meiji period (1868–1912) 95–7; Tokugawa feudal period (1603–1868) 94–5; Western influence 97
crossnational comparisons 116–29; Hong Kong 116–22; Japan 116–22; Korea 116–22; West (the) 123–8
cultural-historical background 17–20
current situation 2–5; female gender roles 81–4

Dore, R. P. 17, 94
double standards; case study 102–4; courtship practices 102–4
drifter sub-culture, male gender roles 60–3

Edo period, courtship practices 94–5
Edwards, Walter 19, 98, 100
Equal Employment Opportunity Law
    (EEO), feminism 35–6
expectations of marriage 16–27; *see also*
    perceptions of marriage
extra-marital births 16

family institution changes, industrialized
    countries 7–8
family system (*ie seido*) 17–18
farmers unable to find a bride 3
fathers, poor relationship with;
    case study 86
female gender roles; bonding with
    mothers 85–6; case study 85–8;
    current situation 81–4; female labour
    pattern 81–4; female textile workers
    77–8; 'good wives and wise mothers'
    76–7, 78–9; historical background
    73–81; ideological perspective 76–7,
    78–81; labour force 74–6, 81–4;
    M-shaped curve 81–3; motherhood
    ideology 76–7, 78–81; 'myth of the
    first three years' 80–1; part-time work
    83–4; productive labour/reproductive
    labour 74–6; role conflict 87–8; wife/
    mother 73–88
feminism 28–53; 'academic feminists'
    36–7; case study 48–51; characteristics
    37–44; delayed marriage 44–8;
    Equal Employment Opportunity Law
    (EEO) 35–6; historical background
    29–37; 'housewife feminism' 38–40;
    limitations 37–44; magazines,
    Japanese women's 45–7; Meiji period
    (1868–1912) 30; militarism 30–1;
    motherhood 37–8; negative image
    40; occupation, post-war Japanese
    31–2; reproduction and rights 43–4;
    sexual autonomy, women's 41–3, 131;
    state and 40–1; travel 47–8; Women's
    Liberation Movement (1970s) 32–4;
    Yomiuri Shinbun 43
first marriage average age 3–4
first marriage timing 113–14, 117–18, 130

gender and marriage, theoretical and
    comparative perspective 6–13
gender gap, Bridegroom School 71
gender inequality, within marriage 9–13
gender roles *see* female gender roles; male
    gender roles

gender views, Bridegroom School 63–4
generation gap 132
'good wives and wise mothers', female
    gender roles 76–7, 78–9
Goode, W. J. 7, 130
Goodenough, Ward H. 6

Henshall, K. G. 56
Higuchi, K. 65–6
Hong Kong; crossnational
    comparisons 116–22; industrialization
    120–1
'housewife feminism' 38–40
Hurst, G. C. 56–7
Hutter, M. 90

ideological perspective, female gender
    roles 76–7, 78–81
ie 138 n Intro, 2
ie seido (family system) 17–18
ie system (feudalistic family structure)
    1–2; case study 48–9
implications 132–3
individualism, growth 8–9
industrialization; Hong Kong 120–1;
    Japan 119; Korea 121–2;
    mate-selection 122–3; timing of
    marriage 118–22
industrialized countries; family institution
    changes 7–8; marriage institution
    changes 7–8
inequality, gender inequality within
    marriage 9–13
interview questions, appendix 135–6
interviewees profile, appendix 134

Japan; crossnational comparisons 116–22;
    industrialization 119

Kanai, Y. 37, 38–40
Kelsky, K. 47–8, 52
Kinsella, S. 112
Korea; crossnational comparisons 116–22;
    industrialization 121–2

labour force; female gender roles 74–6,
    81–4; M-shaped curve 81–3; part-time
    work 83–4
Lee, K. K. 121–2
legislation, Equal Employment
    Opportunity Law (EEO) 35–6
lifestyles, alternative, case study
    104–13

M-shaped curve 81–3
Mackie, V. 36
Macklin, E. D. 128, 133
magazines, Japanese women's,
    feminism 45–7
male gender roles 54–72; Bridegroom
    School 63–71; *bushido* 56–7; drifter
    sub-culture 60–3; marriage difficulties
    for men 3, 65; motorcycle gang
    sub-culture 58–60; non-mainstream
    discourses 58–63; salaryman 55–6,
    57–8; social stigmas 62–3
marriage; age, first marriage average 3–4;
    arranged marriage 17–18, 90, 92–9,
    123; case study 99–113; defining 6–7;
    expectations 16–27; first marriage
    average age 3–4; first marriage timing
    113–14, 117–18, 130; gender inequality
    within 9–13; lingering popularity
    of 23–6; love marriages, shift from
    arranged marriages 92–9; perceptions
    16–27; prevalence 117–18, 125–8;
    theoretical and comparative perspective
    6–13; views, case study 49–51;
    West (the) 123–8
marriage and gender; gender inequality
    within marriage 9–13; theoretical and
    comparative perspective 6–13
marriage difficulties for men; Bridegroom
    School 65; male gender roles 3
marriage institution changes, industrialized
    countries 7–8
mate-selection; *see also* courtship
    practices; industrialization 122–3; post-
    war Japan 97–9; pre-war Japan 93–7
Matthews, Gordon 63–4
Meiji government's policy, female gender
    roles 77–8
Meiji period (1868–1912); courtship
    practices 95–7; feminism 30
men's perceptions of marriage 22–3
men's studies, Bridegroom School 64–5
methodology and the field 13–15
miai meetings, case study 100–1
miai or ren'ai? case study 99–100
motherhood, feminism 37–8
motherhood ideology, female gender
    roles 76–7, 78–81
motorcycle gang sub-culture, male gender
    roles 58–60
Murdock, George 6
'myth of the first three years', female
    gender roles 80–1

negative image, feminism 40

Ochiai, E. 3, 73
Okano, K. H. 60

part-time work; female gender roles 83–4;
    labour force 83–4
perceptions of marriage 16–27; men's
    22–3; post-war cultural-historical
    background 18–20; pre-war
    cultural-historical background 17–18;
    today 20–3; women's 20–1
post-war cultural-historical
    background 18–20
postponement of marriage (*bankonka*) 2–4
pre-war cultural-historical
    background 17–18
prevalence, marriage 117–18, 125–8
Prime Minister of Japan and His Cabinet 18
productive labour/reproductive labour,
    female gender roles 74–6

ren'ai or miai? case study 99–100
reproduction and rights, feminism 43–4
reproduction, views, case study 49–51
reproductive labour/productive labour,
    female gender roles 74–6
Riviere, Peter 6–7, 10
role conflict; case study 87–8; female
    gender roles 87–8
roles, gender *see* female gender roles;
    male gender roles

Sakamoto, K. 45–7
salaryman, male gender roles 55–6, 57–8
Sato, I. 58–60
Schak, D. C. 91
sexual autonomy, women's, feminism
    41–3, 131
sexuality, views, case study 49–51
social stigmas, male gender roles 62–3
Spanier, G. B. 91–2
state, and feminism 40–1
surnames, choosing 1–2

timing of marriage, industrialization
    118–22
Tokugawa feudal period (1603–1868),
    courtship practices 94–5
Tokyo 21st Century College,
    appendix 137
travel, feminism 47–8
Tsurumi, E. P. 78

Ueno, C. 36–7

West (the); crossnational comparisons 123–8; marriage 123–8
Western influence, courtship practices 97
White, L. E. 28, 34

Women's Liberation Movement (1970s), feminism 32–4
women's perceptions of marriage 20–1

Yomiuri Shinbun, feminism 43
Yorburg, B. 53

CPSIA information can be obtained at www.ICGtesting.com
Printed in the USA
BVOW02s1023270114

342971BV00004B/23/P